Praise for Fly Free

In this beautiful and moving memoir, Dami Roelse tells the story of love—love stretching across a life of raising children, global adventure, and searching for deeper meaning in a world of change. A must-read for care-givers, freedom-lovers, and spiritual seekers from all walks of life.

    —Devon Hase, author of *How Not to Be a Hot Mess: A Survival Guide for Modern Times*

We're all pilgrims on the path of love. Dami Roelse's journey took her around the world where she met Ram Dass, Neem Karoli Baba and Goenka. Meeting with great teachers doesn't just end the seeker's journey, it starts a journey of one's own. Dami's journey in *Fly Free* is a heart-rending account of finding and losing love, and devotion to a practice of mindfulness. In the process of losing her husband to Parkinson's disease and dementia, she finds connection with herself and the universal love available to all of us on a trek in the Himalayas and a visit to Maharaj-ji's ashram in Kainchi where it all began. A read that tugs on the heart and takes you on a far-away adventure.

    —Krishna Das, Kirtan /Chant Artist and author of *Chants of a Lifetime* and *Flow of Grace*

Fly Free is a memoir by a woman who started walking a spiritual path as a youth and has continued to do so through the vicissitudes of a difficult and adventurous life. The book carries us from Dami Roelse's family home in Holland, through her youthful quest in India her adult years in California as a married women, working wife and mother of three, to her remarkably hardy journey in Ladakh. Throughout, Roelse writes unguardedly about her thoughts and feelings, with greater attention to honesty than to any need to project a self image. The manuscript tinkles with vivid details of Indian food, California rain or Ladakh spiritual seekers. Her life takes us from the early days of hippie westerners in India, to post modern spirituality that consists of an evolving discovery more than a particular belief. This is the autobiography of a traveler, an adventurer, a lover, and a person who seeks to find meaning while transcending loss. Her readers are also introduced to famous spiritual leaders whom Roelse met, like Ram Das, Neem Karoli Baba and S.N. Goenka. Like myself, there will be many readers who find in this vividly detailed book memories of their own youthful adventures, and telling questions about their mature life experiences.

—Paul R. Fleischman, M.D., Yale trained psychiatrist and author of *Wonder, when and why the world appears radiant* (2013), *An Ancient Path* (2008), *You can never speak up to often for the love of things* (2005), *The Buddha taught Non-Violence, not Pacifism* (2003) and many others.

Fly Free

A Memoir of Love, Loss and Walking the Path

Dami Roelse

NEW SARUM PRESS

UNITED KINGDOM

FLY FREE

First published by New Sarum Press September 2020
Copyright ©2020 Dami Roelse
Copyright ©2020 New Sarum Press

ISBN: 978-1-9162903-9-6

NEW SARUM PRESS
www.newsarumpress.com

Contents

Dedication

To my children Yaro, Quinn and Leela, who each carry on with a part of my life's quest for meaning, showing their own undaunted passion.

Born a Wanderer

The way-seeking mind is the conviction to fly like a bird in the air and enjoy our being in this vast world of freedom.

Suzuki Roshi[1]

I was born a seeker and wanderer. My baby wanderings took place out from under my blankets in frigid temperatures and out of my clothes as I stood naked on the tray of my highchair, my arms stretched out like the leafless tree outside the window with its branches reaching out. As a result, my parents tied me in my bed at night so I'd stay warm, tied me in my highchair so I'd be safe.

At three years of age I went in search of frogs my brother had told me about. We were living on the outskirts of a medieval city in the southwest of Holland. The inner city was surrounded by a bulwark and a moat, with sixteenth century city gates and bridges to allow entrance into the town. A police officer found me standing on the edge of one of those bridges peering into the dark water in the moat.

After that incident, my mother limited my outdoor range by staking me out in the backyard like a goat, one end of a long rope around my waist, the other end connected to a spike in the ground. Later I saw a picture of myself staked in this fashion, leaning my face into my four-year-old boy-cousin's ear. I was staked out. He was not. Was I whispering something about pulling up stakes together and exploring the world?

I don't remember if I felt imprisoned by my mother's safety measures. I do remember feeling my penchant for other places go up a notch when I listened to my first-grade teacher telling us about her

---

1. From a lecture in March 1996. This transcript is a retyping of the existing City Center transcript. It is not verbatim. The City Center transcript was entered onto disk by Jose Escobar, 1997. It was reformatted by Bill Redican (10/30/01). File name: 66-03-26-A: *The Way-Seeking Mind* (Not Verbatim).

travels to the mountains in Switzerland. She showed us a postcard of a landscape foreign to me. Green alpine meadows against craggy mountains covered with snow. The colors, the landscape called on me to explore. With six-year-old logic I decided I would become a teacher and thus travel to great places.

I was born into a large extended family with two sets of grandparents, thirty-some aunts and uncles and forty-seven cousins, who all lived on the island of Walcheren, in the province of Zeeland, Holland. Travel in my postwar family life meant taking a ferry to another island. Travel was cumbersome for my family as we didn't own a car in my younger years. On Sundays we bicycled along a canal road to another town to visit relatives. In summer we bicycled to the beach and gathered with aunts and uncles and cousins. Having such a large family meant that I always had playmates, always had adults looking after me, always had someone with whom to compare my academic abilities, my dresses with my cousins', my childhood manners with the grown-ups. It was a world where fitting in was important, and where exception was frowned upon.

To satisfy my curiosity, I read books. Fairy tales, stories with humanized Easter bunnies as the main characters, stories about children traveling with gypsy wagons. I discovered that there was more to the world than noisy family dinners, gatherings on the beach, cows in green meadows surrounded by dunes. There were deep green forests and tall snowcapped mountains somewhere. I discovered that there were mansions and luxurious rooms, large beds with fluffy covers. The bed I shared with my younger sister flailing around at night, felt crowded.

My curiosity about other worlds, and my observation of the world I was born into, fueled thoughts about my origins. Around age nine I started doubting that I belonged to the people who claimed to be my parents and decided that I must have been adopted. I didn't speak to anyone about my discovery. I'd lie in bed and imagine my "real" parents. I would see a graceful mother and handsome father who'd bend over, listen to me and kiss me goodnight before they went off to a dinner with other equally elegant people in an unknown place.

My fantasies didn't match reality. My mother's smooth face, red from leaning over the washing machine, her hands swollen, feeding one hot piece of wet clothing after another through the manual wringer, warned me that beauty can be lost. The first streaks of gray in her dark curls, the belly bulging as another baby would soon join the family told me that our family outings would be Sunday afternoon walks with the baby carriage. No faraway places for me. When do we begin hiding those deepest wishes from ourselves, those deepest wishes that make our heart jump?

I became a teenager, a dutiful older daughter, a good student, a fair athlete. I helped hang out the endless loads of laundry on cold misty afternoons, watched over younger siblings when my homework allowed me free time.

In turn my mother sewed much-desired dresses for me, and my father praised me over a sports game well played, a top grade earned. I knew the names of all the countries in Europe, their capitals and major rivers. I knew when the wild haired, club-wielding Batavi had come coursing down the Rhine on their rafts to occupy the Lowlands. I knew the names of kings and queens, who had lived in castles and palaces and killed each other for a seat on the throne.

The first break-down of my secure and comfortable world happened in my last year of high school. It was dead quiet in the classroom where gray light fell through high windows onto our heads, bent over the silky thin pages of Homer's Odyssey. There were more than a thousand pages of Greek script in an inch and a half thick volume, telling the stories of gods and men, war and love in a strict pentameter. The Odyssey was our staple for our senior year Greek studies. Five more months before state graduation exams. Hands were flipping pages in the dictionary to find the meaning of the Greek text as we prepped a piece for translation into Dutch for an oral test.

Noise in the distance was coming through an open top window. A tram sounded its squeaky, metal glide over the tracks, a megaphone shouted out instructions to the university crew team on the river. My mind wandered. What should I wear to the party on Saturday? I'd worn all my dresses, nothing new in the closet.

3

The teacher called my name to give the translation. I couldn't figure out the text. All the alphas and omegas were running together. Mister G.'s encouraging voice, "Try again, I know, you know what this means," sounded far away.

No, I didn't know what this meant. Why was I trying to make sense of a long-dead man's interpretation of the world of the gods? I didn't want to do this, be here. I felt I was drowning in text, words. Help! The silence of the class waiting for my answer slowly lowered its pressure bar. I couldn't take it anymore.

On impulse, I stood up; wordless my body walked out of the classroom. Ten pairs of eyes stared at me. Down the big staircase, out the front doors of the school. I ran to the bicycle shed and pedalled away along the river that ran in front of the school as hard as I could. Where should I go? I couldn't go home, Mom wouldn't understand. I didn't understand.

I cycled into the town to my brother's student apartment in a house in the historic market of Delft. The front door was open, I climbed the stairs to the second floor where his room was, looking out over the narrow canal at the back of the house. I opened the creaking door with the rattling handle. My brother wasn't there, he must have been in class or at the lab. All I could do was wait.

I sat there, cold, on the lumpy old red velvet couch. I stared at the sandwich makings on the coffee table, bread in a bag, a tub of margarine, some bologna on a plate with crumbs and a knife, a cup with the dredge of cold coffee. I wasn't hungry. The newspaper, half folded, hung over the arm of the couch, a sweater sleeve caught in its folds. The late, gray, morning light undressed the furniture's flaws, showed the unvacuumed rug. I kept my coat on, it was cold, I couldn't relax.

Finally, my brother came home from his lectures at the technical university. Surprised to see me, he asked what the matter was. Overwhelmed by my own mood, I sobbed. He listened to my outburst. "I hate Greek. I'm not smart enough to figure out the translations. I don't know how the others can remember all the conjugations, all the rules."

My brother made me a cup of tea. He called my parents.

4

I got a week off from school. "Stressed out," they said, "Some rest and sleep will make you feel better." I couldn't sleep. The exams loomed. I had to pass. Wim, my brother, passed last year.

I swallowed hard, and after a week went back to school.

I passed my exams, all thirteen subjects, even Homer, although I had not an inkling what the piece for interpretation was about. The state examiners, old men, must have liked the blue dress with white collar I was wearing (I'm told that "men like blue"), and gave me a good mark as I babbled about ancient gods and their influence on Greek society.

The second break-down of my carefully constructed world happened six months later. I had entered university to study biology. Biology would explain things, I thought. My high-school biology teacher, an older woman, graying hair in a bun at her neck, glasses hanging on a necklace, had told us stories of her time in an Indonesian concentration camp during World War II, while we dissected earthworms and frogs pinned on small wooden boards. She had survived awful things in a place faraway. A faraway place I could only dream of visiting. True to my first-grade conclusion about teaching and travel, I decided to study biology and become a biology teacher.

I attended morning lectures in the dark wood-paneled halls of the old university of Utrecht. My mind wandered to scholars long ago, scholars raised in the church. What was the basis for their knowledge? The bible, or observation and experiment?

Afternoon labs were held in light-filled concrete buildings among new high-rises on the outskirts of the city. Could modern science propel me into the world of scientific truth?

I spent evenings at the sorority house, serving senior students, becoming a freshman clone of these future well-to-do eligible women. But I didn't quite fit the pattern: my hosiery always had runs, my pearls were fake, and my cashmere sweater itched so much that I wanted to scratch. What was I doing there?

At the lab we studied the cell structures of sea-urchins, a life-form that first appeared on earth 450 million years ago. The cell slices on the glass plates under the lens of the microscope became beautiful abstract paintings, as the purple dye injected for observation distributed itself throughout the cell membrane in swirling colors, from lavender to deep purple. The cell slice was a creature dismembered and used for parts.

I diligently drew the lines, the parts, named them and wrote them down in my lab notes. Tedious, categorising work. Was this going to explain life, I wondered.

After the lab session I rode my bicycle back into the old part of the university town. The question, *What is life about, what is the reason for living?* repeated itself with each push of the pedal.

I attended organic chemistry lectures. Two hundred students sat on long wooden benches—remnants of the days when the academic class was made up of priests. My eyes traveled across a blackboard the width of the lecture hall. I stared at a blur of symbols on the board. Everyone around me seemed attentive, writing furiously. *What did it all mean?*

Class over, I bicycled to my student rooms, climbed the three flights of stairs to my attic apartment. The landlady looked at me questioningly from the second landing. I wasn't going to make small talk. I reached the top storey, with its window looking out over the red roof tiles, and yellowed wallpaper smelling of dank dust. The big brown desk with the coursework book sat in the corner, reminding me of the organic chemistry test I had to take. *I would never get this.* I packed my weekend bag, to take the train home to my parents' house. I didn't want this course of study. I didn't want to stay on here.

I stayed at my parents' house, dropped out of university. I spent the long dark winter nights, the gloomy days, in my little room on the second floor. My mother's eyes were red from crying over me. I felt so alone. She didn't understand what the matter with me was. I didn't want to be there, I didn't want to be anywhere. I couldn't do what was expected of me. I wanted to disappear.

Through the window of my room, I watched icy drops slowly slide off the dark, naked tree branches, cold, like the frozen thoughts in my mind. Questions. I had nothing but questions about life.

I didn't believe my mother's religion. Be good so you can go to heaven after it's all over? Why not get the reward while living?

I couldn't accept my father's atheism either. He said we were here, born for no reason to die at some point. That was it? Why was he working so hard then? Why did he care? There must be a reason for living. Why was it all so hard? I didn't belong here, I wanted to die.

I didn't die. I watched the winter sun touch the red roof tiles. The light bouncing back against the icy drops on the tree branch spelled beauty. Then I thought, *If there is beauty, there must be a reason for living.* I was tired of feeling depressed and dejected. I would live and find out what life was all about.

Journey of Love

Chapter 1

Irecognize him. I've met him once before at a relationship workshop. He attended the workshop with a woman. I was with a man.
Standing here at the big country-wedding of my best friend, Doyle is
taller than anyone. He wears a crown made of gold paper on his dark
curly hair, a gift from the children's craft table; and a vest made of colorful, old dress ties, his personal fashion statement above worn jeans
with red suspenders. He's standing a short distance from me, arms
crossed over his chest, observing the ceremony.

The bride, dressed in a gauzy flowing dress, summer flowers
crowning her long hair, and the groom, dressed in a silk shirt, long
hair tied up with a headband, face each other while a friend ordained
by an online church, the Church of Light, asks them to speak their
vows. They're signing a contract of property ownership, not a marriage contract. Like so many who've moved to the country, trying to
escape what they call "the System", they're making their own rules
around cohabiting and ownership. They are living off the grid, on
land far away from town, accessible only by dirt roads and four-wheel
drive vehicles. Still the system is extending its legal tentacles with a
partnership contract into my friends' home, built without a building
permit and on the county's red-tag (illegal) list. For the purposes of
the law they're sharing assets, red-tagged or not. The words, *I see
God in you, you see God in me* [2] are not a password for overruling society's laws. These words remind me of another gathering at an ashram in India, where I, along with other young white-clad Westerners,
expressed my devotion to the master, the guru with powers beyond
the powers of society—or at least I thought so.

India, so far away. That search for meaning and for another society to belong to seems a lifetime away—more than the actual nine
years ago.

---

2. A reference to the extended meaning of the Indian greeting, *Namaste*.

* * *

Alan, my American boyfriend, and I had been traveling for almost a year around India looking for teachings and mind-expanding methods to get a glimpse of what Buddhists and Hindus called enlightenment[3], a state of being where you've overcome all suffering and you no longer accumulate negative karma. I believed it to be a state of eternal happiness. After a year of attending meditation courses, trying drugs and watching Indian gurus bestow their blessings on their devotees, we were tired of spiritual seeking, and cynical about the glamour of the guru scene. A travel companion and friend had encouraged us to try one more time and go see what they referred to as a "man in a blanket".

It had been a cool morning. Alan and I had taken the taxi from Nainital to Kainchi, where Neem Karoli's ashram was; the ashram Ram Dass[4] had told us about when we met him in Delhi nine months earlier on our travels. On this visit to the ashram we wanted to attend our first morning *darshan*[5]— the time the guru meets with his devotees— and find out more about this supposed holy man. On our first attempt to enter the compound Mahara-ji had waved his hands calling a loud *Jao!* ("Go away!"). I learned later that he said this to most visitors.

3. Enlightenment: The eastern philosophical concept of enlightenment as discussed in this book refers to a state of awakening, or insight. Some say that this can only be achieved by seekers and practitioners of certain meditation practices, as exemplified by Gautama Buddha, who allegedly achieved the awakened state sitting under a Bodhi tree in India. The state of enlightenment is often described as liberation from suffering, through an understanding of the arising and ceasing of craving and a non-attachment to emotions and thoughts as they arise and pass. Even though the literature is full of stories about the enlightened ones—those who have attained buddhahood —I believe that few actually reach this state in their lifetime, but I have not ascertained this by impartial investigation.
4. Ram Dass: Richard Alpert, a Harvard psychology professor turned spiritual seeker, teacher and author of *Be Here Now*, published in 1971.
5. *Darshan*: from the Sanskrit word, to see, referring to a holy person or religious statue/object.

Nevertheless we had returned, and I was sitting at Mahara-ji's feet in the front row of devotees, Indian and Western, surrounding his dais. We watched the coming and going of Indian and Western people handing Mahara-ji fruits or flowers, which he tolerated with a wave of his hand, a sideways shake of his head in the *achcha* (all is good) motion. Leaning on his elbow, he looked around the group of people in front of him. I wondered what would happen here: would he speak? Would someone translate? After a few devotees talked to him quietly, he suddenly looked at me, bald head tilted, wrinkly face smiling.

"You come from Holland?" he said in English and winked. How did he know this? I had told no one. Somebody from the hotel in Nainital must have told him. "What's your name?"

"Nellie."

"No, no." He shook his head up and down, which is the Indian way of indicating *no*. He looked at me again and picked up a deep pink flower from a bunch of the offerings of the day. He gently laid the flower on my head, and said,"Damayanti".[6] Then he looked at the surrounding people.

"Sing, *Aarti,*[7] sing!" he commanded.

The group of Westerners and Indians around the dais got up and started singing. The lilt and pull of the sound melted the wall of disappointment in my heart—a disappointment that left me feeling lost over not finding answers after almost a year of traveling in India. I started to cry—I couldn't stop myself. I closed my eyes, cried and listened to the music. My whole body relaxed as the tears rolled down my cheeks, I lost all sense of reality around me, and floated in a dream-like state. Later Alan told me I'd sat there for two hours unmoving, oblivious of what was going on around me as I traveled in my mind.

In my mind I saw shapes of people, light-beings. I followed them and there were what looked like lit-up cities, light-shows everywhere. I heard sounds of flutes, and violins. I felt as if I knew everything that had been and would be. The shapes of beings and buildings had

6. The princess in the famous Indian love story, *Nala and Damayanti*, discussed in more detail further on.

7. *Aarti* is a Hindu ritual of waving lights and chanting before a picture or statue of a deity or holy person.

morphed into floating angels and fluid mountain-like forms, all connected in one sea of vibrating energy. I was one with the energy. I was just energy.

That was bliss.

Later, devotees gathered again after lunch and sat at Mahara-ji's feet in a little room. I sat close to him. He looked at me, head tilted, smiling. I didn't know why, but I wanted to touch the soles of his feet. I felt love, waves of love open inside me. I fell into that love completely and without resistance.

I was high on love.

The next day, back in the village where Alan and I were staying, I wandered around small shops looking for English books to read. I saw a stack of colorful comic books, magazines printed with images of Hindu gods and goddesses, billed as Indian classics for children. A title caught my attention: *Nala and Damayanti*. Who was this person Damayanti? And why had Mahara-ji given me that name? I bought the little comic book, looked at the pictures and read the story, a re-telling of a story from the *Mahabharata*, a Sanskrit epic of ancient India. Damayanti was a beautiful princess who was wooed by a prince, Nala, from a foreign country. I realized if I spelled Alan's name backwards it read Nala. Did this story apply to me? Did Mahara-ji know what would happen in my life? The story talked of Damayanti's noble character and how her prince fell prey to gambling and lost everything he had. Ashamed, the prince left his wife. Damayanti was inconsolable and pined away waiting for her husband to return. After many adventures and a deep inner change, Nala eventually found his bride again, and they lived happily ever after. An Indian fairy tale. Would it hold truth for me? Was I going to have a difficult, but long-lasting love?

* * *

From my vantage point at the wedding site I watch the bride and groom embrace and kiss. Will theirs be a long-lasting love? I see Doyle walk up to them and hug them as newlyweds. Why do I feel so attracted to him? How will the love story of Nala and Damayanti play out for me?

* * *

After that Himalayan ashram visit, I followed Alan from India via Holland to Northern California where we joined other hippies living a free and simple life in the country. But paradise in the California countryside didn't last. Economic reality set in for us. We had to find work, a place to live for the winter. Our little orange travel tent set up in a meadow wouldn't do. What about finding bliss? Through the spiritual grapevine, I heard that Mahara-ji had left his body in September 1973. I wanted to go to New York and sit with Ram Dass. I felt I'd made a mistake, should have gone back to India instead of going to America. The thought depressed me. Would I find inner peace by myself? Ram Dass had sent me a letter with a strand of Mahara-ji's blanket. I carried it in a pouch around my neck, but I didn't know how to find bliss and universal connectedness in the garden of a homestead.

Winter in a small logging town on the West Coast of America was a wet affair—90 inches of rain. Hankering back to the freedom we had had when we traveled, we tried to keep some habits of an Indian way of living alive in our own life: we had a low dais for a couch; we ate vegetarian food, and we practiced the meditation we had learned at a Vipassana[8] meditation retreat. We tried to keep our equanimity as our money dwindled and jobs were nonexistent. Alan smoked weed to stay mellow. I wrote to a friend in Holland about our situation; she responded by sending money. We decided to accept the money—use it for spiritual practice and go to a retreat center for a month. We learned about a retreat center in Colorado. It wasn't a Vipassana retreat, but it should mean some progress toward enlightenment. Unemployed, we escaped joblessness and spent a month at a retreat site in Colorado with Chogyam Trungpa, a Tibetan lama with a large western following.

I sat, and my mind was distracted. After I ran through a review in my mind of the journey across snowy passes to get here, after processing the ins and outs of the retreat site and comparing its workings with the Vipassana retreat center in India where we had taken our

---

8. Vipassana: I was first introduced to Vipassana meditation by Mr Goenka, a Burmese businessman who taught his first courses in India in 1970. directed by his Burmese teacher Sayagyi U Ba Khin. Goenka became a popular teacher with westerners traveling in India in the early seventies.

first meditation course with Mr. Goenka[9], all that had popped up in my mind were thoughts about babies. Did I want a baby? No, I wanted to become enlightened. Relentlessly the thoughts kept coming like biological clockwork. Sitting meditation, walking meditation, sitting meditation. I still thought about babies. Breaks for food and sleep were a distraction. After a month I had no clarity on the baby subject.

After the retreat was over and we were on our way home, I talked to Alan about what had been going through my head.

"No, not now, no babies, maybe never," was his answer.

Back in our country rental home, we found work, we gardened. I baked bread, started a food coop. Morning and evening I sat before my home-made altar with pictures of Mahara-ji and Goenka. What did they want me to do? Live a householder's life, of making money and raising a family, or devote myself solely to my spiritual practice?

Four months later, I made up my mind, no babies, I wanted to follow the spiritual path, whatever that would be.

A week later I found out I was pregnant.

We had a baby son and named him Ya⁻ro Ram. This was a personal spelling of the yarrow herb which is used with the I-Ching[10], and Ram,[11] in honor of the beginnings of our spiritual practice started in India. Divination aside, Ya⁻ro changed the course of our life dramatically.

Work and money became even more important. Alan changed. He cut off his hair, wore Red Wing work boots, checkered flannel shirts, straight out of a logging magazine. He drove a big, gas guzzling truck. Started a woodworking business. We had trouble making ends meet. We argued. Frustrated with the realities of starting a business from scratch, Alan was easily angered. He drank beer and smoked

---

9. There were over 200 meditation centers based on his teachings by the time of his death in 2013.

10. *I-Ching* or *Book of Changes* is a Chinese text at least 3,000 years old. While it is used for purposes of divination, its commentary is based on philosophical, cosmological and cultural tenets that have influenced thought and expression globally.

11. Ram is a Sanskrit word for God, used in daily life and in chants, mantras and scriptures throughout India.

reefers with friends. I didn't know this American man anymore. As Alan drifted away from the spiritual habits we had adopted on our travels, I tried to hang on to a taste of the bliss I experienced in India by maintaining a practice of meditation and chanting. I chanted my son to sleep singing *kirtan*[12], a faraway cry from my guru and the bliss I had experienced there.

I let my mind circle back to Mahara-ji's name for me and that Indian fairy tale. In the story of Damayanti and Nala, as the *Mahabharata*[13] tells it, Nala travels to a foreign country to find his Queen. So he did. Maybe Alan didn't go to Europe to find a queen, but he found me. When Nala returns to his kingdom he gambles with a friend for entertainment. Alan joined forces with a friend in the wood-working business. We invested all our money in making redwood hot tubs, a gamble of sorts. King Nala slowly gambles his riches away to the friend, who mercilessly throws Nala and Damayanti out of the kingdom, taking over as King himself. Alan and his friend's business did not bring in enough money. The friend liked a more leisurely life, not the hard work necessary to make a new business thrive. We were struggling to make ends meet for our small family in our rented forest home. Had fate thrown us into this forest, stone broke?

In the story, Nala is cast into the forest with Damayanti. Ashamed of what has happened to him, he leaves her in the night. Here we were, living in a forest. We fought over money. Alan was unwilling to accept help from his parents. He escaped in daily marijuana smoke. I didn't want to change reality with drugs. I wanted to feel bliss through love. I wanted Alan to deal with his escape into drugs. Like the royal couple in the story, we separated. Had Mahara-ji foreseen all this when he gave me my name? More than ever, I wanted to sit at his feet and lose myself in waves of love. Could I reach Mahara-ji in his Maha-samadhi, his state of blissful energy?

I remembered how, in the story, Damayanti travels to her country to wait for Nala. After Alan and I separated, I traveled to the Old

12. *Kirtan* is the singing or chanting of devotional hymns or chants, often in Sanskrit or more modern Indian languages

13. The *Mahabharata* is an ancient Indian scriptural epic that contains the famous *Bhagavad Gita*.

Country, to Holland, with my two-year-old son. My parents wanted me to stay in Holland, start a new life close to family. Help me raise my son. "No, I have to go back," I told them, "I'll see if we can make it work between us." I could see the worry in their eyes over me in that big, big country so far away. I went back and tried to be with Alan again, we didn't make it. Divorce and a two-year-old boy. How enlightened was I going to be?

* * *

As I'm watching the wedding celebrations unfold in front of me, I wonder if love will return to my life. No guru, no husband. All I have is a meditation practice and the memory of a guru who is no longer alive. After my divorce from Alan I found a dome where I could live rent-free, in exchange for caretaking a forty-acre property. It was close to where Alan was living, so Yaro could go back and forth between parents. Others joined me on the land, and we lived communally, hippies in the country. We added teepees and yurts and worked for peace and nuclear disarmament. We chanted in a circle on Sundays. We started a school for the children, who carried names such as Parsley, Sage, Cinnamon, Skye, River, and Yaro. We gardened and worked in the local businesses; we started our own businesses and made ends meet. We were optimistic—an optimism that came from believing that we could create a New Age, new selves.

We processed our childhood neuroses in New Age workshops. Personal growth was the order of the day. We did primal scream therapy, sat Zazen, Transcendental Meditation, and made love in the fields. We believed that we could undo all the parental and societal damage. We believed that we could be new people, have open, unconditional loving relationships with our children—children who could talk about their feelings and be kind to one another.

We thought we could be free from the System.

It had been nine years since I found Mahara-ji. I had wanted to stay at the ashram, float around in love and bliss, but Mahara-ji sent me away.

"*Jao!* Go! Go to the West, go do your work!" he had said and

18

waved his hand in dismissal. What work it was, I didn't know.

Watching my friends sing songs of Dervish origin and doing middle eastern dances, I fumble with my necklace that holds the strand of Mahara-ji's blanket. I've been meditating, doing yoga, and reading spiritual books, but haven't figured out what my "work" is, aside from trying to attain the elusive state of enlightenment. I didn't know what enlightenment was, but in reading about it I made my assumption that it was an imperturbable state of happiness you could attain by practicing meditation, yoga and certain ways of living. I read about different ways to attain this state. I meditate, but not enough, I work, odd jobs to keep my head above water, but am not selfless about it, and relationships haven't worked out. No, I haven't found my path yet.

I walk away from the ceremony up to the grassy hillock where Doyle is standing under the oak trees freshly in leaf, with mountains undulating all around.

"Hi Doyle, do you remember me?"

"Yes." He turns to me, his green-gray eyes with long dark lashes catch my gaze.

I don't hear what he is saying next. I hear his voice, but I'm distracted by what's happening in my field of vision. It's a clear day, with an unbroken blue sky, and yet, a bright light is coming from nowhere, creating illumination all around him. The light draws me in and I hear words in my head: *You will marry this man.* Light, voices. I'm seeing light, hearing voices. I'm not stoned, I'm not crazy, what's happening to me? Does Doyle hear it also? He stands in front of me talking, curly hair blowing around in the breeze.

Guitar music and songs bring me back to the reality of the country wedding.

"I'm sorry, I got distracted. How'd you end up at this wedding?" I ask.

"I came with Susan, a long-time friend of the bride."

"Ah, yes, you were with her a few months ago at the relationship workshop." I wonder if they're in a relationship. Susan is a friend of the workshop leaders, Carol and Peter. Almost twenty years my elders, Carol and Peter are serious practitioners of Buddhist meditation. They have practiced at the San Francisco Zen Center. Carol has done a winter-long retreat where she practiced meditation instead of sleeping at night. I admired the discipline and stoicism in her practice. They are close friends with the other people on the land I'm living on. Many of the wedding guests, including the bride, lived in a commune in Willits, California, a few years back.

"Are you still living in Ashland? I live in a dome a few miles from here with a bunch of people; if you ever need a place to stay, you're welcome to stop in, there's lots of room."

"Thank you, yes I still live in Ashland, I might do that when I go south to visit my kids in San Diego. It's a long trek from Ashland to San Diego and it would be nice to take a break from driving." Doyle turns toward where the music is coming from. "Let's dance."

Chapter 2

It's late afternoon on a warm August day and living on the land means gardening, watering and letting whatever cool air there is come in through the open doors to the deck of the 32-foot diameter dome-home. A faded red VW bug comes up the long driveway that winds through the woods. I go out on the high deck doubling as a carport to see who's coming. Doyle parks close to the deck, gets out and calls up.

"You're home. Is it OK if I stop in?"

"Of course, just walk around up the hill to the back door." I'm surprised, but excited to see him again. I hadn't expected to see him so soon. A nervous tingling flushes my skin as I walk inside to open the back door for him. What will happen now that he's here? His large torso straightens up in the open space of the large dome.

"What a great space you have here," Doyle says as he looks up at the dome's structure of cork-covered triangles mixed with plexiglass ones to let in light on all sides. "Finally, a space I fit in."

"Yes, you won't bump your head here. I like the openness of the space, the plexiglass triangles let me look up at the sky. The dark cork makes it seem like a night sky in the evening when the stars are out. This dome isn't mine you know, I'm caretaking it for a friend who lives in LA" I explain.

"Do you have time for a visitor? I'm sorry I didn't let you know I was coming, but I don't have your phone number. I'm traveling south to drop off this car for my son."

"Yes, I have time for a visit. I just dropped off my son with his father in the village. I have a week without him."

"Are the other people who live in the teepee and the yurt around?" Doyle is referring to the land partners who share the forty acres with me.

"Yes, actually we have plans to go swimming in the river in a

21

while. It's hot today. Do you want to go?"

"Absolutely, I can use a cool-down." Doyle smiles, wiping the beads of sweat away from his dark, curly sideburns.

We swim, we talk, we meet other local friends at the river. Doyle seems intelligent, social and easy-going. As evening sets in we drive back to the dome, make a communal dinner, drink beer, have a smoke. When the land partners drift off to their sleeping quarters, Doyle and I stay up, sitting outside on the large balcony overlooking the gardens below. Doyle's presence so near makes my skin buzz. Do I care what he thinks about me? Does he have any other intentions than a mid-way stop on this visit?

"Isn't it a lovely evening?" I sigh feeling expansive and free from responsibilities. "I don't have to work this week, so I can do whatever I want."

"Do you feel like taking a trip?" Doyle asks.

"A trip where?" I'm up for an adventure.

"My drive south would be much more fun with company, we can take the coast road, take a few extra days and stay on the beaches."

"Sounds enticing. I never do anything on the spur of the moment, but I really have nothing that holds me here this week." I feel my spine straighten with anticipation and sit up in my chair while my thoughts flit around the excitement of adventure. What am I thinking, though, taking off with this man? A man I'm attracted to. I don't know if he has a girlfriend. I'm a free person, but that doesn't mean he is. But we're adults, we can make our own decisions. If he wants me along, why not?

"How are you coming back?" Despite the beer and the smoke, there is still a practical part of me ticking.

"I'm gonna stay a few days with my kids and then fly back." His plan is set.

"I don't have that much time, but if you drop me off in Santa Monica with Ron, the owner of this land, he'll put me on a plane back. I visit with him every so often to talk about what he wants done here. I can make it a check-in visit." I feel smart about my solution, turn to Doyle with a smile and lay back in my chair. Doyle nods.

"Good solution."

We raise our beer bottles and clink. Our adventure has begun.

We're driving, talking endlessly, filling each other in about our lives. The wind is blowing in from the Pacific Ocean through the rolled-down windows; life is all smiles. It feels good to leave the stressful exchanges with my ex over our four-year-old son behind and pretend I'm a free woman. Doyle and I share our woes of kids and ex-partners, our dream of living in community, working creatively. We buy food and make sandwiches sitting on a dune, or on stones by the ocean. Doyle shows me his former home, a houseboat in Point Reyes, California, and introduces me to his friends there. Once we're south of San Francisco we sleep on the beaches with the waves crashing at our feet, dew on our faces—and why wouldn't we share the sleeping bag?

Four days later, with sand in every crevice, wrinkled clothes and in need of a shower, Doyle drops me off at Ron's house. We say our goodbyes, no promises, just a *see you later.* We had a great time, an adult fling, but I'm still smiling. After a brief visit with Ron, clean, in respectable travel clothes, and an assignment for arranging a kitchen remodel in the dome, I board the plane back to my life up North, a life of idealism, work, motherhood and spiritual seeking. As Mahara-ji had said, *Go home, go do your work.*

I look out of the airplane window, into the empty clear blue. What is my work? A failed first marriage, an open-ended search for meaning, a place far away from my home country. Where and how do I belong? I'm not a whole lot further in figuring it all out since that bus ride in Afghanistan in the fall of 1971. I remember finding what felt like a fateful blue book, *Be Here Now,*[14] that reverberated so deeply with the quest I was on. The plane vibrates, shakes; it feels a bit like the bus, where the blue book that led me to Mahara-ji fell in my lap. I close my eyes and let the images and memories from the past take me back.

* * *

---

14. *Be Here Now* by Ram Dass, 1971, published by Lama Foundation.

The engine of the bus was revving, shaking the bus. A jerk, a shriek above the din of road noise and chickens, and the bus taking us from Herat to Kandahar in Afghanistan came to a clunky stop. Alan, sleeping with his heavy head slumped against my shoulder, woke up and lifted his head. My shoulder felt wet from his sweat.

"What's going on?" Alan's voice sounded startled. Turbaned Afghans hanging on to the back of the bus jumped off, making the bus bounce as they did so. The hot, dry wind coming over the empty, beige desert blew through the open window and made my back stick to the plastic seat.

"I don't know, I guess the bus broke down." The last words caught—the dry dust mixed with the acrid exhaust had tightened my throat—and I coughed to clear it.

"It may be more than nine hours to get to Kandahar today." Alan leaned forward to stretch and get the kinks out of his back.

The bus driver got out, gesturing and speaking rapid Dari, pointing at the engine. He opened the hood and climbed underneath, while everyone else got out and squatted down on the dirt by the side of the road.

"We might as well get out for a while. Is there any water?" Alan stood up and nudged me to get up.

Another long-haired American across the aisle behind us got up too, grabbed a book with a blue cover while greeting us.

"Hey man, what's happening?" The meaningless international greeting took on actual meaning at that moment. We were on a lonely road in the Afghan desert. I always thought desert meant sand dunes, but this was just beige, bare dirt with an occasional bush and tree. *Pomegranate trees*, someone said. I had never seen one before.

"I'm cool, but the bus isn't," Alan answered.

"I'm Jerry, you wanna share a smoke?" The American pulled the strap of his hemp bag over his head and shoulder, hanging it on the beads dancing in the opening of his Afghan shirt. He pulled his long hair up from under the bag strap and tied his hair in a knot.

We stepped out of the bus and joined the lineup on the side of the road. Some Afghans had wandered south toward a settlement I could see in the distance, taking their chickens and bundles with them. There was no traffic, just a long and winding road stretching northwest to southeast. What if the bus driver couldn't fix the problem? Nobody seemed concerned. Would we all sleep on the bus until somebody came to fix it?

Jerry started talking again, holding out the book with the blue cover. "You've got to read this! It's a far-out story." Jerry handed it to me.

"What's it about?" I asked, while Alan pulled out some papers and tobacco as a contribution to the "smoke".

"Drugs and enlightenment," Jerry answered.

I stared at the square blue book in my hands. On the blue cover a twelve-point star was drawn in white. White lines crisscrossing from each point to the opposite point in a circle forming a web. The words *BE HERE NOW HERE BE NOW BE NOW HERE NOW BE HERE NOW BE HERE NOW* surrounded the circle. The word *REMEMBER* was printed on all four sides of the cover, creating a mandala.

"Is it a manual on how to get high?" I had met enough Americans by now on this trip overland from Amsterdam to know that they liked their drugs.

"No, actually, the opposite." He grinned with the lightheartedness of a man loving life.

"Is it about mandalas?" I asked again. Maybe it was about meditation, focusing on a mandala. I was curious about meditation. When I had announced to my family that Alan and I would to travel to India, I hadn't told them I wanted to explore different spiritual practices. My father would have smirked, my mother would have warned me to be careful. I had told them I wanted to visit my friend Wim, who was studying music in Delhi, and that I wanted to explore Indian theatre.

"No, it's about a holy man who can do amazing stuff."

"So it's not about drugs?" I said. Jerry handed Alan a chunk of dark brown hashish. Alan crumbled it on the tobacco and rolled the joint. The Afghans looked on. Were we going to share this joint with everyone?

"Yes, and no. This guy gave 900 micrograms of LSD to a holy man.

It didn't change the holy man. Can you believe it? *900µg!"* A shake of his head loosens his long hair again. More hot air coming my way.

I opened the cover of the book with the word *REMEMBER* on four sides. On the first page the face of a gray-bearded Indian man with a white paste marking on his forehead, a checkered blanket around his shoulders, stared at me, a finger raised. Remember, what? The next page showed me a picture of a kneeling Indian God-man in a loincloth with a monkey face and a lion's tail, hands folded in prayer mode. Below it the words: *Lama Foundation, 1971, year of the earth monkey.* It was October 1971 as we were traversing the desert. The book must have just been published. The next pages showed me the monkey-human-god figure upright on the left page ripping his chest open, blood dripping down, revealing two figures in the place of his heart. *Pretty far-out art, can't be real.* On the page to the right another circular form, a labyrinth with a Sanskrit *OM* sign in the center, the words *JOURNEY* at the top, *THE TRANSFORMATION* at the bottom of the labyrinth. At the bottom of the page it said: *Dr. Richard Alpert, PhD, into Baba Ram Dass.* I didn't know this guy, maybe Alan would.

"Al, do you know Richard Alpert, aka Ram Dass?" I waved the book at him.

"Yeah, I've heard of him. He introduced the world to mescaline and LSD. I have some with me." *Now he tells me!* I thought. What if they had searched our packs in Turkey or Iran? Visions of jail time on the border of Turkey and Iran floated through my mind. I remembered how scary the border crossing had been, even without knowing we were carrying drugs.

However, this was Afghanistan and drugs didn't seem to be a problem. Alan lit the joint and took a drag. The Afghans smiled. One of them broke open a round dark red fruit and handed us each a piece, its red seeds shining inside the yellow flesh. Was this an invitation to trade joint for juicy fruit? I took my very first juicy bite of the pomegranate, for that's what this desert fruit was, tasting its sweet-tart flavor.

"Delicious." I smiled approvingly at the Afghans.

"Are you going to share your joint with them?" I asked Alan

as Jerry took a drag, held his breath and let the smoke sink into his lungs. Jerry handed the joint to me, but I declined. I preferred not to get high on the road. After an unpleasant experience of being grabbed in a bazaar, I didn't want another encounter with male dominance and needed to have my wits about me. The only women I had seen so far were shrouded in their burkas, moving stealthily along the walls of village compounds. I didn't know what Afghans thought about women smoking, but assumed the women didn't have much freedom. I wanted to know if we would get to Herat today. What would happen with the bus? There were tools spread out on the ground, several men had their heads under the hood. It looked like it would take a while.

"Call me when there's action." I stood up, glad to stretch my legs. I hadn't mastered squatting like the Afghans yet. "I will take a little walk. Find some shade while you guys have your smoke." Alan and Jerry were passing the joint back and forth between them and the Afghans. Even though it was October the hot midday sun felt relentless on my scalp through my fine blond hair. I wasn't wearing a burka for protection either. I took the book with me.

The empty desert spread out in front of me. I wandered south. All there was, was heat, dryness, the open sky shimmering above the exposed empty landscape. *People lived here in this hole of nothingness. What a life! I better find some shade, or I'll get too thirsty*, I thought. *We only have one canteen of water each. I don't know when we'll get more.*

I found some dappled shade under a sparsely leafed tree and sat down to read the blue book. I read about this guy Richard Alpert, renamed Ram Dass, and how he found what he was looking for in life as he devoted himself to his guru. *I'm so ordinary*, I thought, *I'll never find a guru*. Sweat beads dripped down my neck. The place was a slow boil. It was so quiet, I could just drift off into nothingness. What if I was all alone in the desert?

"Hey, wake up!" An anxious voice pierced the silence. Where was I?

"The bus is leaving, hurry!" It was Alan. I opened my dust-encrusted eyes. My neck hurt, slumped against the rough trunk of the tree. I remembered: empty desert, bus broken.

"Give me a moment."

"There is no moment, do you want to be stuck out here?" He sounded angry now.

"Oh, OK, won't they wait for us?" I heard engine noise in the distance.

"What do I know? Afghans do what they want. They don't care about us." Alan now sounded worried. I was up and able to move my legs. "Let's run!" He grabbed my arm and pulled me along, dust flying. I dropped the book, reached for it.

"Just leave it!" Alan commanded.

"No, it isn't mine." Useless retort in the situation. I grabbed the book.

Alan started yelling at the top of his lungs. "Wait, don't go!" Wait!" The bus noise got louder. Could they even hear us?

We ran. The noise got louder. I heard laughing. Were they laughing at us? Were they going to leave us behind and laugh about sticking one to the foreigners? I saw movement in front of the bus, a person, shirt flapping, arms waving wildly. What was this guy doing? I ran faster, my hot breath scraping my dry throat.

Then I saw who it was. Jerry, it was Jerry jumping up and down in front of the bus, arms flailing, water bottle in hand.

"Goddamn, Jerry's blessing the bus, smart guy!" Alan sighed and slowed down a bit, letting my arm go. "Wouldn't you know, this crazy dude comes through?" As we came closer, we saw that Jerry was sprinkling the last of his drinking water on the engine compartment. The Afghans were laughing, hitting the side of the bus, slapping Jerry on the shoulder. They were thanking him for his ritual. The bus would be fine now. Everyone climbed in. Some climbed on top of the bus where they sat among the luggage. We had never asked, but I assumed that those were the cheaper tickets. Out of breath, we slid in our seats, Jerry behind us again with a wide grin. The bus started moving.

Alan turned to Jerry. "Thanks for saving our butt, man, I wouldn't have wanted to be stuck without my pack in that sandbox."

"Hey, no sweat, what a kick." Jerry, with bloodshot stoner eyes, grinned from ear to ear.

"Let's blame this," I added, waving the blue book. "Reading it, took me far out." My pun was wasted.

"Good, we didn't get stuck there, in Far-Out Land. At least we're on our way to Delhi again," Alan added.

"You guys going to Delhi?"

"Yeah man, we have enough money for almost a year. What about you?" Alan turned around.

"I don't know, I'm avoiding the draft. Don't know if I can go back until things die down in Vietnam." Jerry shrugged his shoulders and let out a sigh.

"Oh wow, you just left the country without signing up?" Alan said. "I was lucky in the lottery, didn't get drafted. Still, what a mess at home, eh?"

"What are you going to do in Afghanistan?" I asked him.

"Score some hashish and travel on to where it'll be warm. Goa's warm and cheap in the winter; will make this last longer." Jerry patted the bulging travel pouch hidden under the front of his shirt.

"Is that all? Just hang out?" I wrinkled my nose as I tried on this notion while my goal-oriented Calvinistic upbringing oozed out in my voice.

"Just read the book, woman. There isn't a lot more to do in life." Jerry shook his head in a patient, fatherly motion.

I had my questions about what to do with my life. I thought I had to do something, something meaningful. Doing the expected thing of getting a job after graduating from the university didn't appeal. Teaching? What was there to teach, if I didn't know what life was about? My degree was in Dutch language and literature. Literature had only added to my questions. Theater? At least that allowed for posing questions on the stage.

"Does this guy Alpert figure out what's important?" I had to ask.

"Oh, yeah, he's a researcher, can't help himself. I can figure it out without doing the research, eh, eh!" Jerry laughed.

The image of propping my eye over a microscope in the lab at my university appeared in my mind. "I don't think it's that simple,"

I retorted. "People have been debating the reason for living since the ancient Greeks and probably before that. Religion has made a mess of it all, unless you like giving up control to some people who interpret the scriptures for you." I turned towards him in my seat to give emphasis to my statement.

"That's exactly it, nobody really knows. When I'm high at least it feels like I know what's going on. This guy Alpert found that out too. Then he gave up his control to this holy man. Now he's high from meditation or something. You should read the stories about this guy, Mahara-ji. He can be in two places at once. He can change shape. Can you believe that? What a trip!" Jerry let out his fascination with the magical.

"I'm not so sure that getting high is the way to get answers. Do you remember what you thought while you were high?" The word *REMEMBER* on the page of the book took on a new meaning. Maybe there was more to remembering than recalling thoughts and events, maybe there was another dimension of "memory".

"Can I look at the book again?" Now I wanted to know more about this story.

* * *

As I recall what had happened in Afghanistan, my body shakes in the seat. The plane jerks as it gets ready for landing, shaking me out of my reverie. I'm in a plane approaching San Francisco, not in a bus in Afghanistan. Such a short flight, now I still have the bus ride up north back home. Home? What is home for me? Here I am, living in a strange country, in a dome surrounded by people who want to explore altered realities, who believe in psychic phenomena, who have left the status quo behind, and who want to live the simple life of living off the land in cooperation with others. It all sounds so good, but I can't escape my need for order and security, even if I get high at times, even if I go on a weeklong adventure with a relative stranger. I haven't found the bliss I experienced with Mahara-ji. What is the work Mahara-ji wants me to do? I know how to work hard, but where do I put that work energy?

"Mom, I have a new hammer!" I hear my four-year-old son's excited voice as he tumbles out of his father's truck. My arm around his lean muscular body, bones and muscle all reaching for new heights, I reach with the other hand for the bag my ex hands me.

"Good week?" I ask, while my son wriggles out of my embrace, ready to try his new hammer on some wood laying by the back door.

"Yes, he's fine, just had a run in with Laura over leaving mud in the house."

Damn the new woman. Why does a strange grown-up have to raise my child?

"I'm sure I'll hear about it tonight. It always comes out the first night he's back."

At dinner Yaro is hanging crooked on his chair, poking his fingers in a slice of bread. He's not responding to my repeated admonishments to mind his manners. I'm tired of this routine.

"I have an idea. Let's play a game that you're the parent and I'm the kid" I say.

My son grins. "Yes, let's."

I put my elbows on the table, slurp the vegetable soup and start whining, "This is too salty, I want different soup."

"No, you have to eat it, like it or not." Yaro's eyes bigger than usual with his new power, he stays firm.

"I don't want to, I'm not eating it." I pretend to cry.

"Don't cry, it's not that bad, it's all there is to eat tonight." Yaro falls out of his role. "Do we have anything else to give you?" I shake my head.

I whine-cry, "But I'm hungry, and this has tomatoes in it, I can't eat this."

My son sighs, looks at me and says, "I don't like being the parent. Too hard."

"Mmm, it's hard sometimes, but it's also good to love someone so much that you want to do the hard stuff for them."

"Good, because I want you to be the mom again."

We hug, we have an amicable meal. Yaro even eats his bowl of soup.

My thoughts go to the last week's travel with Doyle. How would I add another person to this relationship with my son? It's difficult enough to be the two of us. Could—would —Doyle want to be part of this? Would I want him to?

Even though I don't want to go through life as a single woman, I don't know if I'm ready for a new serious relationship. I'm 33 and have much to explore. One thing I'm clear about, though: Yaro and I are a team forever.

Chapter 3

Two months later Doyle's back for a visit. It feels good to have his interest and I let myself open up to new possibilities of relating. Yaro is staying with Alan for a week, so Doyle and I have the freedom to focus on each other. We don't go anywhere; we hang around the dome, on the couch, in bed and in the kitchen, talking endlessly. We talk about what we want in life. Doyle tells me that his girlfriend was in Europe while we took our little trip down south. *Hmm*, my sixth sense knew there was somebody else. He also tells me he's broken off the relationship; he is fifteen years older than she, and it's too much of an age difference. He must think beyond a fling if he tells me this. We're four years apart in age and we both have children from a first marriage. Does that make us more compatible?

"I've been here for a little over a year now," I say as I lean over the back of the couch and look out of one of the triangular windows where the trees are turning color.

"Winter is coming and I wonder when the others living in tee-pees will tire of that living situation. I'm comfortable here but it can't be permanent. I can't afford to buy this property and Ron may want to sell at some point. It feels like my life is an experiment, not just because we're living in community, but also because we're exploring different ways of relating with one another, more honest both emo-tionally and ideologically." I sigh and let my body rest against Doyle's next to me on the couch as I think about the difficult personal growth work we've been doing as a community. I look up at the vaulted ceiling and wonder what direction my life will take.

Doyle puts his arm around me.

"My communal experience was in France where I lived for a few months with others in a house," Doyle says. "Point Reyes was a semi-communal experience; we were all close friends and hung out a lot. One of my Point Reyes friends helped me buy the land on Tyler

Creek in Ashland."

"You've lived in many places since you left your marriage and kids in San Diego. Is Ashland where you want to live?" I turn to him to see his face. He's told me he's moved at least every four years in the last ten years. Is he a drifter?

"I want to live in community. I bought the land on Tyler Creek in Ashland to find that, but there are no people to do it with," Doyle says as he looks at me.

"I don't have land or money, but I have the people here, there are six of us doing it on this land and then another five more on another property further up in the mountains." Would he want to join us?

"What we're doing here is an experiment, but one with a school, a weekly peace council, a commitment to a lifestyle of openness and sharing." I lay out the model we've developed. "We've been doing it for a year and a half on this land now. I don't know where it's going, it's hard to meet everyone's needs and wants, but the kids bring us together." I refer to the six boys among us who need schooling, and playmates. "We want them to grow up with a deep connection to nature and to know themselves that way. Living in teepees and growing food helps us learn about our connection to nature. Doing personal growth work changes our relationship to ourselves and others and has been one of the driving forces that has pulled us together," I tell him

"Are you guys open to having more people?" Doyle asks.

Even though I would love to have a partner in our community experiment, I might want to hold off and see if we're compatible. I'm tired of the string of loose relationships I've had in the last two years and don't want to ask the others in our community to accept another someone who has trouble finding himself.

"What do you mean? Do you want to live here?" He doesn't seem like someone who sticks around for very long.

"Yes, I want to get to know living in community and getting to know you."

Hmm, I think, *what comes first, the community or me?* Still, it doesn't matter what comes first, as long as we can work it out together.

"How do you see this happening?" I ask.

"I have a project designing a house for my sister in Southern California. I could work anywhere I can put my drafting table, as long as I can travel down south to meet with them," he adds more of his plan.

My heart leaps. Here is this gorgeous man, with a real profession that makes money. He's not just another marijuana grower, and he's interested in being with me! With me and my ideas of living. He even has meditated a bit and wants more of this way of life.

"You do? Really? Stay here? Live here for a while?" I can't believe it. I reach for him and hug him. When we end our hug, Doyle gets up from the couch.

"Yes, I can bring down my drafting table and set it up." Doyle walks toward the space behind the stairwell and spreads out his arms. "There's enough room and light here to work, if it's OK with you."

We start our experiment of living together. Yaro gets to know this new man in our life. Community living has made Yaro flexible with living arrangements and he seems comfortable enough with this new person. I watch the two of them as Yaro's blond head and Doyle's dark one bend over a woodworking project, Doyle holding the piece, Yaro swinging the hammer on the nail. They're cut out of the same cloth.

I walk around feeling expansive, everything I do seems to be OK. I don't have to give up who I am. He likes me just the way I am. My abundant energy doesn't bother him, my cooking delights him, my intense feelings don't scare him. His quiet, slower manner calms me down. He can pick me up, literally, and I feel weightless, I feel held completely. I feel as if I've come home. I work my job at the food-buying co-op I created a few years ago. Doyle is there when I come home. Doyle sits on a high stool at his drafting table behind the stairwell next to a large window section of the dome and draws pictures of a very large home. I stand next to him, leaning in, watching his strong hands hold the pencil and make the lines, write his even architect script. An artist and a practical man all in one.

It's a cold day in November. The big cast-iron buoy-turned-wood stove is loaded with wood, the flames are curling up along the inside. We're standing around with a cup of tea in hand after morning breakfast, a moment of warming ourselves by the fire before getting on with the chores of the day. Doyle, in his checkered lumberjack shirt, while his faded beanie keeps his balding head warm, leans up against the ladder he's put there to fix the damper higher up.

"I want to ask you something," he says.

"What is it?" He sounds so official, why doesn't he just ask what he has on his mind?

"Do you want to marry me?" Without introduction Doyle pops the question.

I'm stumped, not expecting this yet at all. Thoughts of *It's too soon, we've only known each other for six months and lived together for three,* and *I haven't thought about this,* race through my head. My body buzzes, my mouth opens, and I say, "Yes! Of course!"

Our embrace is warm, excited. What does this mean? My first official marriage proposal, and I said yes!

"Let's tell the others and then go to the coast to celebrate." Doyle grins and takes my hand.

I hesitate, feeling a little unsteady as my mind races to grasp what's happening.

"I'm nervous about this, I have to get used to the idea." Do I know him well enough to make a commitment? I'm not the one in control here, he has a big impact on my life. Doyle lets go of my hand and says:

"You don't want to tell them?"

"Well, yes, but I just have to sit a bit to let this sink in. I'm going to get married! What does that all mean? Can we give it some time before we have the wedding?"

"We can set a date later. I'm just so happy you said *yes.*" Doyle gives me another hug. I feel my body relax against his torso, feel the trust I have in him. It will all be OK.

We finish our tea grinning and moving the words marriage, husband and wife like new flavors around in our mouths. I realize the idea won't become any more real until we tell others. So we walk down to the teepee to tell the land partners. The non-stop grin on my face is making my face stiff. No-one else seems to be surprised, they're happy for us. There are hugs and cheers all around. After a while we drive off in the yellow VW to the ocean where it all began four months ago.

We set a date for the wedding seven months out. We choose the summer solstice and plan a country wedding, homemade music, homemade food, homemade brew, and a homemade place to hang out under a large parachute stretched across the meadow. As our wedding day approaches, it's hard to believe that only a year ago we watched our friends say their vows from a knoll under delicate green oak trees, while we barely knew each other. And now it seems I've known Doyle forever. Our lives have blended seamlessly this last year; we're both ready for a commitment, we both want family and community. We both want to become better human beings, to continue the exploration of our spiritual practice, to find out what meditation can add to our life and what it means to become an enlightened being. We have shared a year of seasons, rainy weather, mud, potholes in the driveway, time away from each other because of work, soft spring mornings together out on the deck with yellow blossoms of spring bursting into fragrant bloom, gardens that need tending, gardens with poison oak blistering Doyle's skin. We can do this, we can make a life together.

Friends and family arrive and camp out on the land to help with preparations. We take walks in the woods with our resident marriage counselors to define our commitment, to write our vows. We turn the large meadow behind the dome into wedding grounds. There is an area for children's activities, a stage for our community band, a bathtub to hold drinks on ice, long tables for community food offerings, a homemade altar—a small table and some stones—in the center of the open area that can hold the large circle of friends and family who will be brought together by belly dancers and drummers. Our marriage counselors and friends, Carol and Peter, a lay Zen couple, marry us, brushing our seventh chakra with a twig, as we say our vows to each other, *I will be there for you, for the rest of our life.*

My father, mother and two brothers have come from the old country to add their blessing to the wayward daughter's new beginning and welcome this man into the family. My father works hard with his speech in English, telling those gathered in the circle about the value of marriage. He speaks about the importance of a community to support a marriage as he's experienced it through his longtime membership in the water-polo and swim club at home. My mother smiles and nods, not understanding what he says, but agreeing with him anyway. My brothers take care of my son and shoot pictures of the event.

I have stepped out of the forest of nonbelievers in the system society has created, and entered the institution of marriage, not just a contract for living together as my friends signed a year ago, but a legal government ordained marriage. I'm choosing to belong to this man and find my bliss with him. I want it all, the path of unconditional love, marital bliss and spiritual growth. Do I have Mahara-ji's blessing? In the story of Nala and Damayanti, the King changes personality while roaming the forest and comes back for his Queen. In the story Damayanti lived happily ever after with her King. Is Doyle the King returned to me? With Doyle I have found an electric, soulful connection I have not known before. As I look into his eyes when we say our vows, I feel a big *Yes* sound inside me: this relationship will be my vehicle to enlightenment.

Three months after our solstice wedding, we attend a meditation retreat at a Boy Scout camp on the Pacific Coast. Doyle is eager to meet Goenka, my meditation teacher, who's come from India to the United States for the first time to share the teachings, forty miles from where I live. Doyle has told me he has experimented with Transcendental Meditation but hasn't had any formal instruction. This retreat will change that. I tell him that in India Mahara-ji sent all his followers to Goenka to learn to meditate. Now Goenka is here. Is Mahara-ji taking care of me, as Ram Dass had said he would? Is it a coincidence or providence? I take note.

After ten days of sitting in silence, practicing the technique and listening to Goenka's daily discourses, Goenka ends the retreat by giving Metta[15]. He chants the familiar chant with his wife Mata-ji, as he returns to his quarters. Tears roll down my cheeks, I feel deeply united with the wholeness of the universe after ten days of silence and observation of the basic rhythms of living, and breathing. I walk

15. Metta: the practice of developing loving kindness. Offering metta is sending thoughts of loving kindness into the world.

out from the female section of the meditation tent with all its rows of meditation cushions, empty now, onto the central lawn of the camp. The men come out of their section of the meditation tent. According to the practice tradition men and women meditate separately and all maintain the vow of silence during the retreat. On the tenth day they allow us to mingle and the vow of silence ends here.

I look for my new husband. I haven't spoken or interacted with him in ten days. How was it for him? Will he accept my practice? He comes out of the big circus tent, walks towards me, our eyes connect, asking, how was it? A big embrace. A silent *wow!* The practice unites us.

* * *

This was a practice that started ten years ago for me in Alandi, a village near Bombay, when I traveled with Alan around India; a practice I hadn't been sure I could remember or maintain. I had heard about Goenka, a Burmese businessman turned spiritual teacher, from other young western travelers. They had told me that his meditation course "rocked" and was free to boot. We had been traveling for four months, and I secretly had been hoping to find an answer for the nagging question that had plagued me since my first semester at the university in Holland: *Why are we living? What is it all about?*

Sitting ten days in retreat I learned that I was nothing but a bunch of decaying cells in an enormous universe. Since Goenka was a teacher who was supposed to know something, I gathered up my nerve and posed my question to the teacher in an interview. "Why are we here?" I blurted out. "Is there a reason for living?" There! I said it, the pressing question that would help make sense out of what I was doing. Goenka-ji answered with a benign smile, "You'll know when you no longer have the question." Puzzled, I got up, bowed in respect and carried this answer inside me. My throat felt tight; it felt like I'd swallowed bitter medicine. I felt ashamed I even asked. How long would I have to wait for the question to disappear?

* * *

And now I'm here at the end of another ten-day retreat. I feel good, blissed out from the silence and focus on my breath. I still have my questions about life. Will being with Doyle help me answer the questions I have carried for so long? If we practice together will we figure it out together? Being here is a good start. As Goenka said after chanting at the beginning of each meditation period, "Start again, start again."

Four months later, Doyle and I are standing in the dome's kitchen. Light streams in through the plexiglass triangles all around, creating a dancing mosaic on the Mexican tile kitchen counter. Yaro is playing on the other side of the kitchen counter. I'm mixing the batter for Saturday morning pancakes, holding the bowl on the shelf of my belly growing with our child. I became pregnant right after we returned from our ten-day retreat together. What was it with retreats and babies for me? Even though I had not been thinking about babies during my retreat with Goenka here in California, I became pregnant as soon as we got home.

"I'm thinking about getting a motorcycle, what do you think?" Doyle says.

Out of the corner of my eye I see the bright blue of Zeus, the work truck, sitting outside, flashing in the sunlight. Why can't this larger-than-life vehicle carry him up and down the mountain to his current building site? We have enough expenses already. How are we going to save for a trip to my parents in Holland, if we spend our money on more modes of transportation? We're living on borrowed land. How long will that last? I stop stirring as I look at Doyle.

"I don't think anything." I point at the blue truck sitting outside. "How is a motorcycle going to get you up Spy Rock?" I say.

"I'm not getting it for work. You are having a baby and I want something too."

With lightning speed my blood boils, my face heats up. I throw the bowl and its contents at him screaming, "*We* are having a baby! I didn't ask for a baby for me. We made this baby together." I wake up from my New Age dream of shared responsibility in relationship, with the splatter of pancake batter all over the black cork walls, dripping slowly down to the floor and over my husband, his face, part of his torso and hands covered with the beige whole-wheat mash as he ducked too late to avoid my wild attack.

"Whoa! Easy, I'm only asking." Doyle, wide eyed, wipes the batter off his face.

"Now you have a mess to clean up, Mom," my five-year-old son comments from his play corner. *Touché*, I think.

Our commitment to each other bridges the chasm caused by words. Together we clean the batter off the wall, talk, and agree about the baby, *our* baby, and the motorcycle.

Doyle buys a Honda 500 and takes it out for pleasure rides. I ride with him sometimes. The last time I ride on the back of the Honda, my arms around Doyle's warm torso, is a warm summer day, after a leisurely swim in the Eel river. Swaying with the motorcycle as it moves on the road reminds me of the ease of floating in a body of water, the comfort of having a homestead given to me for shelter, and the connection with a man I love—all the important elements of living are here like they were in India when Alan and I had moved to the tropical environment of Goa for the winter months.

* * *

There were grass huts on the beach, blue water, waves for body surfing, a house for rent shared with other travelers, cheap food. Goa let us get away from heat, flies, the hustle and bustle of Bombay. A respite from the beggars, and diseased people dying on the sidewalks—images I still carried in my head. I was wondering if I should give them my money so they could live another few months longer or let their suffering take them away sooner? I was looking for a respite from the tug on my heart and the relentless waves of powerlessness to change the world, which were washing over me. Goa, with its tropical beach, the sparkling coconut water from green coconuts fresh off the trees, had been a paradise. We rode bicycles on the beach; I learned to body surf in the warm waves. Life seemed endless ease and yet I was on this trip to sort out what I wanted to do with my life. It seemed a perfect time to take the mescaline we'd been carrying around for the "right" time.

Waves of color, sparkles, feelings of love and bliss coursed through us for hours. We went swimming while we were high, as the sun set low over the Indian Ocean. The waves carried my body in a long-lost experience of utter wholeness and comfort. I felt connected with everything, felt like I was getting a taste of enlightenment.

* * *

The drug wore off. The feeling of enlightenment, of connection to *all that is*, didn't last. Maybe it was too good to be true. Maybe I was too ordinary a person, not enough of a spiritual seeker. I didn't want to become dependent on drugs for my belonging. I decided my new meditation practice would have to be the way to get there.

And yet, though the living seems easy here on the land, I'm a long way away from finding enlightenment through daily meditation. I'm living a householder's life, raising and taking care of children, developing a business with my husband to help us survive, with only moments on the meditation pillow. I put my cheek against Doyle's warm back as he shifts into a higher gear and we ride home in the wind.

That night I go into labor with our baby girl. We become responsible parents. Motorcycle rides in the wind give Doyle an occasional feeling of freedom, an antidote for the stress of being a father and sole provider for now. I embrace motherhood.

Chapter 4

O K, I'm willing to look at real estate and see what's available," Doyle says as he drives down the long boulevard.

We're visiting Ashland, and exploring a move to Southern Oregon, where Doyle once lived and owns property. Community living on the land in Northern California has become complicated as we want to make improvements in our living situations but have no legal ownership. Home schooling works for a while, but Yaro already needs more than we can offer. The small local school cannot meet his needs either, so we will need a place with good education for the kids. A place away from the booby-trapped marijuana growers' world. Some friends who lived in Willits have moved here in the past and I feel a sense of acquaintance, a family of sorts.

"You know, I can build a shop in a short time on the land at Tyler Creek. Then we can live in it until the house is complete." Doyle is trying to warm me to the idea of moving to the ten acres outside of Ashland in the mountains.

"I don't want to live on the land. I know how that goes. Remember how long Joe has lived without running water, using an outhouse and storing food in a cooler in the ground?"

Doyle nods. "I can guess. But I won't let it take that long."

"We don't have the money for putting in sewer and water lines. So how will we have those basics? Seventeen years from now, we'll still be living in the shop. Look around where we live in California, isn't that what's happening? I need running water, a washing machine. If we want another child, I'll be doing diapers again. Washing diapers by hand isn't how I want to spend my time." Our two-year-old daughter, Quinn, is sleeping peacefully in her car seat behind us. "I want a yard for the kids to play in. A place to ride their bikes." I'm listing the family's needs. Were three years of living in community not enough for him?

43

"That means we must live in town, or close to town." The enthusiasm is draining from his face. His gray-green eyes withdraw behind the long dark lashes as he leans his tall torso into the driver's seat. He struggles to let the property go—in his mind, at least. Property he bought only five years ago in the foothills of the Siskiyou Mountains, half an hour's drive from Ashland. Before we met, he had lived for a few years in the little valley of Tyler Creek. For him it was the start of living on the land, with a small community of neighbors who had become his friends. He then continued it with my land-living community, and he still likes the idea.

"Let's at least see what's available," I say, putting my hand on his thigh as he drives on.

"All right, I know a realtor I trust." At least he's open to the idea.

We buy the cheapest house in town, a rambling concoction of add-ons, interior walls covered with barnyard siding, exterior walls covered with plywood, painted barnyard red. Wood-framed windows reclaimed from other buildings are covered with plastic to keep the cold from seeping in as the wind comes howling over the mountains in winter and hits the two storey part of the house. The house is like the country houses in northern California, built piecemeal—off the grid but legal—there is running water and a bathroom. It feels like we can feel at home here with a mix of country living and urban amenities. The windows give us sweeping views of the valley, Grizzly Peak, and even a view of Mount Ashland from our upstairs bedroom. There is land, grass and garden space. The downtown area is only a ten-minute walk. The house sits on a quiet paved street, where the children can play safely, ride bikes and push go-karts. The back yard holds a shed and sauna heated by a wood stove. There is a bank of rich mushroom compost, used to grow hallucinogenic mushrooms by former occupants. It's the house known as the "hippie house" by people in town.

A year later we move to Ashland, when our second baby, Leela, is two months old, and begin our small-town life. Doyle rents a garage at a friend's house to set up his shop. He works in construction to earn the family's bread. I'm home with the three children. Yaro lives full-time with us and no longer has to go back and forth between us and his father. In the backyard of our new house, the motorcycle sits next to the rabbit hutches and chicken coop. It is now gleaming after we overcame the divisiveness it once caused— it comes out for spring rides when Doyle goes out with a friend for a day of riding and letting his hair down. He loves to experience the excitement of power and freedom a motorcycle gives to the adventurous at heart. I love his adventurous side, even if it means I'm home with three children while he rides out. My turn to feel my freedom will come. Stirring the soup on the stove, I look out the window into the street where Yaro is riding his bike.

* * *

I think of the time when I was a teenager: my mother was home with three small children and my father was away all the time. To meet the costs of our large family, my father was working two jobs. Had they taken care of their relationship needs?

My father had given my mother a television so she wouldn't feel so alone in the evenings when he was at work. My father would spend his sparse free time at the local swimming pool with his water-polo comrades. He would bring club members home on Friday and Saturday evenings after training sessions. My mother would serve coffee and beer until she went to bed, while club members entertained each other into the wee hours with water polo stories. On Sundays when there were tournaments my mother would send the little ones with my father to the pool and she would stay home and find an escape in romance novels.

At age nineteen and still living at home, I wanted to escape the smallness and predictability of my family home, the debates my father liked to have with us older kids.

"If you're so set on equality and socialism, how come you don't accept the view of the Christian parties," I challenged.

"Yes," my mother piped in, "you think religious thinkers are stupid."

"You don't know what you're talking about, you don't read the papers. You can't mix religion and politics." My father moved his hand in a dismissive gesture toward my mother and turned toward me to give his "educated" opinion. I hated my father when he did that. I was angry with my mother for blushing and bowing her head under the gesture. I hated the Sunday conversations that always turned into debates, a battle over who was "right", who was "wrong".

To escape the empty conversations with my mother over the noise of the television on evenings when my father was working late, I'd go out into the wet, misty night, large winter coat wrapped around me, swishing footsteps on wet pavement. In the chilly spaces of the empty train station, where wind always blew cold, I'd wait for the last train of the day to take me to my boyfriend. He was a student at the Technical University in Delft, the nearest town.

Once there, I walked through the narrow streets. Cobblestones led me past buildings that carried history on their facades. Facades of lives full of ambition, dreams, adventures, and war. The scars were there, the new beginnings were there, the old ambitions, dreams made manifest. Such was the taste of Old Delft. The train station with its red brick and tile front stood with unassuming pride, covering the grimy gray train yards.

Along the canal where the dirty water stared dark at me, I found my way to the bridge with curling iron railings painted farmhouse green, ready for leaning over on a sunny day, and spitting into the freight-laden barges that would float underneath. I walked under the spire of the Catholic church hanging crooked on its sagging frame, its foundation slipping into the sea. The arch of a gothic window looked in the direction of the abbey, old in style but, with new brick mixed in with the old, restored again after the ravages of so many wars.

The cold mist would follow me in the arched through-way of the abbey, the walls heavy with history. Prince William of Orange had walked through here four hundred years ago, and was shot for being who he was, a freedom fighter, a man tired of waiting out a seventy-year-long war. The bullet hole, marked by a plaque, formed a relief print on the wall. War, hadn't we had enough of it to last my lifetime? I was waging my war inside myself, as the different parts of me argued for position. Was there a God, or no God? *For God and Country* the plaque said; what good did that do for William of Orange besides giving him fame after his death? Dying for a country that could be occupied by the enemy in a heartbeat, just as it was in WWII? No! I wanted life, aliveness.

Eager for human connection, I climbed the rickety stairs to my boyfriend's attic apartment. We sat in the windowsill of his attic window and listened to the church bells ringing the midnight hour, always a few minutes later than the town hall bells on the market square. The night was still young. I would let my boyfriend's tall body wrap itself around me and thought I could find aliveness with him. Beers in our hands, we talked. We breathed in the freedom of possibilities. So much better than the arguments I had with my parents at home about their rules, their suffocating proper view on life, better than the empty conversations with a mother whose husband didn't talk with her. He gave her a television instead of his company.

* * *

I hear Leela stir in her little rocking cradle in the room next to the kitchen. As I walk into the room to pick her up, I have to admit that Doyle can make more money than I do, the children are small and one of them is still nursing. After getting my Oregon massage license, I work part-time in the bodywork practice I developed when we were still living in California. I had trained with a Rolfer in San Francisco and a Reichian therapist in Los Angeles and added other New Age therapies over the years. I use a form of mind-body treatment to alleviate physical tension through mindful exploration of sensations while using breathing. I offer a series of sessions to re-align the body through deep tissue work. Even though we hire a babysitter to fill the gaps, the cost of babysitting outweighs my income.

And so, life with children evolves. On Friday nights we are both too tired to go out. On weekends, as the children get older, we attend school-related and sports events. In springtime when Doyle goes out for rides on his motorcycle with a friend—I'm not invited. I stay home with the children who play in the yard. This is how we allow our lives to separate us—the assumption is that one of us needs to be home with

47

the children, while the other pursues their own interests. Why did we not share? I now wonder why didn't we prioritize time to do things together, just the two of us? Our shared meditation practice slows to a trickle with occasional attempts to sit, but we don't schedule time to sit formally, as family life and work demand our attention. I attend Sunday morning "sits" with our friends Carol and Peter, who've moved to Ashland as well and have set up a meditation yurt on their land. After one of the sits, I take a walk with Carol on their land on the east side of the valley just above Ashland.

"How are you?" Carol asks, peering at me in her uniquely attentive manner. Carol has a way of making me feel "seen" without being intrusive; as if I matter in her life.

"Oh, family life is busy and Doyle and I are not getting much quality time together. I wished he could come and sit also, but one of us has to be with the kids, so that won't happen."

"Don't you have a sitter?" Carol refers to our college-age babysitter. She's great with the kids, but also a college student and I have to respect her time constraints.

"Yes, but Jessica helps us out when we both have to work. Paying her to sit increases the costs and we don't have much to spare."

Carol shakes her wrinkled face and curly head in agreement. "Hang in there—your time together will come again. At least you're getting some sitting for yourself."

Carol, who has been a long-time meditator and is my go-to person for spiritual wisdom, adds, "Just sit with *what is*, and the stress will fall away."

"Yeah, it's all temporary, we'll sail through this." I say.

And so our family life continues and daily stress does its slow work of eating away at our relationship while we're not paying attention.

One Sunday evening after a busy weekend of running around to sports and school events, I find a quiet moment on the couch to fold laundry and wait for Doyle, who's on the phone in the kitchen with his project partner about the coming week's work. I feel the distance between us as we operate in our separate daily worlds. I wish I could do more than watch what's happening with detachment as Carol had advised me.

* * *

I remember another relationship I had as a student at the university, my first serious one. A serious relationship that was undermined by adventure and led to another relationship. I was living and studying in Amsterdam. Bob, my boyfriend, had encouraged me to make the leap and leave my family's home and live on my own, go to school in a more exciting town. It was the late sixties in Amsterdam, students in Paris had revolted against the establishment, radicalized the university system, and the students in Amsterdam were following suit.

"Here, hand these out!." My friend Thea shoved a stack of pamphlets into my hand. I was leaning over the edge of the stone balustrade of the university administrative building in the heart of Amsterdam.

"Do you want me to scatter them on people's heads?" I looked down on the sea of heads filling the street below, as a throng of students was making their way into the building. Loud shouting—"We are Academia, We are Academia"—filled the air.

"No, don't waste paper, go down there and put them in people's hands," Thea's voice barely reached me over the din.

"OK. Where are we meeting again?" Now that I had found my way into the center of rebellious activities, I didn't want to let go of the excitement. Who could have thought that the roles of authority and student would be reversed?

"The pamphlet shows where the meetings will be. I'm going to the psychology building. The meeting for the literary folks will be at the Keizersgracht. We can meet at my house for dinner."

Thea and I had become friends in a theater class, rolling around on the floor, exploring improvisation and new ways of communicating. Thea was smart, adventurous, petite and pretty. Every time she showed up for a workers Marxist meeting, people did a double-take. What was this pretty, blond girl doing, wanting to work in a factory? Thea didn't care what others thought of her. She wanted to make changes, break out of her current status of the pretty housewife with an academic career. I wanted to break out of the status quo for women but didn't know how. I followed her around.

I waved Thea goodbye and made my way down the marble stair-case. A loud crashing sound from outside made me run faster. What was happening?

Out in the street, I saw torches reaching for the scaffolding that had been installed to make repairs on the building. The banner draped along the balustrade, proclaiming the slogan of occupation, had caught on fire, and some boards on the scaffolding had caught fire, and crashed down on the throng of students.

"Fire! Fire!" People yelling, running, the crowd dispersed. This was getting too crazy. This was like Paris last year. A siren was coming down the Singel Canal. People were climbing over piles of bicycles, cars, to get out of the way. I was going to stay away from this mad-house. I walked across the bridge to the other side of the canal where small groups of students were watching the scene. I started handing out the pamphlets.

A week later we sat in a circle, fifteen senior students, one profes-sor. We were holding a meeting about the objective of the course, *The love poetry of Hooft*[16]. We decided, by consensus, what we wanted to study, and how we would grade ourselves. The professor nodded, and even though he had agreed to this new education format, he couldn't help arguing, "I do have to see papers, to see what you know."

"There are other ways to share our knowledge," a student piped up.

I wanted to form a small study group, read the material, discuss it and make a comparison with the Italians. Let's forget about writing more papers that would get lost in archives. I wanted to know how we apply this knowledge to our current life. The professor agreed. The consensus circle closed.

I went home to my houseboat on the Prinsengracht. I kissed my boyfriend, who was sitting at his drafting table peering over drawings

16. Pieter Corneliszoon Hooft (1581 -1647) wrote a history of the Netherlands (*Nederduytsche Historiën*), inspired by the Roman historian Tacitus. His focus was primarily on the Eighty Years' War between the Netherlands and Spain. In 1947 a literary prize was instituted by the Dutch government in Hooft's name. It is awarded on the basis of a writer's lifetime work.

of a bridge.

"Are you going to make one of those?" I asked.

"Maybe, eventually. It's all theoretical now." Since he was at the university, my boyfriend's practical bent was limited to connecting hoses from the spigot on the canal's edge to the water tank on the roof of our barge and from there to the kitchen sink to give the appearance of running water.

"Today we decided the coursework of our graduate course in love poetry." I took off my second-hand fur coat and draped it over the one armchair we had. "I wonder if anything really has changed in the world of love since the sixteenth century." I walked over to Bob again and raked my hands through his curly hair and bent my head to smell its scent. "It seems stupid to be studying this old stuff. But I do like to find out what people in those days experienced with human emotion." Would it help us now? I wondered. Why was I still looking at history for answers about my life? Bob and I were struggling with our relationship, how to keep "love" alive. What was love about anyway, we wondered?

I kissed his hair and said, "I'm going to pack and change. It's time to get to the railway station." I was about to leave for my weekend job as hostess on an international train to Germany, Switzerland, Austria and Italy.

"Wow, it's the weekend already," Bob answered. "I'll go hang out with Thea and Paul, while you're gone, catch up on the ins and outs of the proletariat." Bob had joined them in organizing factory workers.

"Don't share too much. I have limits about sharing bodies". I grabbed my stewardess uniform off the clothing rack Bob had installed in the boat's hull and wriggled my body into a tight skirt and tailored jacket. My paisley tablecloth-turned-miniskirt lay crumpled on a chair.

"Let's talk about all that when you come back Monday." Bob stretched his long torso back in his chair, tipping the chair against the portholes of the barge. The water of the canal sloshed against the glass above his head.

When I came back the following Monday, I was tired from a

weekend in Bolzano, Italy. Conductors, worried about rules, had kept me up at night. Uniformed border officials thought they could have a little more than mere friendship from a young woman and hadn't left me alone to explore the town. I hadn't had any rest or relaxation. I just wanted to sleep.

I woke up when Bob walked in with a man who looked like a blond Jesus. An American.

"This is Alan, I met him on the Dam.[17] There were demonstrations again," Bob announced and found a beer to share.

I wrapped myself in a robe and made some tea. "What are you doing in Amsterdam?" I asked.

"I'm traveling but am tired of being on the go all the time. I'm staying at the youth hostel for now." Alan pointed out the window up the Prinsengracht. "There are a lot of Americans staying there. America's a mess. The Vietnam draft is in force, students are protesting on campus, and there's violence between police and students."

"We've taken over the university here. We're running things now." I struck a match, lit the two-burner propane stove in the kitchen area and put on a kettle of water.

"You guys are lucky—such a small country, so reasonable," Alan said.

"You think so? You have so much space and freedom. It's so small and constricted here." I thought back to my visit to the USA two years ago, when I spent two months on the East Coast as an *au pair* with a Belgian family. "I was in the US for a few months. There is so much wild nature."

"Yeah, nature's beautiful, but people are power hungry and intolerant," Alan said.

After Alan left, Bob and I had our talk about sharing our relationship. It didn't go well. Bob said he wanted an "open" relationship. I just saw him wanting to sleep with my best friend.

I ended up breaking up with Bob, who was much too morose, too

---

17. The Dam—Amsterdam is a centuries-old open gathering place and trading center in Amsterdam. It is remembered as the site of the shooting of unarmed civilians by German troops at the end of WWII, after German forces had capitulated.

confused for me. I left our houseboat on the Prinsengracht and moved into a room in a "kraakhuis,"[18] where some of my street-theater friends were squatting rent free. Finding regular housing in Amsterdam with postwar baby-boomers coming into adulthood was impossible.

Alan came to see me at my new home, with his friend Pete. I made tea, Pete strummed his guitar and Alan played Bob Dylan tunes on the harmonica.

Pete pulled out cigarette papers, some tobacco and a stick of a brown pasty substance, pressed into a bar. He crumbled some of it on the tobacco and rolled it into a cigarette with the ends twisted together. He lit what I later learned was a joint, and passed it on to Alan. Alan handed it to me and said: "You want to try?" I didn't know what it was, but was up for trying. Following Alan's example, I inhaled the smoke, held my breath and felt the rush going to my head. The music sounded better. I dared to sing along. We laid back on the makeshift couch and watched our minds produce images and thoughts. We laughed until the munchies[19] for bread, cheese and cookies set in. As the high wore off, we drank more tea. Pete left, and Alan stayed.

* * *

I finish folding the laundry, Doyle is still on the phone. I'm going to bed, I think. Other relationships, other times, I remind myself. I was young then and commitment was a fluid concept. It's different now. Doyle and I have committed to being together until death do us part. Commitment will take temporary feelings of separateness in its stride, won't trip over differences, but help us work them out and bring us back together. I believe it: my parents have been together almost forty years and found new adventures and happiness with each other as they grew older. Besides, we have so many more relationship tools at our disposal. Everything will be fine.

But it isn't all fine. We need help to work out our differences. We do some relationship work with a male counselor. I walk out of a session, furious over the patronizing tone. Doyle talks with his men's

18. Kraakhuis: a condemned home, due for demolition. No relation to the contemporary "crack house".

19. "The munchies"—a food craving caused by marijuana ingestion.

group. I talk with a friend. We try to implement some well-meant advice to improve things; we learn listening skills, make I-statements, set time aside for intimacy.

It's another tired Friday night. The kids have gone to bed after watching The Cosby[20] Show. We're sitting on opposite ends of the couch, the middle vacated by the young ones, a representation of the week's divide.

"Is there anything interesting on TV?" I ask.

"Let's see," Doyle flips the channels.

Why doesn't he reach for me, I think. Why is he so passive, flipping channels?

"Not much there". Doyle looks at me with a "Now what?" expression.

"Not much between us either, is there?" I say. "Are we going to continue like this?"

"You look at me for initiative all the time," I keep going. "It seems like you spend all your creativity on work projects and have nothing left for us. Well, I'm tired of moving our relationship along." I feel energy rising in me when I say what I think. Confrontation does that to me.

"I don't know what you want from me." Doyle pulls his head back.

"Maybe I'm ready to give up wanting; I may as well live my own life." I let my thoughts go. Would I really want to live my own life separate from him?

"You want to separate from me?" Doyle's eyes get bigger.

"Well, are you happy with how we're getting along?" I feel a belligerent tension in my hands.

"Hmm, a divorce?" Doyle's voice rises as if he's trying on a new taste.

"You have any better ideas? We've done counseling." My energy plummets with the lack of solutions. I yawn and feel like the whole week of work comes crashing down on me.

"I need to go to bed, I'm too tired to think." I get up off the couch.

"No, don't." Doyle grabs my arm and pulls me over. "Come sit with me." I let him pull me on his lap and my head falls against his

20. The Cosby show. Ironically, Bill Cosby was later convicted of sexual assault, despite his role in the show as a figurehead for family values.

chest. As he strokes my leg, he says:

"We're both tired. Let's be tired together. Let's not make any rash decisions we'll regret."

I snuggle up against him, smell his familiar smell and all my belligerence melts. Why does it take a stand-off before we can come together?

We don't get a divorce. Our non-verbal relationship is too strong. Stronger than communication strategies, stronger than misfirings in our attempts to know the other, strong enough to carry on.

Chapter 5

Five years have passed. It's Labor Day Monday. The phone rings. I pull my hands out of the bread dough and pick up the receiver on the wall phone. The wall no longer has wood shingles as it did when we moved in ten years ago, it now has wainscoting and wallpaper to surround the dining area. We've juggled jobs and remodels as our children grow up, we've forged bonds in their school community and developed our individual and couple friendships. Doyle is part of a men's group, where he bonds with friends through talk and action. I'm part of a women's group where I find support for marital issues. Yaro is ready to go to college in a few weeks, Quinn is a horse-riding teenager; Leela is the only one who still enjoys being at home with me, playing in her make-believe worlds.

"Is this Mrs. Brightenburg?" A man's voice.

"Yes, this is Dami." Is this a telemarketer, I wonder? I don't have time for that.

"I'm calling from an ambulance. Your husband and daughter had an accident." The whirr of an engine sounds in my ear, competing with the man's words. "They rear-ended a car with the motorcycle." My brain comes to a grinding halt as I hear the words. The voice continues: "We're transporting them to Rogue Valley Medical Center. Can you meet us there?"

"Are they—" My words stop, but the screaming sound does not come out, freezes around my mouth. Lips numb, I stare at the beige wall phone, the receiver with the extra-long cord dangling, left, right, twist, left, right.

"We're taking good care of them. Come to the emergency room." The ambulance voice becomes silent.

"I'll be there." I hang up the receiver in slow motion. I turn, my eyes follow the late September morning light as it passes through the kitchen leaving its shadowy yellow trail, my hands on my apron, sticky with dough. I have to wash these, I think. I walk over to the sink and turn on the faucet. The water, slow to warm, runs cold. The soft sticky dough rolls up around my fingers like glue.

Oh my God, rear-ended, blood everywhere, helmet head into smashed window, the images are swirling in my head. *Quinn, what happened to her, did she hold on? Young body splayed out on pavement, arm twisted, neck contorted.*

Go, the voice in my head. Everything is so slow, what do I do now? The car, I have to drive to Medford. I can't take Leela, she doesn't need to see this. She needs to go next door. *Make a call.*

My body takes over, I dry my hands, I move through a mist to the phone again. I remember the neighbor's number and make the call; I speak, explain, "An accident, no, I know nothing. Yes, can you take her? I'll let you know, thank you."

The yellow Volvo, our family road tank, barrels up I-5. My hands are on the steering wheel, my feet moving the gas and clutch pedals automatically. Thank God I can drive. What did he do? Did he lose control? Cars are zooming by in the left lane. Speed, what speed was he going? The impact, I don't remember how much distance you need to avoid dangerous impact, one car length, or two? Slow down, you want to get there. Hospital sign, first exit.

What happened? Was he distracted? I should not have gotten on his case for being so involved in his projects, not paying enough attention to me, he was doing it for the family welfare, not just for him. What a stupid argument. What a way to spoil a morning walk. Never part while you are angry. *An accident, oh please, let them be OK!*

"Thank God, you're breathing and awake, are you OK?" My knees are shaking, will I hold myself up? "Where's Quinn? Is she OK?" I ask, my voice directed at anyone.

He cringes, eyes wider. "I don't know, I think so, she was right next to me, in the ambulance, she was crying."

A nurse, speaking softly, appears from behind a screen and calls me with her hand motion while she says to someone else, "Your mom is here, it's all right."

I walk around the screen. Quinn is awake, dark curls, big eyes, her 12-year-old budding body laying innocent, good-girl-trusting, under the white hospital blanket. This love, this body from my body, torn up by the road, machinery, how dare they? I feel heat rising, crawling up my arms.

"Mommy!" Her soft hands reaching.

I look to the nurse, questioning. "Can I hold her?"

"Yes." A nod.

My arms around her, lifting her gently, oh so gently. Her tears flood my pounding heart.

A few minutes later a forty-something man, dark hair, balding, with black eyes, looks around the screen and asks me if I am family. Can he speak with me? I stroke Quinn's hair and lay her down again on the gurney and answer him, "Yes". Why do I notice this guy's head? Doyle is balding, he wears his beanie cap most of the time. Helmet, oh, yeah, he had the helmet, they both did.

He looks at me, holding a clipboard with forms; scribbles, a pen in his hand. "Can I tell you what happened?"

"Yes, please". I need to know. Do I want to know, though?

"Step over here, please." The man guides me to a couple of chairs away from the gurneys, tells me his name. I immediately forget, except now I know he's an EMT.

"She went flying", the EMT's voice.

"What do you mean?" My mind in overload, visions of Quinn with a sheet for wings.

"There was a doctor who was driving right behind them and saw it happen. Your daughter flew right over him—your husband, isn't it?" The EMT lines up the facts for him and for me. While holding the chart in his hand he looks me in the eye. "The stuffed backpack saved her when she landed on the pavement on her back. Apparently your husband tried to avoid the car. Grazed it as he rear-ended. Slid the motorcycle into the berm. The doc found him with his leg under the motorcycle in the dirt. No protection for his leg." He grimaced as he described what had happened.

Yes, he had worn a helmet, and I had seen them riding off, Doyle in shorts, light blue denim shirt flapping in the breeze. A man and his motorcycle, a lifelong love. A late summer day, a treat for riding in the breeze, taking Quinn to the horse-riding barn.

"He's lucky," the EMT reports, "that there was a doctor right there. The doc called the ambulance, gave him first aid, tied off the artery."

I'm seeing Doyle's blue shirt, red blood and black dirt all swirling in my head. I shiver for a moment, it's cold in here. Pay attention, stay alert.

The attending doctor appears and shakes my hand. "I'm Dr. H., we will take care of your husband. He lost a lot of blood, it's serious. The damage is mostly in his leg. His head is OK, the helmets protected both of them." The attending doctor peers at me through reflecting glasses.

"What about her?" I cannot believe that this is happening. Both Quinn and Doyle, maimed, crippled?

"A crack in a vertebra, no broken bones. Some bruises, nothing else. With rest she'll heal. She doesn't have to stay here." The buzz of ER machinery mixes with the voices as the information is loaded into my brain. The good news is like morphine for my nervous system. I feel lighter. Quinn will go home with me. I shiver again. I have to pee. Where is a bathroom?

In the bathroom, I sigh, let go of bladder tension, wash up, look at my face in the mirror. Who is this? A forty-seven-year-old, grayish blond woman, a wife, a mother, and in a matter of seconds this accident has changed the whole game of cards in her life. Was it my fault, was there such a thing as fault? Whose fault was it? The face looks back at me, wrinkles around the eyes, eyes watery, no message. I leave the bathroom unmoored.

While the nurses tend to Quinn, I move to my husband's gurney and sit down.

"How is she?" His head turns in my direction.

I touch his hand, the long strong fingers, the beautiful square palm. "She will be OK" My eyes well up, voice thick with tears. "She can go home with me." I can barely tell him the basics.

"I will make it." Morphine and shock give him a "can do" expression. This is the man I married, always working out the kinks in life.

We're a team, maybe it won't be so bad.

"Yes, you'll get fixed up. I love you." My soft palm touching his. I can't tell him that he almost bled to death. That he's living on someone else's blood, five pints of it.

"We'll take him into surgery soon," the nurse checking his drip lines.

"I'll be back when you come out of surgery. I'll take Quinn home and take care of things." I have no idea what is ahead.

That afternoon at home, as I'm busy telling friends on the phone I need help, my eighteen-year-old son Yaro walks into the house and says: "I'm OK."

"What do you mean?" He looks OK to me, but the fact that he's announcing it means he must not be, or he had a close call. Am I having hallucinations? Is he really speaking to me?

"I rolled my jeep on the freeway, as I was driving to Medford. The jeep is totaled. The roll bar, that roll bar you thought looked so silly, so macho, saved me." Yaro stands tall, all six foot three of him, blond, blue-eyed Viking, wondering why I just stand there, staring at him, my arms limp, my mouth open, silent.

Behind him, out of the window I can see a tow truck driving up with the smashed-up motorcycle. My frozen throat tightens.

Chapter 6

The accident changes everything, except we don't realize it — not yet. We see it as a temporary setback and put our strong shoulders and minds under this challenge. Five surgeries and three weeks in the hospital have given Doyle a semblance of a leg, wrapped in a cast to his groin, ready for the healing work to begin at home. A fungal infection, picked up from the soil as his leg grazed over the berm after he slid off the pavement with his motorcycle, has raised his white blood cell count to astronomical numbers. He arrives home from the hospital with a drip infusion that is supposed to kill the infection. He'll get the drip until his kidneys can't take it anymore. The side-effects of the medication make him throw up all the time, and after three weeks of this routine he looks like he came straight out of a concentration camp.

We turn our sunny living room with the window seat wide enough to accommodate a full-size mattress into a hospital room. Since Doyle can't go to the office, his office comes to him. His fellow designers and builder friends traipse through our house to meet with him between nurses' visits, and visits from others. The constant flow of people not only supplies a positive atmosphere, it also demands constant cleaning up, coffee making, and re-organizing to accommodate Doyle's medical needs. I'm *busy*! Self-employed as we both are, there is no family sick leave and neither of us are making much money.

People want to help. Work partners and members from Doyle's men's group turn out and build a deck with ramps to allow him to get around in his wheelchair, and later on his crutches. The ramp allows him to return to work in his home office in the new addition to the house. Friends organize friends and acquaintances who want to help. For six months they deliver meals for our family as we battle the fungus, the surgeries, the exhaustion.

It's the end of a long day. I'm getting Doyle ready for the night. I give him his medication, adjust the pillows under the cast that reaches to his groin, massage his back, sore from laying on it all day. I clean his face and his hands one more time. I stack reading material in case he can't sleep, put away the remnants of the meal. I still have the dishes to put away, check on that paper Yaro wants me to edit for school, arrange a ride for Quinn to get to the stables so she can ride her horse tomorrow. Did I get the laundry out of the dryer? I walk into the kitchen as my mind is checking the endless list of tasks generated by a family with two teenagers and a younger one who's waiting to be tucked in with a story.

"You're so distracted," I hear his voice from the other room.

"What do you mean?" I walk back in.

"You don't take time to hang out and be with me. You just go, go all day. I want some time with you to be a couple." His voice raspy, he stares at the dark evening outside the window.

Guilt and overwhelm surge inside me. I know we haven't been intimate; I know I'm just pushing through the piles of work every day, waiting for him to get better, for things to get back to normal. Why do I have to give more, when I'm not getting much from him? I try to hold back my irritation, but tiredness from weeks of care-giving let me lose control.

"I can't believe you're complaining. I work and work to keep the show running here, work to pay the bills, be a mother, be a nurse, and now you want me to lay around and be romantic also? I haven't heard a thank you in four months." The months of worry, anger and frustration are spilling out. I stomp around.

"Do you think I don't have any needs? I can barely catch my breath and get a rest to even think about being romantic. You're lying there all day, visiting with people who come to see you and care for you. I clean up after them. I clean up so they can sit here with you. I clean up so you're presentable. I clean up so you stay alive! I clean and clean and what do I get from you?" Suddenly I feel how exhausted I am. I can't face another task. Doyle turns his head to the dark night outside, the schism between us palpable.

I feel the tears inside me, tears of exhaustion, tears of loss, tears over the chronic pain he has, tears that need arms around them to let them flow. The daily family busyness with little time for us before the accident hasn't helped me feel warm and fuzzy about him either. Our relationship has rolled from doing our individual tasks into the intense relationship of patient and care-giver. We have no choice but to carry on, do better, be better, get better.

Four years later, after thirteen surgeries by a skilled orthopedist who installs pins, replaces Doyle's knees several times, gives him an ankle fusion, and a lift in the shoe, and Doyle is walking and bicycling with both legs. Doyle experiences depression at times, which we attribute to the trauma of the accident, and there's medication for that, so he is taking an anti-depressant to lift those low moods[21]. I've switched to a job in a residential treatment center for emotionally disturbed youth. This job provides me and the family with health insurance. It's a job I can leave at the office and don't have to be involved with out of hours. Doyle's business is flourishing. What he's lost in physical achievement is transferred to career success. We have re-committed to our meditation practice and go to several Vipassana retreats together.

We look forward to high school and college graduations. We attend the kids' sports events, drive a Ford van up and down the free-way transporting teenagers to and from water-polo tournaments; we learn about crew as my son is part of a collegiate rowing team. The Volvo is covered with "proud parent" stickers. We're overcoming the accident.

"I have an offer to buy into a partnership," Doyle tells me as we're walking back leisurely after having coffee in town across and through the undeveloped railroad land that separates our neighborhood from the railroad district. It's Friday, and I look forward to having our morning together without work, for connecting and maintaining the thread of love that gets worn so thin amidst work and a busy household of five people.

"Is this what you want to do with our time together, talk business?" Frustration rises in my stomach, making me want to grit

21. I'm adding this footnote to foreshadow the increased libido and impulsivity Doyle will experience later on when he starts taking Sinemet (levodopa/carbidopa), with its resulting looking "elsewhere" for satisfaction.

my teeth. I see a much-wanted feeling-connection evaporate for the morning. I have felt distant from him. He's been absentminded, preoccupied with a project deadline this week.

"It's simple. Not much to talk about. We can buy in with $25,000, no other costs involved. I have my mother's inheritance." Doyle recently received money after his mother passed away. Doyle is wrapped up in thought; his body sways, as he takes big, uneven steps. I have to push myself to keep up with him.

"Instead of spending that money, it would be good to finally have some savings for emergencies." I'm thinking about the bigger picture for our family. I don't want to think about the expansion of his business. I want to *feel* him, not *hear* him. I grab his hand.

He slows down a little. "I have my worries about the business, it needs to grow. This building would add exposure and reliable income. The four of us, partners, would buy that undeveloped lot on A-Street. We'll get a construction loan and build a mixed-use building. Offices downstairs, one for me too, and apartments upstairs. The rents will pay the mortgage. It'll give more visibility for the design business."

Now we're talking business anyway. He's right, it *could* be good, it *would* be good. It could lift us out of the paycheck-to-paycheck mode. The warmth of his body near me relaxes my jaw, makes me want more of *us*. Where are the fun times of hiding Easter eggs late at night for the kids and falling into each other's arms, loving endlessly? How else will we make our wishes come true: wishes for more trips abroad, bicycling with the kids in Switzerland, surfing the Atlantic Ocean?

"Give me a day to think about it," I relent. Doyle puts his arm around me, we're a team. Walking home, the sky opens blue. The possibilities of better times float into my mind. I can see it now. We can have it all.

When we walk into our house, the sunlight is streaming into the living room, inviting us to hang out on the window bed and feel its warmth. We talk, connect and love each other. It almost feels like when we first met and hung out on the deck of the dome talking about the shared life we envisioned. Much of what we envisioned then, our partnership, the community ties, work we wanted to do to create a better world, has come to pass. We're still loving each other despite the hardships we've been through. We feel connected to people in our community. Doyle is involved in environmentally responsible building practices; I help families in my work with high-risk youth. Our vision of a good life is expanding with this plan for the office building partnership.

In the years that follow Doyle creates a design group with his architect-partner, a landscape architect, and another young architect. They're housed in the office buildings that we now own. His team creates environmentally sound, community-inspired building projects on the last of the available land in the heart of town. An almost lost underground creek becomes a wetland with birds and tall grasses waving in a pond, located right next to a family medical clinic. Apartments above office spaces provide rooms with a view—and not just any view: buildings with Doyle's designs sit next to a Buddhist temple, acknowledging our meditation practice. The area, with footpaths, invites those who live and work here to know themselves and roam throughout the place they call home. His design work helps to shape the future of this unique small town, a model for balanced living in America. He's in the thick of it and it's exciting; there's no need for a motorcycle to let down his hair: his career is his adventure.

We get involved with a local Vipassana group. We help organize local meditation retreats and bring Vipassana meditation practice back into daily living. It feels good to do the work that Goenka encourages us, his students, to do. I join the Oregon Vipassana Board and with our local teachers we make plans for establishing a permanent center in Southern Oregon. I no longer rely on Carol for my spiritual advice. Carol goes to Ladakh in the Himalayas during the summers. She's deeply involved in the Buddhist culture there and helps establish women's cooperatives. She even brings a lama to Ashland who gives a talk about the spiritual benefits of contributing to and creating centers for practice. He is raising money for a nunnery. I accept his talk as an encouragement to work locally on spreading the *Dharma*. Doyle agrees. Little by little we turn over the stones of loss, pain and distance between us. Equanimity will overcome suffering, we think.

There's a road to happiness in relationship. Bliss is just a stone-throw away. I belong with this man, in this place.

The optimism I feel coursing through our life doesn't let me suspect that something is wrong. I don't know that, in his office, Doyle feels the phone slowly sliding out of his hand. I don't know that he struggles to get a better grip to put the receiver back on his ear. I don't know that he makes an appointment with a neurologist for a checkup.

One day he tells me he's taken out a life insurance policy on himself.

"Why now?" I ask.

"I want you guys to be OK, if something happens to me. I don't want you to lose what we have." I take this decision as an act of caring, caring for our future, not as a warning. We're planning the subdivision of our home property. Finally, we will build a house of our own design. We dream of a cooperative housing situation with the new house and the rambling old home which has evolved into a home with an apartment attached, housing one growing teenager after another.

A few weeks after our conversation about the life insurance policy, when I'm working in my office, my phone rings. The sun is streaking in through the windows. The first words of a client's discharge summary form a dark line on the computer screen. I answer.

"It's me," Doyle's voice.

"What's up?" He rarely calls me when I'm at work.

"I have Parkinson's,[22] his voice calm.

---

22. Parkinson's Disease (PD) is a disorder that affects the dopamine-producing neurons in the brain. It develops slowly and symptoms include tremors, slow movements, rigidity and balance problems. Psychological symptoms include apathy, depression, sleep disorders, loss of sense of smell and cognitive impairment. There is no cure but medication (and sometimes surgery) may delay progression. The chief medication, Levodopa, stimulates the formation of dopamine, while dopamine itself is the "reward" neurotransmitter. This means that a side-effect of taking levodopa may be so-called "self-medication" and the development of impulsive behaviors. There are also dopamine agonists that trick the brain to think it's receiving dopamine; side-effects may be confusion, sleep attacks and compulsive behaviors. Dopamine doesn't only control movement, it's also sometimes called the "feel good"

"What?" I turn my office chair toward the windows and hold the receiver away from my ear to look at it. Did I hear him right?

"What do you mean?" I listen again.

"I saw a neurologist, because I had some strange things going on in my hand. He said Parkinson's disease is affecting my muscle movement." He explains, "I'm relieved, knowing what it is. Now we can do something about it."

My thoughts hover. What is Parkinson's? Another problem? In my mind, I see the pile of physical syndromes of the last five years that I thought was contained, grow a little higher. *Don't panic, keep it together, you don't know what this is yet.* Parkinson's, it sounds official and big. A description of some new development, a process I don't know yet. Don't know if I want to know about it even.

"We can talk more about it later, just wanted you to know. Don't worry, I'm OK." Doyle's deep voice warms my ear. I can tell he wants to end the conversation.

"All right, I'll be home around six."

I come home that night and we sit at the kitchen table after dinner. The girls are doing homework in their rooms.

"Have you said anything to them?" I nod my head toward the girls' rooms.

"No, let's find out what it all means. The neurologist told me that Parkinson's is a chronic disease, not a death sentence," Doyle adds.

Doyle tells me what he's found out. I learn that 85% of the *substantia nigra*, a part of the brain that produces dopamine, which is an essential neurotransmitter, necessary in muscle movement, is gone by the time the symptoms appear. It can be a slow progressive disability. More disability? I don't know if I can handle that; we were just getting a respite, some regular, albeit somewhat limited functioning. There is

---

neurotransmitter; it plays a role in how we feel pleasure. A lack of dopamine can cause depression, anxiety, and hallucinations but when a patient adds an anti-depressant to his or her medication regime the result may be an increase in libido. Doyle used all the medications mentioned here and had a brain implant to slow down the disease. Without our knowledge at the time Doyle experienced all the side-effects, including increased impulsivity and cognitive decline.

medication to help keep control over the muscle movement. Good! *If we can control it with medication that'll work, he's never been resistant to popping pills.* Having Parkinson's explains the depressive bouts he's experienced. There's medication for that too. Why is this happening? Are we cursed? We read and find that yes, trauma can cause Parkinson's. That awful Amphotericin-B, which almost destroyed his kidneys and saved his life right after the motorcycle accident—could it have caused this?

Medication is reentering our life. In addition, we look for and try out alternative healing. Healing is still a possibility, we think. Haven't we beaten the odds on everything so far? We buy a new car, an automatic, to make driving easier. We buy a small sailboat, turn the van into a camper and spend summer weekends up by the lake, just the two of us, reconnecting in nature. Doyle in the driver's seat, teaching me to sail, while the kids, young adults, are off doing their own things. I love having our weekend adventures. It feels like we can have our golden years yet.

The meaning of life has become doing life, overcoming the odds that life will be taken away.

Summer solstice, four years later, we're facing each other on a small grassy area behind our house instead of a large meadow. A circle of fifty friends instead of one hundred and fifty surrounds us. Our grown daughters are catering a lavish spread. Twenty years older, like velveteen rabbits beat up by life and stress, we've become real for each other. We let love shine with hope and determination. Our wedding clothes are still intact, adapted for our changing bodies.

The tears of hardship are welling up in my eyes, tears of sorrow over the man in front of me fighting for life, normality. A normality that's escaping his now constantly moving hands, barely controlled by artificial dopamine. Choked up, I can barely speak the words.

"I will love you for the rest of my life, I will be there for you for the rest of our life." Our vows, checked and re-checked, are still true. Carol and Peter, who married us then, still here to conduct the ceremony of reaffirming a twenty-year marriage. We've brought together old and new community as our witness.

The ridge of Grizzly Peak is looking down on us, lying there with its back so solid, so trustworthy, so reliable. Rain or shine, winter or summer, green with spring grass, or yellow in the heat of summer, Grizzly is our totem, our inspiration for living on.

On this summer night the setting sun strokes the valley and the ridge with golden light as we say the words of our marriage poem, a Manitonquat[23] prayer:

> *Love is life — creation, seed and leaf*
> *and blossom and fruit and seed, love is growth*
> *and search and reach and touch and dance,*
> *love is nurture and succor and feed and pleasure,*
> *love is pleasuring ourself, pleasuring each other,*
> *love is life believing in itself.*
>
> *And life...*
> *Life is the Sacred Mystery singing to itself, dancing*
> *to its drum, telling tales, improvising, playing*
> *and we are all that Spirit, our stories all*
> *but one cosmic story that we are loved indeed,*
> *that perfect love we seek we are already.*
> *That the love in me seeks the love in you,*
> *and if our eyes could ever meet without fear,*
> *we would recognize each other and rejoice,*
> *for love is life believing in itself.*

After the ceremony Doyle takes me by the hand and we lead the dancing on the deck to the music of Bob Marley, the Beatles, and the Mamas and the Papas. Our friends join in and soon we're all humming or singing the familiar trail-blazing words we heard in our youth for believing in life. Doyle whispers in my ear "dream a little dream of me". Love fills my ears, and I let my body sway with his.

I believe in our love, I believe in this man's love for me. I will not let the fear of disease and illness pull us apart. Our eyes will meet

---

23. Manitonquat: 1929-2018. Author and writer on New Age philosophy and community sociology.

without fear, because we believe in life, we believe in ourselves.

Chapter 7

Two years later we're experiencing a cold November in Ashland. I'm unpacking a suitcase as I have just returned from Holland where my parents died only a week apart from each other. Two deaths wrapped around All Souls' Day. I tried to make it back to Holland in time to be with my mother as I knew her health was failing. The news of her passing reached me in Connecticut where I had a stopover to see Yaro before crossing the Atlantic. Yaro had moved two years after finishing college for a job and I didn't see him very often. When my brother called and told me Mother had died that day, I realized how close I had been to making it, to be with her one more time while she was still alive. I was one day too late. What does it mean, I thought, to not see my mother alive ever again? Yaro had suggested a walk in the nearby woods, and I kicked the piles of wet leaves on the path, fallen in their rich palette of decay, red yellow and brown. The light rain fell wet on my cheeks. I didn't have tears—not then—it all had to sink in. That night the ring she had given me for my eighteenth birthday broke on my finger. It was an eerie sign of our broken connection. I shiver and pull the navy sweater, her sweater, the one she used to wear around the house, closer around me. As I continue unpacking, I think back to the last family reunion.

My mother and I stood outside the door of the vacation farm home in the north of Holland where the family had gathered. Doyle was finishing packing the last items in the rental car as we were to drive back to the airport. Mother's back stooped, white hair spun like fairy yarn escaping the hair combs, she reached for the last hug. I embraced her in my oldest daughter strong arms. She cried.

"Why are you crying? We've done this for 30 years now," I said to her.

"It never gets easier to let you go." Her raspy dialect vibrated in the hollow of my throat. When would I let myself really be her daughter? Tears welled up in me, as we stood there holding what couldn't be had.

Now, in the States, far away from the failed relationship with my mother, in the quiet of my home, the memories of our lack of closeness come flooding in. I remember another time when the distance hung between us as we sat together.

* * *

Did she know then, when I was only nineteen years old, that I wanted to escape her, escape the predictable small family home? I had been reading romance novels interspersed with philosophical works on the big questions in life. Questions I couldn't talk about with her, religious and church-going as she was. I wanted to be loved by someone who understood me. Did my father understand my mother?

On nights that my father was working late, I would sit near my mother on the couch for a while. As we drank coffee, we made small talk. I could feel her hunger for connection, but I couldn't—wouldn't—fill her emptiness. I would slip away when I could take the opportunity, up to my own room, my own thoughts, my own fantasies.

I knew my mother waited. Waiting had become living for her. Waiting like a tree in the forest. Waiting for my father to come home? Waiting for all six children to grow up and leave home? Waiting for the day to be done?

At eleven o'clock I heard her climb the stairs, turn into the hall to her room, where she would wait for sleep while her body warmed up the cold bed. As she laid there, the small sounds in the house, the soft breathing of the little ones in the room next to hers, the water filling up the tank of the water closet, empty after her last use, filled up the silence of the hallway. The sounds outside, an occasional car driving by, footsteps of someone walking home, a call out goodbye were markers of a late night. My father was still not home.

Everything was dispersing, slowly fading away in the silence. What were her thoughts as the silence became emptier? Did that silence allow for greater spaces between thoughts, spaces that filled up with feelings? Was she lonely?

I was nineteen years old. I didn't want to wait; I was impatient; I didn't want to feel the loneliness that lurked in the shadows of my mind. I wanted to live; I wanted to get away from the stillness, filled with her empty words. I would find a love that would give me that aliveness my mother didn't have.

* * *

My mother is dead. The words sound in my head and accentuate the stillness that hangs in the kitchen where I'm unpacking. Here in a far-away land, what is my aliveness? Where's my love?

My mother's candle had burned low during the last year as she weakened with congestive heart failure. Phone calls had been short. I'd scheduled my yearly visit and wrote what turned out to be my last letter on a yellow legal paper to her: "Thank you for giving me my freedom, the freedom to study, to explore, to go where I needed to go. Thank you for bearing the loss of an oldest daughter."

My father, in denial of the obvious reality of her decline, burned himself out living for both of them. My mother's death was expected. My father's death came without warning a week later.

We'd taken my father to the hospital when it became obvious he was much sicker than he wanted to admit. I spent the night with him in his hospital room. We talked about the necessity of being there, the medical interventions he needed as pneumonia blazed through his lungs. He slept fitfully. In the middle of the night, as I was dozing, he pulled out his IV and, delusional, got out of bed to get dressed. I called a nurse who persuaded him to go back to bed. She cleaned up the mess, blood spatters everywhere, but didn't connect him to the IV.

"We'll do that in the morning," she said.

The following morning after his bath, in new fresh pajamas, which Bram, my younger brother, had left for him, his breathing became more labored. He fell asleep after eating a little breakfast. The sun was shining in through the high windows. A sunshine mixed with dampness and haze hanging over fields where crops hung limp after a first frost. Looking out at the frosty fields, I thought about my father and our last time skating together.

A farmer's son living between high rises, my father used to check the temperature gauge outside the big picture window every morning. The temperature only mattered to predict the possibility of skating. He was 74 years old the last time we went skating together. It was January, just before my mother's seventy-fifth birthday. Wetlands frozen, ice clear and black before anyone had skated on it, he moved in front of me. He made the familiar long skate strokes, with his hands folded on his back covered with his old wool sweater, his nostrils dripping into the cold cloud of breath hovering in the air. The sun shone low through the spare trees and bushes that formed the horizon of this water land. I had to reach far back in my brain for my balancing skill on skates. It came back with each stroke as I followed him. Childhood memories, love for country and father all rolled into one rush as my blood warmed and let me live those moments.

When I came back to the reality of my father in his hospital bed, it was an ordinary day. Nurses were checking on their patients, doctors were doing their rounds, people were going to work, kids going to school. My older brother, Wim, called from the polders[24] and said he would come by the hospital in the afternoon when his meetings would be over. My father slept. I left the room to make some phone calls and tell my sister Liesbeth how my father was doing.

When I came back into the room, a stillness in the air put me on alert. My awareness was paying attention beyond the ordinary. The rhythmic gasps between my father's breaths connected me with a primitive knowledge of life and death. I slipped into universal knowledge and knew to stand back.

On one of his visits to my home in the States, he had wanted to swim across Emigrant Lake.[25] We had told him he shouldn't be doing it alone; he was sixty-six and anything could happen. He had looked at me with that determination in his eyes that had come from surviving a hard childhood. Feelings of pain turned into passion for living. I had told him I wouldn't stop him, and dying while doing what he liked, wouldn't be a bad way to go.

That was when I let him go the first time. He swam across the

24. Low-lying land reclaimed from the sea or from other bodies of water.
25. A reservoir five miles southeast of Ashland, Oregon, USA.

lake and came back that day.

In the hospital, I went looking for someone to tell them what I thought was happening. I couldn't find any nurses or doctors. Things were different there than in the hospitals in the States. Nurses were having coffee in the break room. I walked up and down the shadowy gray hallway, cold white doors everywhere, metal supply closets, a nurses' station without nurses, just a telephone. Where was everyone? Someone was dying... was everyone too busy to notice? I was so calm, time was suspended. Was I in a dream?

My body did what it knew to do. I used the telephone to call my younger brother and tell him to come over. My sister would be on her way by now.

I sat in the chair by his bed remembering the day after he had arrived from his eighteen-hour overseas flight and drive to my house on one of his visits. He had risen as usual at 7:00 AM. He had come into the breakfast room in his jogging clothes to do what he always did on Wednesday, jogging. I wasn't surprised, as I was used to his regimented life. It was 95 degrees Fahrenheit already at 9:00 in the morning. A hot summer day. He left for his jog and time went by. When three hours passed, I noticed the clock. I had said nothing to my mother, who in her state of jet lag wasn't aware of time. After four hours I was still as trusting as ever.

Just as I decided to get in the car to start looking for him, he came walking down the street. Pale and slow he had reached his physical limits after an hour and a half in the sun. Six miles away from home, he had given up the jogging and pushed his body in slow motion home.

It had never occurred to me he wouldn't make it back.

I stepped out of the room and paced the hallway waiting for someone. The nurse was done with her coffee break and came with me to the room. They'd told me the doctor would stop on her rounds between ten and eleven. It was almost eleven. The gasps were bigger, startling him to open eyes, no words, no recognition. My brother and sister showed up, and we walked the hallway as we took in the reality that our father was on his way out, dying. It wasn't supposed to be that way. With my mother gone, I wanted some time with him. I wanted him to come to my home and live in a warm climate to ease the stiffness in his bones. I wanted him to myself.

When I was twelve, the doctor had ordered my mother to stay off her feet and sit in a chair for six months. Danger of blood clots, the doctor had said. My father and I did the housekeeping in the evenings after he came home from a day at work. He had no flair for cooking but managed with bookkeeper precision to produce the daily fare of meat, potatoes and vegetables. We hung out the laundry on cold misty evenings, exact, in closet order. He reached for the high lines; I handed him the clothes and pins. We became a team that winter. I watched his enduring energy. He didn't complain. He would work until he was done and fall into his chair, where he buried himself in the newspaper.

I waited in the room by his bed. When the doctor finally showed up on her rounds, she took one look at him, then looked at us and we knew. There was a flurry of orders, stethoscope dancing on his chest. Then, nothing. My sister stepped into the hall with the doctor and came back. No, no life support, he didn't want that. Just let him go. Suspended in time and place I accepted the procedures of the world I found myself in. No longer a familiar world. Time had eaten the connection between worlds.

We gathered around and waited. My first death watch, I was fifty-six years old. Curiosity mingled itself with stunned automatism.

It was all over in a half-hour. No goodbyes, just breathing out the breaths left to him. The breath became less and less, breathless moments more frequent. My hand was on his chest, feeling the rising and the heartbeat. I leaned over and told him in his ear, "*Ik hou van jou,*" I love you. I wanted him to hold those words if there was a journey remaining for him. The girl, arms wrapped around his waist on the back of his bicycle, the teenager next to him hanging up the laundry, the young adult waving as the ocean liner moored on the homeland quay—I would be left behind in a world that he and I no longer shared. There would only be memories to keep the *us* feeling alive.

When I turned six, I had received a birthday letter, my first letter ever. It was from my father who was working in another city three hours away by train. He'd written the letter on lined paper, his even handwriting jumping off the page to let me know he hadn't forgotten me. There was a book also, and I indulged my newly found reading skills in a world of humanized Easter rabbits.

Dreams are made of memories. When you die you are easily forgotten—you live on for a while in those that carry your blood. Not long and then you become emptiness. I carried my parent's memories in my blood.

What dream of my father was I living out? Was it the dream of being connected with the mystery of living, buried too deep for him to know? He had lived his commitment to my mother loyally. His values were of the mind. He followed his reason. He rarely shared from his heart. It must have been beaten out of him by his father, when he was little. I had wanted to be his feeling connection. I had wanted to be the catalyst for his emotional freedom.

My mother's dream had been about enjoyment. Children, material things, a good family life. She hadn't asked difficult questions. She believed there was a heaven, an afterlife.

My sister and brother cried. The whole transition slipped by on us. How could we have just let him go? Was it a mistake, a bad movie? It was sinking in that we had let it happen, there was no return. I folded my thoughts inside me and watched as his face smoothed and he became the young man my mother had chosen so many years ago.

I called Doyle six thousand miles away.

"He died?" he asked.

"I can't believe it. It wasn't supposed to be this way. He was going to come and live with us for a while." I had shared the plan I had concocted with my father, after my mother's funeral.

"I'm sorry." His voice empty over the line.

"I will stay here longer. I must change my ticket. I'll let you know when I'll come back home."

Doyle didn't offer to come be with me. The tears were stuck in my throat. I needed someone. Why couldn't he be there for me? But my initial reaction turned to reason—I wasn't surprised. Travel wasn't easy for him. After five years of living with Parkinson's, his movement had become dependent on medication. Medication that made him sway and make strange dancing moves in public. Medication that seemed to make him high and uncaring, focused on *his* needs.

I called Yaro in Connecticut.

"Opa is gone." I could barely say it.

"I'll come out to be with you." No hesitation on his part.

"I need to change my ticket, maybe we can come back together after it's all over."

"Give me your info and I'll see what I can arrange." Young voice of confidence. "I love you Ma, I'll see you soon." The phone clicked.

The next Saturday we had another memorial gathering followed by condolences, a lunch for the family traveling from far away. November sun lit up the golden trees lining the narrow driveway from the funeral home out of the graveyard compound. The hearse with my father's body slowly drove away to the crematorium. He would come back in an urn to rest his ashes on my mother's grave. A burial plot he had bought for her a week ago. His last gift.

Yaro and I flew back to the States over the Atlantic. The flight attendant handed me a Dutch newspaper. My eyes scanned words, flipping pages for something of interest: *De zin van het leven*, an article about the meaning of life according to a modern Dutch philosopher. I'd never heard of him, but that didn't surprise me since I had not kept up with philosophy in Holland. *Why did this show up today?* My life still had meaning, I still had my husband, my children, a community where I felt I belonged. Then I saw a headline, "artificial diamonds, the process of creating diamonds out of carbon, ashes". For 10,000 Euros I could wear my parents on my finger in a blue diamond. I could have them with me always....

Home in the States, far away from the actual place of loss, winter weather matches the darkness in my heart. We shouldn't have let him die, we should've hooked him up to a lifeline. He didn't want to die. My sister on the phone disagrees. We cry.

My new, busy job at the correctional facility which I had started in the spring distracts me from thoughts about my parents during the day. The commute home at night on a quiet freeway brings the loss of family and the emptiness of being far from my siblings to the foreground. I work a four-day week and am home when Doyle goes to his office. I sit in the living room staring out of the picture window at the mountains across the valley where the first snow has laid its white blanket of cold fluff. The thirty-six Buddhas on the Tibetan thangka on the wall stare at me with their equanimous smile. Easy for them to be with the silence, I think, they have lifetimes of practice. I still need to process my feelings. I want to talk about my parents with someone who knew them. I want to relive the story of their passing. They didn't suffer, no prolonged suffering, I tell myself over and over. But Doyle doesn't have time for talking about death. Doyle has immersed himself in a new building project, doing a small housing development for a woman who has settlement money from a divorce. It's all he wants to talk about. The man who only wanted to work part-time when we married, to have time for relationship and adventure, is now losing himself in his work, a place where he can function and ignore his limping body, pain and his progressing illness. It feels like I'm losing him, losing him to an illness. So I spend the winter grieving my parents alone, letting my meditation blanket embrace me when I sit on my cushion.

One dreary winter day, my friend Carol, who had traveled to Ladakh in the summer, invites me to a gathering at her house. A lama she met in Ladakh is visiting and he will give a talk about practical Buddhism. Not wanting to talk to many people about how I'm grieving, I slide into the back of the crowd already gathered at her home and settle in to listen. A Tibetan-looking monk, with shaven head and in a maroon robe, addresses the group.

"To support meditation practice, helping others to learn about practice is a good thing," he says with a beatific smile. *Is this man truly happy?* I wonder. *Has his practice brought him this joy? Can I feel joy again?* I look over the crowd as Geshi-la points at a slide of a village in high mountains with a monastery perched against the rocks and verdant green fields of barley terraced at its base.

"We want to build a nunnery for women of the village." Another slide of young women laughing while walking on a path near the monastery. "Women are not allowed in the monastery, they need a place of learning. Will you help?" Geshe-la put his hands together in prayer mode and bows to the audience. Carol and Peter step forward and explain more of the project for building a nunnery.

I feel touched by Geshe-la's smile. Yes, I'm helping others learn about meditation through organizing Vipassana courses locally, but it won't hurt my karma to contribute to this project. I pull out my checkbook and write a check. Doing good for others will make me feel better.

It's January and I'm at work. I call Doyle with a question for him. He doesn't answer. It's Sunday evening, and I wonder why he isn't home. Later when I get home I ask, "Where were you this evening?'

"Meeting with my client."

"On a Sunday?"

"Yeah, I had some questions about the project. We ended up watching a movie."

The project meetings continue, too many meetings. Too much involvement. As we drive home from a routine appointment with the neurologist regarding his ongoing treatment, I let my thoughts roam as the green fields zoom by. The project pops up in my head, and I wonder why he's so engaged in this. I ask, "What are you doing with her? You're spending an awful lot of time together."

"It's just work. We can make this development a real success. She needs me to help her figure it out. She's a nice woman, she's always friendly with me." Visions of nurses in the hospital who became friends with him, the image of his secretary who seems to dote on him, bring up an undercurrent I have given little credence to until now. *Does he flirt with these women? Why do they flock to him?*

"Friendly, huh? I don't believe you." I'm yelling the words, since the car window is slightly cracked, and the rushing air drowns my voice. "I don't want you to have her as a friend." Doyle shrugs his shoulders as he turns the wheel to pass another car.

"I can be friends with a project partner. I don't see the problem. John and I have been friends through all of our projects together." He refers to his long-time contractor friend.

In the following weeks I fret, I grieve, but I trust; he won't do that to me. Remember, *I'll be there for you for the rest of our life.* He said it too.

It's late February, a cold, sunny day. I'm home, Doyle isn't. I have not been able to let go of thoughts of him with the woman I haven't met. Why isn't he introducing me to his client?

I call him on the phone: "We need to talk, I'll meet you by the railroad tracks."

"OK, what about? I have little time right now."

"I'll tell you."

I walk and meet him on the path, carved out from foot traffic crossing the fields and the tracks into town. He's walking in my direction from his office, showing that uneven movement with his damaged leg. The clouds are racing in the sky, spring is around the corner. This is the last undeveloped land in the heart of town. The place where we have walked the dog, picked blackberries, walked the children to school, had morning meanderings as we planned business deals and travel trips. This wild piece of land that has shrunk as he developed and designed the A-street district with his partners. When we meet, I blurt out what's been building inside me.

"I want you to stop seeing her." My voice is high pitched.

Doyle stops, looks at me and raises his open hand to explain.

"I can't, we need to work together."

"Put it on hold, for me." I feel tears of worry, mistrust and loss well up.

"No." He shakes his head. He just stands there and doesn't reach for me, doesn't comfort me.

"Are you are telling me you're not willing to put a 'friendship' on hold for the sake of a twenty-year marriage, our marriage?" I'm louder now, my disappointment that I can't make him take my side switches to anger.

"I'm not giving up this friendship." Doyle holds his ground. *What's going on? Why doesn't he listen to me, what is he getting from her he's not getting from me?*

A dark cloud races across the sky above his head darkening Doyle's face, making me feel the chill in the air. I don't want to be let down, don't want to feel so vulnerable.

Abruptly I turn and walk away, my voice screaming in my head, *He's betraying our relationship, he's betraying me!*. When I get to our house and walk in, the warmth and comfort of home wraps itself around me. The protection of home makes me want to protect myself. How can he be chasing another woman?

I call him later, and tell him I don't want him home, he needs to find another place to stay for now.

It's April, I'm walking through the park. I see Doyle up on a grassy slope above the road. He's dancing, shirt off, arms flailing, body swaying. A younger woman sits in the grass watching him, laughing with him. Is that "her", the woman he works with and who gives him too much attention? I don't want him to see me walking by; I don't want him to know that I see him in this uninhibited state. Shame made me hasten my steps as much as I could, while remaining unnoticed. *How can Doyle do this? How can he spend our money on her? Invest in her project?* A week ago I found out while checking our accounts that he had taken out a large sum. When I confronted him about doing that without my consent, he said it would come back; it was an investment. *Investment, yeah right! Investment, my life, my future.*

Spring is around the corner, new life, new blossoms are opening in the garden. I normally relish the hard work of spring time, to get the garden ready for the full season, for the new growth I help create, I don't want to be in a life where there is no-one but me to eat the produce of the garden. Where there is no-one but me who needs the money I earn to survive. Clean house, dirty house, who cares? Who will chase me out if I don't pay the bills? I hate my body, hate that it gets hungry, falls asleep, has habits I need to tend to. My parents are in their grave, my husband is living elsewhere. My children are off to college and new careers.

I'm living in the house of our past, where the wood-filler patches on the door to the living room tell me he would finish sanding them before I would paint. I lay on the window bed made for two, and feel the cold near the window, the hollow space next to me. My legs carry me to the fridge for something to fill that hollowness, the hole in my life. My daughter's hand-drawn magnet of her dog on the fridge's door reminds me I need to walk and feed the dog. The dog, her dog, left for me. I don't want to fill the hole inside me with a dog.

I don't know what to feel about Doyle. We continue living separately. We have a family therapy session in which the children find out what's been going on and express their disbelief and feelings of betrayal. Doyle ends his involvement with the younger woman. The project with her is finished. He gets the investment back, barely and without interest. I let him move back into the old house, so he can be close to the building of the new house—the one he started designing last winter for the subdivision of our property. Is it going to be *our* house? Shall I let him back in my life, and does he even want to be with me? Can we work through this distance, this schism of disease, desperation and mistrust we're in?

We muddle through another winter. I help choose colors for the new house interior, have my say about the layout of the kitchen. It doesn't feel like my house. The house is Doyle's, built to his specifications, built for his disease. Doyle moves into the new house in the spring. He doesn't ask me to move in with him; I'm not ready. The first colors of spring warm my face. I don't want to feel. I'm living next-door to my husband of twenty-two years. Is he still my husband?

I remember the barren rock walls of the slideshow I saw at the gathering at Carol's house with Lama Geshe-la when he gave his talk about supporting spiritual centers. The slide show of a trek to a village called Lingshed in the Himalayas, at least five days' walking from any motorized road, where they wanted to build the nunnery. It showed me steep rock walls, torrential rivers, and endless stretches of trail with very little vegetation. Maybe I can lose my numbness while walking an endless trail and figure out what to do with my life.

I had read a book about this place called *Ancient Futures* by Helena Norberg-Hodge. It's about Ladakh, a country annexed by India on the border with China and the Himalayas I trekked around when I was twenty-four. The Himalayas where I found bliss and unconditional

83

love. Ladakh is a place where community means survival. Ladakh is a place with Buddhist values which might help me deal with what isn't happening here. Maybe, in this land with towering rock walls, and endless stretches of trail, I can get away from the hole I feel in my life.

I mention to Carol that I'm thinking about visiting Ladakh. She asks me if I'll go to Lingshed and bring back pictures of the nunnery built with funds we raised in the West. In return she will introduce me to her network of friends in Leh[26], including Karma, a monk turned householder she had met on her travels there. Karma, an ex-monk practicing human kindness, will surely help. She gives me a mission, and I accept it as medicine for my soul.

---

26. Leh: made famous by Rudyard Kipling in *Kim*.

Chapter 8

At work, I ask my boss, Randy, for a meeting. We sit down across from each other in his office.

"Don't mind the mess around here," he says as he straightens his crumpled shirt and leans back his office chair to give me his attention, "I've been unpacking and organizing the materials for our staff training; it's still a work in progress." He waves his hands to the stacks of handbooks on the floor.

"What can I do for you?" He rubs his scruffy gray beard and his eyes smile at me through his glasses.

"I have a request," I say. "I'd like to take some time off."

"Go ahead, fill out a vacation slip and we'll see if it works with the schedule of the other therapists." Randy shuffles some papers.

"Actually, I want to ask for sick leave," I say.

Randy looks up, raises an eyebrow. "Are you not well?"

"Hmm, you could say that; I'm not physically ill, but my home life is in shambles and I need some time off to figure how to move on. I've been seeing a therapist but talking isn't helping much." I sit back to see how he would take this information.

Randy leans forward and puts his elbows on his desk and says, "We'd have to justify sick leave, or family leave. Can you get a referral from your therapist?" I could kiss him for his flexible stance.

"Yes, I probably could," I say.

Randy opens a binder and leafs through the pages until he finds what he's looking for. He pulls out a paper.

"Give your therapist this form and have him fill it out; we'll make it work. Anything I can do for you right now?" Ron asks.

"No, I'm functioning. Knowing I can take some time off will make a huge difference. Thank you so much!" I give a sigh of relief. Now I can prepare for a trip I want to take and leave my life here for a while. I walk back from Randy's office through the double secure doors to the locked part of the facility where I have my office in one of the units that houses the youngest inmates. I will get a break from my role as therapist for these unfortunate youths and take care of myself full-time. I'm already breathing more easily as I settle into my office chair to see what my next task of the day is.

When I get home from work that night, the dark windows stare at me as I walk up the path to the front door. The darkness matches the darkness inside me. A darkness I want to run away from. A home I want to run away from. This home, our family home, holds my silent screams, my unshed tears, all our unfinished projects. This old house has become a shell for a life that exists no more. A life that isn't mine, a house where I no longer belong.

I don't know how to feel about what has happened to me, to us. I'm afraid to feel, afraid I'll tear everything around me apart, throw furniture through the windows, become unreasonable, mad. I'm afraid I'll lose it completely.

How can I grab the world by the throat, shake it, tell it to become reasonable, not do this to me? How do I tell the world to give you back to me? I think.

My thoughts zero in on Doyle: You were my anchor in the sea of life. Who pulled the anchor? I'm adrift in not knowing. I have been holding on to this house because it's all I know.. You're living next door in the new house you designed. A house holding your professional dreams, a house built for you, for you and your disease. How did it all happen this way? Did I make a mistake, did we?

I enter the kitchen, clean out my lunchbox and order things in the dishwasher. I go into the living room and lie down in the window seat in the dark with only light from the kitchen shining at a distance. My body feels limp from the left-over tension of the day. I smell the lingering smell of my office air-freshener in my clothes. Hmm, it'll be good to leave work behind for a while. I can see the house next door, where Doyle is living now, through the tall windows around the window seat. The light is on in your living room. You must still be up. What are you doing with your evenings? Do you spend them alone, like I am? I think back to how we had made plans after the motorcycle accident to subdivide our property and create a small co-housing situation, where we could surround ourselves with friends, people who want to age gracefully right along with us. You and me and friends. What was wrong with that? You wanted to design a house with possibilities, a house that would hold our aging, aching bodies. A house that would have room for a caretaker if we needed one.

This old house was meant to be a place for others, friends, a chosen family. The garden that connects the houses would be a shared garden, a place to exchange news, sit in the sun, smell the flowers, grow some food. This is how we would stay ahead of the curve of decline.

Did we really think a new house could keep decline at bay? That friends living around us could help stop the wave from crushing our life?

The changes happened so fast, sped up and you let yourself be swept away by the drugs that kept you functioning. You let impulse rule your decisions, give you a chance at unfettered love.

They say that when a loved one dies, women wail. I have done no wailing. I never got the news that you had died. You walk around still, but it isn't you anymore. You talk but it isn't about us anymore. You plan but they aren't our plans, they're plans for your disease. I can't find you in our daily life. I look for you, in every nook and cranny of our interactions. I look for that great big man who opened himself to me. The man who has always been there for me when things were tough. The man who loves me unconditionally, promised to listen to me with his heart. Did I forget to listen to you? Am I the one who kept you in the straitjacket of normality, pretended that we were OK? OK with a limp, medication, tiredness, side-effects that ate their way into our togetherness?

I shift my body and put another pillow under my head, grab the remote and turn on the TV. Here I am on the daybed where you slept so many a night. First when you came home from the hospital after the motorcycle accident. Later when you had been too restless, too often awake during the night to share a bed with me. Spontaneous expressions of love had become planned struggles for normality as we waited for the medication to kick in so you could move your limbs. I hated it; I hated the life left for us. As you couldn't walk very well anymore, I had found others to go hiking with, play in the snow, make my body breathe hard. I had lost you as my playmate.

After flipping through some channels, I turn off the TV. I can't be distracted. I better go to bed, I'm tired. I enter the downstairs bedroom we have shared since the accident. There isn't a room in this house without memories. I've bought new bedding, changed the colors and bedcover, but it doesn't change what happened here two years ago.

You put your arm around me as we laid next to each other; you cosied up to me. I knew what you wanted, so much more often than before—another side-effect of the medication. I rolled on my side away from you. Not again, I didn't want another struggle to make it happen. Couldn't warmth and comfort be enough?

"Come on," you said.

"It's no fun for me anymore," I answered. I felt your body going slack behind me, the disappointment turning you away from me. You got up to go to the living room, the other bed, where you had the privacy to satisfy yourself. I felt bad and got up to go to the bathroom, wanted to talk to you, but didn't dare go into the other room and walk in on you doing what I didn't want to give you.

Here I am now in this house, this room, by myself. You took the rejection and walked away. Like a tree splitting, the crack between us widened, the weight of each side pulling each half apart from the other half. The heavy crown of branches grown over decades of breathing and living together, separated, falling away from the center, searching for sap on the sides of the split trunk only. Our life has become two separate lives rising from one entwined root ball.

At times I have relished the freedom of my life without you. I don't have to feel your body struggle to move your limbs; I don't have to feel you twitch with pain, your nightly restlessness. I've pretended that we did the best we could. The nagging question, *What if I made love with him that night?* battles inside me knowing that the change, the dysfunction, is getting worse and is irreversible.

I have focused on my work, protected our children's lives. And you, you've done the best you could to keep functioning. You, the man who always had time for adventure and the outdoors, buried yourself at your office, which gave you a last vestige of normalcy. You lived with a fantasy that you could be a partner to a younger, less "demanding" woman. The man who always professed that a twenty-hour work-week was a good goal, spent over fifty hours a week at work, less and less at home.

I sit down on the bed, pull off my socks and start undressing. The phone rings, my youngest daughter, this late?

"What's up, everything OK?" I ask.

"Yes, I need some papers signed for school, can I email them to you; can you return them tomorrow?" Leela's voice sounds pinched.

"Yes, I can, I don't have to be in early tomorrow at work. I'm getting ready for bed, let's talk sometime this weekend, OK?" I hang up and put the phone down.

I remember how I got calls from her late at night because of the time difference when she was in Italy for a year abroad and I had to help her figure things out long-distance. That was a good year for her.

My mind returns to talking to Doyle: I remember how I dragged you along for our last family event, a Christmas trip to Europe to visit our almost grown-up girls as they both were studying abroad. A trip where we could forget the emptiness between us, I thought, amid the foreign distractions.

We landed in Florence where Leela met us at the airport with her host family. She wore a deep maroon woolen coat. "Made it myself, Ma!" she had exclaimed. Her hair styled fashionably, she looked Italian. When she started speaking in Italian with her hosts, the change from a timid high-school girl into a young woman of the world seemed complete. You and I clasped hands in the back seat of the car as they drove us to our hotel. Yes, we had done this together, helped her find her way in the world.

Three days later we arrived in Barcelona where Quinn was studying. We had met Yaro who had flown in for this Christmas get-together at the airport, and we had all piled into a rental car and had driven to the hotel. After settling in, the kids wanted to explore the city and get something to eat.

"Are you coming?" I asked.

"No, I want to stay here," you said.

"But we're just going in the neighborhood, you won't have to walk far," I retorted. The cane you had been using to get around, rested against your chair. "Do you want me to stay with you and get room service?" I offered but didn't really want to stay behind with you.

"No, you go with them, I'll rest," you answered.

So the kids and I went off on an exploration of the city for some good food, Quinn in the lead. It was the beginning of your limited participation in our family activities. You sat on a bench while we walked around Park Guell. You stayed at the house we rented on the coast, while we went down to the beach. Your computer was always next to your chair to entertain you. I let myself soak up the conversations among the children, three young adults now, and watched them be at ease in a foreign setting as I had always wanted them to be. I let you slide into the background.

We came back from that trip to this old house. A house that held good memories. A house you had wanted to leave behind, though, because it constrained you with its low ceilings, and it had too many problems. You had wanted to manifest your dream to finally design a house for yourself, for us. I tried to fit my wants into the design that was determined by your needs, your disease. Then when my parents died, I couldn't think about a move, I couldn't face another loss. As you gave the new house shape on your computer, it felt foreign to me; it didn't feel like mine to live in. You continued to work on the plans at the office, while I dealt with the loss of my parents here in my familiar surroundings.

I slide into bed and pull the blankets up around my shoulders. I enjoy sleeping in a self-made nest of blankets, now that I don't have you to wrap around me. The memories of that gut-wrenching moment come into my mind, the moment that split the foundation of our relationship, broke the trust we had in each other. That moment when I realized that you weren't just at work to work. At the office your assistant had been giving you the loving attention and the admiration you craved. The new project partner had involved you in her world, had invited you to become an entrepreneur, enticed you with the possibilities of greatness, invited you to her home... I hadn't been able to put a stop to what was happening. You didn't respond to my questioning about your interactions with her. I had wondered about your time at the office with your assistant. I had yelled at you, demanded that you give it up. That you acknowledge our long life together. I wanted to be first in your life.

You didn't want to come home to me; you were under the spell of a new relationship, her niceness. I reproached, hassled, wanted you to respond to me. My reproach became my wail...

Then I asked for your honesty. You denied the disbelief in my voice about what was happening to us. You reasoned, told me everything was OK. You wanted everything to be OK. Had told yourself you wouldn't cross the line. I didn't know that you had ignored the pain and dysfunction in your leg by taking more medication. I didn't know that you had ignored the warning signs of your addiction to the medication, your vehicle for normalcy. No one had told us that a side effect of the medication was loss of inhibition.

I didn't trust you anymore. The split between us widened with a loud creaking sound. When I finally asked for that time of separation, time for you to come to your senses, you had agreed to it too easily.

Now separation has become the new normal. I've watched you with my heart ripped open, beating harder than normal, tensing my jaw, shutting my face in a frown. I see that your life became a search for wellness, a collecting of pills to keep pain and dysfunction at bay. I've learned that life for you is about moments, the moments when the medication kicks in. I saw you do strange things. I watched you dance ecstatically, shirtless in the park. That isn't the Doyle I know. But what do I know about you any more? Without my questioning face around, you can do what you want, unrestrained. I see you've bought a new car, even though you are not safe to drive. You bought a new reclining bicycle and people told me they'd seen you riding it among the youngsters in the skateboard park, doing jumps over curving concrete.

The darkness of the bedroom isn't soothing, the nest of blankets isn't comforting, it just brings more memories of the searing split between us. My mind continues talking to him. It's as if I'm stuck in the movie of our separation and like in a nightmare it runs over and over in my mind.

When I was grieving my parents, you gave me a trip for two. You meant well to offer me time away. You said you wanted to take me on that trip, but you didn't do it. Were you too tied up with your new project partner? All I felt was rejection from you. So I went with Quinn to Costa Rica where she wanted to immerse herself in Spanish and I wanted learn some Spanish myself. You took a trip to an esoteric healing center deep in China, to get your health back. You did all the things responsibility wouldn't let you do before, responsibility for me, the family.

Costa Rica and China changed nothing for us. You moved forward with the new house. You involved me in choosing colors and materials as if I would still be the woman in the house. The design held a basement studio space for me. The relationship with the other woman had petered out. I bet she'd just come on to you to get a better deal on the project. Did you still intend for us to live together?

I roll over on my side, maybe sleep will come that way and get me out of this re-run. The yellow light of the street lamp is lighting up the blinds. I better roll to the other side where it's darker. The yellow swirling behind my eyelids brings back the image of the yellow legal pad with my writing on it laying on the kitchen counter in the new house. A kitchen I had carefully scrutinized for all the latest design features. My mind plays out the scene.

"I want to talk about what I want if we're moving forward together." I wanted to broach the subject of our relationship. He was sitting in the chair facing the hearth.

"Oh? What is it?" He turned the chair to me.

"I need some honest answers and an apology for what you did with her," I referred to his project partner with whom he was no longer involved. I picked up the pad. "I've outlined some steps for making amends. Here!" I handed him the legal pad. "I also have some requests for moving forward," I added.

Silently he looked over what I had written. He looked up and putting the pad down, he said: "I don't feel that I betrayed you, I never was intimate with her."

"You don't think wanting it was a betrayal? You don't think using our money without telling me was a betrayal?" I said in a clipped tone. "If she had opened herself to you, you would have gone for it, wouldn't you?" The words hung thick in the warm afternoon air.

"I don't want you to have control of all our money," he brought up a thing I had jotted down. "I want to spend as I wish."

"You're buying all kinds of things we don't need, you haven't discussed any of your spending and it's my money too. I won't let you ruin us financially. This house is a big investment and who knows how long you'll be able to work and bring in money." I ran my hand over the cool stonework of the hearth we had designed together and sat down on the wide ledge that could warm our bodies in wintertime. Doyle frowned at the back of the paper I had handed him, moved his leg around stiffly and said:

"I can't do this. I want to live here without you for now, do what works for me."

The movie stops in my head. My hands are clutching my pillow. Laying here I feel the hole of despair open up in me. Who is this man? Didn't our commitments mean anything to him?

Did he really think we could just walk away from a 23-year marriage? Walk away, build a fence and do our life on either side of the property? Why did he want to live alone in a house?

I'm in this old family house. The graduation pictures of our children stare at me from the walls. Delightful faces I have held, stroked, encouraged, said *no*, but mostly *yes* to. The smiles hurt my chest. I can only feel the stabbing pain of proud moments lost. We enjoyed those moments together.

I don't want to feel the emptiness, now that the last child has moved away to complete her studies. The emptiness of moments gone by, moments we experienced together looking into each other's eyes. I think of when we said: "We did it, they're almost launched! Now it's time for us."

The emptiness has me by the throat.

I roll over again and swallow the big lump of tears, my jaw clamped down on my anger. Alone I can't cry. Without you, there is no-one here to hold me, turn on my tears. I can only cry in my dreams.

I get up, walk to the kitchen to get water. The blue Delft tiles above the sink shine in the under-cabinet lighting. They're a solid, shiny barrier for the splashing water, cultural heritage for cleanliness and neatness, a link to my home country, a reminder of my parents' last visit to the States from Holland.

I remember that it was a hot, sweaty late May day. My parents' visit was only a few days away. I had decided to do the tiling project, so they could see that their gift of five years prior had found a place in my home. They had tried to bridge the gap of generation, wayward child, oldest daughter gone, never coming back. They had tried with gifts of home, my favorite chocolate, cheese, indestructible quality cotton underwear you just couldn't get in the States. They had been more accepting of my wandering ways than I was of my decision to leave my country. Why did I leave? How foolish was I in my youth to think I could maintain a bridge between the new world and the old? Here I am, in a house where I don't feel I belong. Here I am after three decades in a foreign country still holding on to my Dutch origin? How to be me?

I will not have any more visits from my parents. Their deaths, wrapped around All Souls' Day, eighteen months ago, is still fresh inside me, beating in my veins. No-one can hear it, no-one here knows them. They're lying on top of each other, ash over decaying body in a small, cold, carefully laid out plot in the old graveyard of my hometown. Three-hundred-year-old trees spread their naked limbs above those remains. Their limbs reach out in blessing, as the minister did from the pulpit when, as a young girl, I went to church with my mother. My father had picked the spot for her, a family grave. He hadn't known that his ashes would join her a week after he buried her.

I know the trees above their grave will bloom again, taunting death with life.

Life that must go on.

I drink a glass of water, turn on my heels to go back to bed. The ache of imbalance, the feeling as if my left arm has been ripped out of my body, keeps me teetering on the edge of nausea and anger.

Why did you, my other arm, my home away from home, my adventurer, have to get an accident, lose your handyman ability, so you couldn't even do the tile project? You, who always fixed everything in our home? Why did your body have to fail you, so you couldn't come be with me when my parents died? Why did I have to let my son take your place and join me in my grief?

Did you want to ease me in, back during the tile project, already knowing I'd have to do the hard things in life without you?

My rational mind tells me to get a hold of myself. *It isn't his fault.* Still, why is he shutting me out from his struggle with his illness? I want to walk down this road of illness with him. I don't want us to be separate. I don't want to do life alone.

The pit of loss is sucking the energy out of my body, lets me think crazy, irrational thoughts of pounding on him to beat the dysfunction out of his body.

I want to scream at him, "Why can't you be here for me? Our promise to each other, *I'll be there for you for the rest of our lives*— what is it worth now?"

I go back to bed, exhausted from all the thinking, all the memories about a life that is no more. I pull the covers tight around me. Something needs to hold me, give me a feeling of belonging. I drift off into a sleep of exhaustion. Can I belong to someone who wants to exclude me from his life?

The next week my therapist fills out the form for an extended sick leave. He gives me a diagnosis of depression, recommending a change of scene to break out of it. My colleagues at work think I'm off on an adventure. When I tell the youths with whom I work in the prison that I'm going on a trip for a while they look longingly out the windows of their unit to the courtyard, their only break-out place. I have my permission slip to go to no man's land, the barren mountains of the Himalayas. Without knowing if and how Doyle and I will move forward as a couple, I prepare to leave for Europe and India. I look forward to finding a no man's place for my mind, emptiness away from all the confusion. A place where my only function will be to survive the trek. A place where meaning is dictated by the elements. A place I can get lost in, while accomplishing a mission. A place where the emptiness around me can echo my silent screams.

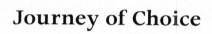

Journey of Choice

Chapter 9

I step through the open door of the small Indian Airlines' plane onto the staircase and take my first breath of Himalayan air. I'm almost bowled over by the negative ions. In my nose is the smell of a hundred freshly washed sheets dried in the open air. Is this for real? The snowy peaks around me confirm the reality of this moment. The last flight was an uneventful two-hour jump from busy, hot Delhi to the calm of Leh, the capital of Ladakh. My excitement about entering the world above tree line goes up a notch with every intoxicating breath.

Carol had told me that I would have to take it easy on arrival. "The change in altitude is hard," she had said, "you'll have to lie around and drink a lot of water for a few days." Slowly I descend the stairs followed by other passengers and walk on the tarmac to the arrival building. Two American college students in need of a place to stay follow me, hoping that they'll be able to stay at the guest house where I've made a reservation. The Leh airport is small. Indian security guards in green uniforms direct a mixture of locals and tourists to the designated lanes for passport checks and baggage pickup.

A crowd of dark-eyed people stare at me as I leave the arrival building. How am I going to recognize my pickup person, a man I've never met, never spoken to? A month ago I made a late-night phone call from my home on the West Coast of the US to Dawa, my guest-house host. Dawa, thousands of miles away in the Himalayas, spoke enough English to let me know she'll have the "sun" room reserved. Her husband Chandar will be at the airport to pick me up.

"Taxi, Memsahib?" four voices call at once.

"No, thank you." I have my driver, I think.

How do I find him? I'm watching people taking taxis and the crowd thins out. I'm a stranger meeting someone in a strange land.

Will it happen? Another arrival in a strange land a long time ago runs through my head.

* * *

I was nineteen years old, sitting in John F. Kennedy Airport after my first ever airplane ride away from Holland. I was on my way to become an *au pair* with a Dutch-Belgian family on Long Island for the summer. It was an overwhelming, strange world. I had never used spoken English. I only knew the English I read and translated in my schoolbooks. I was familiar with train stations, but I'd never seen an airport on the inside until this trip. Where were my hosts? I waited for my pickup, but no-one showed.

My hand clenched the piece of paper with a phone number. *Should I?* The phone booth loomed large and intimidatingly red across from me. I had twenty-five American dollars in my pocket. The instructions for making a call inside the phone booth told me I needed a dime. What was a dime? Should I ask someone? Large African American men passed me by. Women in veiled headdresses avoided my eyes. I heard the unfamiliar sound of cowboys chewing their words. What were they saying? I read the instructions again, walked over to a newspaper stand and asked for "small money" for the telephone. A friendly woman gave me what she called "change". I tried the different coins and followed the dialing instructions. The phone rang.

"Hallo?" a Dutch voice answered.

"Riet? I'm at the airport. There is no-one to pick me up."

"Nellie, is that you? I've been waiting for your call. Planes do not always arrive on time. We will meet you in half an hour." Instructions for where to wait followed. I sat down on a bench, shaking a bit. I wouldn't be lost in this big maelstrom of strange people. Tears wet my young hands as I blew my nose.

* * *

"Dami!" Someone calls my name.

I look around to locate the voice and see a man waving at me.

"Chandar?"

"Yes, over here!" He speaks English. Relief, it's all working out. Within minutes, luggage, the American girls and I are barreling down the dusty road to Dawa's guesthouse. The sun room and a bed are waiting. I've found a home in my no man's land.

The next morning I wake up with a bursting headache, hung over from reduced oxygen. The dreaded adjustment to an altitude of almost twelve thousand feet has begun and I have to wait till my body starts producing more red blood cells to capture the oxygen that's available. I'll follow well-meaning instructions to drink water, lie around and avoid heavy foods. I have no appetite anyway. After I swallow a homeopathic altitude remedy, which I figure may or may not help, I try to get comfortable in my sleeping bag on the hard mattress, I remember the headache I had at the Mount Everest glacier. The headache, the little hut at the bottom of Kala Patar, being a guest to a rag-clad Sherpa, dragging my body one step at a time. I was following Alan on his mission then.

* * *

I remember how the Mount Everest glacier in summer had been nothing but dirty, icy ridges of gray snow, melted and refrozen, forming a linear pattern to greater heights. I had a view of the tallest peaks on earth circling around me, white and towering. I felt so minuscule. My headache then was masked by an altitude remedy a doctor-traveler had given me the previous night. My born-below-sea-level vascular system was straining even after three weeks of steady up and down hiking.

I remember how we climbed Kala Patar, a black peak of gravel in the center of the glacier, 18,000 feet high. I counted steps, twenty at a time, then rest, look around. I was doing the unthinkable, climbing near the highest peaks on earth, thanks to Alan, who had dreamed of this ever since he'd started rock climbing in the western ridges of the Sierra Nevada Mountains in California.

* * *

Lying in my sleeping bag in this guesthouse all I can do is let my mind roam. Back then on Kala Patar my mind was empty, my whole focus was on breathing, getting enough air, while my head was pounding with the heartbeat of my arteries. The mountains had reigned in their imposing silence. Will I find such mountains here in Ladakh? They don't call it Little Tibet for nothing. They say that mountains are the abode of the gods. Do they really live here? I had heard a far rumbling on Mount Everest and the sound had taken my eyes to an avalanche. Had the gods been speaking to me? I thought of the man in rags who'd been living in the little hut at the bottom of Kala Patar; he would've known. He served hot boiled potatoes with yak butter. The best I have ever eaten. Hunger does wonders for appreciation. Does it work for hungry souls? I found a spiritual connection then, but has it served me; could it serve me now?

This is a different time, different guesthouse; I'm on my mission, not Alan's as it had been in 1972. I'm staying in a guesthouse in a small village on the outskirts of Leh. Through the glass wall of windows of the large 'sun' room, my home for the time being, I watch the rising sun hit the mountains across the valley and slowly start its trajectory over a mosaic of green fields with crops in different stages of growth. I recognize that these are the barley fields Helena Norberg-Hodge talked about in her book *Ancient Futures.* Barley, with its short growing cycle, is still the staple of Ladakhi life. Will they feed me *tsampa* (barley flour, mixed with tea) for breakfast? The thought of food turns my stomach and I relive the memory of hiking to Mount Everest and eating *tsampa* on the trail.

* * *

I remember sitting in a tent with Alan. It was still early in the morning. We'd walked our first stretch of the day. We'd been walking in the mountains of Nepal for two weeks, up and down, through forests, villages and high meadows. Our first food supplies which we had brought from Kathmandu were dwindling, and we had to rely more on local fare. On that cold morning we met up with a group of Sherpas who invited us into their breakfast tent. The Sherpas passed a small bag around and everyone reached in and brought out a handful of flour. They passed tea around as well. Alan and I followed the example of the others. Put the flour in your cup, add a little tea, and mash the substance into a ball, roll it, and pop it into your mouth. The raw flour substance stuck to my teeth, the dry taste made me gag. I took another swig of the yak butter tea to create a porridge I could chew. That was a mistake, because the flour expanded and absorbed the liquid. All I could do was chew and chew. I then understood the real meaning of the onomatopoeia, *tsampa*. *Tssa*, push the flour off your teeth, *mm*, close your lips, *pah*, smack the flour as you try to chew. It was cold outside the tent, and my body needed energy to keep climbing. I chewed and chewed and turned off my likes and dislikes for the time being. The brown eyes all around me smiled as they passed the tea. I had become a member of a community on the trail. There was one law: *eat to survive.*

* * *

It's hard to believe that I'll survive the drastic change in altitude and feel normal in a few days here. I look out the window where I see an old woman working the field. Is she old? I feel old: 58 going on 80 today. I sleep some more, but eventually I cannot escape the call of nature and drag myself to the bathroom. The light bounces off the gray concrete as I cross the first storey patio. My head hurts, my nostrils smell smoky incense. A woman steps out of a room filled with religious symbols, religious paintings and bowls for offerings, the *puja*[27] room of the guesthouse. Someone is minding the spiritual store. I hope she prayed for me.

I get dressed slowly and venture downstairs. Westerners are walking around. I see Dawa, a woman of about forty in the kitchen dressed in a *chuba*, the local brown wrap-around dress for women, and a western sweater. I enter. Squatting, she's stirring a pot on top of a kerosene stove that is sitting on the dirt floor. There are no counters, no sink; a refrigerator hums in an adjacent space, where the floor is stacked with dishes, waiting to be washed in a large basin. This is

---

27. *Puja*: ritual worship, often with flowers, candles and chanting.

camp cooking and washing.

"Tea, breakfast?" She speaks softly, looks up from her task and smiles, her face smooth around her dark eyes.

"Tea, yes, I don't know about breakfast." My stomach hasn't straightened itself in my body yet.

"Go into the garden, we'll serve tea there," Dawa instructs and gives me a friendly, illuminating smile. I think I'll be able to get along with her.

I go outside, bright light, high altitude light, I want sunglasses. The American girls, who came with me off the plane yesterday, are sitting at a small table surrounded by plastic chairs looking out over the terraced fields below the house. I sit down, am introduced to other guests and given tidbits of information about places and travel. There is bread, jam and tea on the table. A young dark-haired girl asks if I want eggs. Good, no *tsampa*, this is tourist catering. The sun warms the tension from my head. The tea energizes. I might just take a few steps today into the village.

Each day I'm able to breathe more easily and walk farther before the heavy altitude tiredness settles in my muscles, forcing me to rest. I walk along narrow trails criss-crossing the fields to town. The few unpaved main streets of Leh are lined with rows of what look like storage units, their corrugated doors open to the street in the day-time, displaying cottage industry items for sale, teashops, small internet businesses and tour offices. Only the bank is a "proper" building with a front door, a hallway and teller windows. After getting the lay of the land in Leh, I venture out into the surrounding neighborhoods and villages, climbing winding dusty alleys and country paths to a higher elevation. A two-hour walk here feels like a day's hike at home in Oregon.

On one of my walks in the villages, I come across a little white *stupa*, a Buddhist shrine containing relics. Decorated with gold paint, it sits in the enclosed yard of a small building, surrounded by a lush flower garden. The afternoon air is quiet and warm. I perch in the sunshine on the low wall of the garden, imagining life if I were the nun who takes care of this place. How I would do the daily ritual of opening the puja room, lighting the incense, reciting the chants? Most of all, I imagine the peace of mind that might come from knowing my work would be securing me a better place in a next life. A peace of mind, a purpose I haven't found yet. Could I take up the spiritual life and find peace of mind if I leave behind my worldly life with all of its loss?

Ah, the clarity in living that comes with conviction! At twelve years old, I knelt every night at my bed and prayed. I wanted to become a missionary and save my father from his atheistic downfall. The Buddhist monk who lives here has his convictions. Does he have peace of mind?

I climb on the narrow road from this small spiritual center to the outskirts of the village. As the road climbs I see fewer and fewer houses. Rocks dot the landscape, rocks stacked in little piles, marking the now invisible trail up to another *stupa*, sitting above and away from the village and town life.

I sit on the windswept wall around the pure white dome of sacred energy and look out. There is no green out here anymore. No signs of life, just rocks and sand in varying colors of gray. I'm all alone in this rock desert far away from home and family. No-one knows where I am right now, not even Dawa or the temporary friends in the guesthouse. The thought that I can walk off between those mountains and no-one would know, no-one would know where to look for me, holds my attention. I could walk out of my life here. The temptation hovers around my loss and confusion. I wonder how long it would take to die out there. I sit and think, but I don't walk out into the mountain desolation.

When I walk the road back to the guesthouse in the afternoon, I have to cross a bridge over a river. The river is gray with silt from snow melt, flowing full and fast. People are putting sandbags along its banks. What a difference, I think, between the small stream this morning and this wide body of water working its way up the banks and over the bridge as it roars down to a lower elevation. I watch the sandbagging for a while. Nobody seems to panic, this must be normal spring flooding, I guess.

When I reach the guesthouse Dawa tells me that Karma, my friend Carol's contact for me in Leh, is sitting in the guest dining room waiting to talk to me. I enter the dining room and Karma's dark eyes in his broad face turn to me with interest.

"Hello, are you Dami, Carol's friend?" he asks.

I nod and put my hands together in greeting, "Yes."

"How is Carol-Ma, is she well?" He uses the sufffix of respect and endearment for an older person as he refers to her.

"She's well. Do you want to see a recent picture of her?" I reach for my journal in my bag where I keep a little photo album of pictures from home.

"Yes, very much, it's been a while since I've seen her." Karma's English is quite fluent. When I show Karma the picture, he nods and smiles.

"I help Carol many times, she's a good lady."

"Can you help me, maybe? I want to meditate for a few days at a retreat center while I get used to the altitude before I go trekking." I share my plan to retreat from the world without telling him I want to ponder my wish to escape life. Karma tells me about Mahabodhi, a Buddhist monastery where they hold Vipassana retreats, an hour bus ride south of Leh.

"That's wonderful!" I feel amazed and lucky to find a center in the Vipassana tradition.

"In two days retreat starts; part-time attendance is allowed, so you can be back in a week to organize trek," Karma explains. I give him a big smile, elated that plans are unfolding so smoothly.

I disappear in a meditation retreat. My last retreat was for three days in Oregon in the depths of winter after my parents died. It had felt good to wrap myself in a blanket, be silent and let my loss unfold with each breath. This time, following the routine of sleeping in a cell, waking before dawn and sitting in meditation either in my cell or the meditation hall, the retreat gives me a momentary reprieve from the search for new meaning. The monastery holds the meaning. I do the prescribed "body sweep", moving my attention from the top of my head to my feet, noting each part of the body and its sensations with varying focus, bringing my attention back to sensation when I'm aware that my mind is wandering. My mind is focused on numbness, every bone in my body hurts.

On my slow walks around the compound during breaks, I can see the snow line on the surrounding peaks receding more every day under the summer sun, inviting me to trek into this formidable vastness of rock and scree. My breath is deepening. In the quiet of the retreat, I hold my back straight as I sit on my cushion and start to feel my energy flow. I observe my body tingling and notice renewed strength as the tiredness lifts. I'm adjusting to living at high altitude. The quiet well-being I'm experiencing is producing thoughts about giving back to this place where I'm able to find my center. Maybe the person in charge of this monastery could give me some direction as to how I can do so. Maybe he can teach me something about living a spiritual life.

I request an interview with Sanghasena, the Abbot of the monastery. He is a well-traveled monk whose entrepreneurial spirit has turned this large, high desert piece of land into a tree-lined site, holding, besides the monastery compound, a hospital, a small restaurant, a nunnery, a boys' school, an old folks' home and a new school for young monks.

The evening before my departure from the retreat I'm given entry to the Abbot's quarters by a monk who looks to be 30 years of age. Age is hard to guess in this country, with harsh conditions and often insufficient nutrition. The room I enter is large and the walls are covered with *thangkas*, painted Buddhist wall hangings, and Chinese damask draperies. A multitude of carpets hide the floor. There's an assortment of low furniture with cushions in all colors. From the ceiling hang banners, ribbons, and Chinese lanterns that light the room. I feel as if I've entered a fantastic cloth store, where I can order royal outfits to adorn me as I'm getting ready to take off on a magic carpet. Very different from the small, dark, smoke-filled rooms I entered years ago in small monasteries on my trek to Mount Everest. This is monkhood in the fast lane, unafraid of material display. I sit down on one of the settees and study a colorful, glossy brochure about this monastic development.

After a little while, Sanghasena enters in red and ochre robes,

Western style glasses, an ochre wool cap and a gleaming watch on his wrist.

"You come from Europe?" he asks.

"Originally, yes, but I live in the States."

"I have been in the States and in Holland," he replies. "Not for a while though; I've been too busy with this property. In the last six years we've built many buildings. I go to Bangalore now and then to discuss financial matters with headquarters." He waves his hand to a picture of a large monastery with a golden pagoda and monks in ochre clothing lining the paths.

"I noticed that the old people struggle with their eyes. Only a few seem to have glasses. Can I help? Make a donation, maybe?" I notice I'm speaking in simple sentences after the silence of the last five days. I want to explain the idea that came up while I was sitting comparing life in this monastery and life in the prison where I work. "You're doing a great social project. I work in a facility that rehabilitates criminal youth. A monastery of sorts, except the youth do not get Buddhist instruction."

Sanghasena smiles as I make the comparison.

"I wonder if the young monks here can correspond with the youth in my facility in Oregon."

"That will be good; they will practice English." Sanghasena picks up one of the brochures on a table next to him and hands it to me.

"I'm working on developing a Vipassana center east of Leh, a new meditation center." He talks about his next ambition, as I just experienced the benefits of meditating for six days. Smart man. The interview turns into a well-couched pitch for donations to expand his projects, rather than a spiritual talk about the values of living according to Buddhist principles. The tradition of seeking sponsors for enterprises has a strong hold. I recognize this Asian form of lobbying. A conservative view on development, where religious dominance means power and economic progress.

Seeing the display of Buddhist politics in front of me, I let my disappointment take hold of my judgment. I won't ask this man for spiritual advice regarding the mess in my marriage. What does he know about marriage anyway, except that it's an economic institution, a lower form of spiritual work than he's doing? Ladakhi of origin as he is, he belongs here. He's doing good work for his country and his people. Can my social work with people at home be enough for me? If I break up with Doyle, can work be the meaning of my life?

"I'll make a donation tomorrow when I leave."

Sanghasena smiles, "I will instruct my secretary to write you a receipt."

When I return to my spare quarters in the meditation compound, I stand outside my room and look up. The stars are brilliant in a dark blue sky. I'm no longer bound by the familiar, simple routine of responding to the meditation gong. I'm on my own again to decide what my practice is. The desire to live in a monastery I had on my first trip to India so long ago, is gone.

Staring at the stars, I wonder what I'll do with my spiritual aspirations of the last thirty years, now that my life as a householder trying to incorporate a meditation practice is falling apart. What will I do with my ideals about society, the wish to live a harmonious and shared existence, implanted by my socialist father? What will I do about waking before dawn and feeling my unmet need for connection, now that Doyle is living apart from me?

Will this place of barren snowcapped mountains, thin air, lush gardens and friendly people show me how it all can come together?

Chapter 10

After the retreat I go back to Dawa's guesthouse to plan my trek to Lingshed. Dawa tells me Karma has sent a message asking me to go see him at his office in downtown Leh with an invitation to visit his family and have dinner with them. Dawa gives me directions and the next day, after walking into town from Dawa's guesthouse, I wend my way through the small center of Leh with its tourist shops to a street with markets for locals, a bakery with Indian sweets stacked behind a counter and a butcher with meat hanging from hooks outside, flies buzzing around it. Seeing the meat I'm glad I've decided to eat vegetarian on this trip. Outdoor vendors, mostly women, sit on the street with small displays of vegetables on a piece of cloth or cardboard. They must come from their farms to make some money in the city. As I turn the corner to find the courtyard behind the buildings where the entrance to Karma's office is supposed to be, I see an open area full of secondhand clothing, western secondhand clothing. *Hmm,* I think, *so Goodwill must ship its overflow here.* I walk past and see a door that leads upstairs. That must be where the office is.

I peek through the open door of the office. A small woman stands in the middle of the room speaking rapid English with a French accent. Karma sits at a table with a computer with his back to me. There is not much else in the room except for a filing cabinet. I step inside.

The woman says: "Phillippe's not coming out this year, the money isn't there. You must make the tour on your own this summer since I'm going to see Helen next week and stay in the mountains. We just have to wait and see how much they want us to do."

Karma nods, looks over his shoulder and smiles in my direction as I enter, and says to the woman: "I haven't been able to organize the trip. The computer's been down a lot, and I haven't organized the data yet. It's time to go to Kazai region, the snow's melting and plants are blooming."

"Well, I'll see you when I get back from Hemis, for the summer training." The woman nods at me in greeting and takes off, scarves flying behind her.

"So this is where you work?" I say, as I look into a small room to the side where a young girl is asleep on the couch.

"No, just the office work, the French company that hires me rents this office. Volunteers who help with the work come here too." Karma turns to me. "I work in the field also to teach *Amchi*, Tibetan herbal medicine, to villagers who don't have access to western medicine. I document the work we do and organize trainings here in the office." My friend Carol in Oregon had told me that Karma worked for a non-profit organization and sometimes traveled to Europe for his work. That must be why his English is so good, I think.

Karma turns to me and says: "That was Marie. She's lived in Leh for eight years, off and on. She doesn't officially work for the organization anymore, but she stays involved. There is no money to pay her, but her contacts are valuable to get things done. I'm sorry to have to tell you I can't leave to go trekking. I have to stay in Leh for the summer training. I've asked my nephew to be your guide instead of me. Tondup will be a good guide. He has finished school for the year and wants to go back to see his home and family."

"Too bad, I would have liked your company on the trek." Even though I don't know Karma well, I've taken a liking to him. What will his nephew be like? "Does your nephew speak English?" I ask looking out of the window over the mosaic of rooftops at the Himalayas with all its unknowns. I wonder what I'm in for now. I'll have to trust that Karma has the best in mind for me.

"Tondup speaks English, he's trustworthy and strong. He will take care of you. I will tell him." Karma takes a last look at his computer screen and shuts it down. "I'm not getting anywhere with this project today. Let's get some food to take home for dinner." He steps into the side room and gently wakes up the girl. Sleepily she looks at me.

Karma says something in Ladakhi, pointing at me. I hear my name. The girl smiles. I smile back.

"This is my daughter Dechen, she goes to school all day and gets tired," he explains. She waits here after school until I'm done with my work." This must be Karma's daughter from his marriage to his brother's wife Dolkar. Carol had told me that, after the death of his brother and in line with local customs, Karma renounced monkhood in his early thirties to marry his brother's wife and care for her and his brother's children.

Karma picks up his bag and helps his still sleepy daughter up. We step out of the office, Karma locks the door and we walk to the local bazaar. The bazaar is a narrow passage between two sides of vendor stalls displaying wares, a passage full of people chatting, drinking tea, and shopping. I like the bustle of people doing their shopping, not paying much attention to me. I feel like I'm part of daily life here, walking with Karma and his daughter. Karma stops at a produce vendor and buys some vegetables and mangoes. He squeezes the mangoes to test their ripeness and quality. "You want the mango to be soft, so you can suck out the flesh," he tells me and hands me one. I've never eaten a mango that way and enjoy the sensual slurping as we slowly make our way through the throng of people to the bus station.

It's almost five o'clock, the end of the workday in the city, and many locals are waiting for buses to take them back to their villages. We sit down in a tea shop to wait for our bus. I give Dechen a cookie from the bag I've brought as a dinner gift. Dechen looks at me with big brown eyes, smiles and nibbles her cookie slowly. When we finish our tea, Karma looks at his watch and says: "Time to go to the bus stop; the bus will be here soon." We join a crowd of waiting people on a platform. When the bus arrives, I'm the only Westerner boarding the bus, and all, mostly male, eyes are on me as I make my way to a seat Karma has found for me. I feel awkward, and know that I stick out like a sore thumb with my blond-gray hair and blue eyes among the black hair, brown skin and dark eyes of the locals. Being different makes me feel like a target, an object of exploration for everyone around me. Memories of being ogled take me back to a bazaar in Mazar-I-Sharif on my way to India many years ago.

* * *

I remember craning my head to see why the small crowd had gathered in the narrow, covered bazaar. Alan and I had been on a treasure hunt among oriental carpets, jewelry, and fragrant wood products mixed with wafts of shish-kebab and spicy sauces. My blond, long-haired, six-foot-three American boyfriend towered over the dark-haired crowd. Then I felt it. The hand softly stroking my back. Was I making it up? Definitely not, the hand was traveling down to my buttocks and not so subtle anymore. My anger flared. My fresh convictions about women's liberation wouldn't let me cower. I turned and grabbed the man, yelled and gave him a piece of my mind in English while pushing him hard. Before I knew it, the crowd had turned toward me. My boyfriend swept me away before things could go further.

"Walk!" he insisted in a low voice. "Are you crazy? We're in a Moslem bazaar." He had a firm hold on my arm showing the crowd he had control of me.

"But... he was touching me!" I defended myself.

"Yes, and you are just a woman here. A foreign woman at that!"

"I hate it, I don't want you to have to protect me. I want to be free to be me as a person." The whole mess of watching my father diminish my mother in her traditional role in the marriage flushed through my brain. I had gained the freedom to travel, but I needed the man next to me to be safe. Would I ever be really free to move about?

* * *

Back in Leh again—the male eyes in the bus follow me until I sit down. Dechen sits down next to me. Will I have to deal with male cultural biases here too? Do I have Karma's protection? Karma stands in the aisle. Once I sit on the seat in the back of the bus, it seems I become just part of the crowd. No-one pays attention to me any longer. I can sit here and observe people moving about in their day and make up stories in my head about the local people and school children as they board the bus and get off at different stops. The young man, proudly wearing his starched shirt, probably works in a bank. The girl waving at her friend as she gets off the bus hopes that her family can pay for the new shoes she wants.

From our stop it's a short walk through the newly built neighborhood to Karma's house. There are no paved streets separating the houses, just dusty roads and alleys, wide enough to let a car or water truck through. The square houses are all built with locally produced mud bricks. A small yard surrounded by a low mud wall lies in front and to the side of Karma's house. We enter the barren, dusty yard and walk the few steps to the front veranda. Karma introduces me to his twelve-year-old stepson, Kalsang, and says something to the boy. He comes back with water in a shallow basin. We wash our hands and go inside where Karma introduces me to his wife, Dolkar.

Dolkar greets me shyly with a few English words, while putting her arm around Dechen. I smile to make up for my lack of skill in her language. Dolkar motions me to her kitchen where she makes butter tea for us in a long tubular wooden holder resembling a Western butter churn. The cabinets above the kitchen counter are filled with Chinese porcelain cups, bowls and plates. When I point at the porcelain ware, smile and raise my thumb in sign of approval, Dolkar gets up and carefully takes out a cup and plate and hands it to me with a head movement to take them and inspect them. She stands by smiling and nodding as I look at her treasures. Karma says something about Dolkar spending too much money on luxury items as he waves me to a low seating area covered with a Tibetan rug. While Dolkar makes tea, Kalsang comes over and sits with us. He shows me his homework for the day, algebraic equations neatly written out in a notebook. I comment on the difficulty of the problems for someone his age. He smiles and in English says that it's hard, but good to learn. Karma explains the subjects they teach his son in school and I tell him how they resemble an English boarding school program rather than what I expected a Ladakhi public school to teach. Karma agrees but notes that Kalsang has to learn these things to be able to pass entrance exams to the university in India if he goes there.

As I hesitantly and slowly drink the salty broth that is butter tea, Dolkar, with help from Karma, explains her work as a public health educator. She travels regularly to outlying regions to educate village dwellers on health issues and to provide them with access to hygiene products. While talking, Dolkar deftly makes noodles from scratch, kneading the flour ball and pinching off little pieces that she stretches and shapes into a shell-like form. Karma cuts vegetables and starts cooking the broth for the traditional dish we're having, a form of dumpling soup. He brings out a German can of meat, and explaining how some of his trekking clients had left it for him after a trek, he adds it to the broth along with the vegetables. I'm relieved that I can break my no-meat rule without worrying about the source and cleanliness of the meat. Karma says again how sorry he is he can't accompany me on the trek to Lingshed.

"I want to go see one of my teachers in Lingshed. I haven't seen the monastery teacher in three years," he says wistfully.

"Is there any way you can avoid the training?" I have a glimmer of hope.

"No, I'm organizing most of it, and will host the trainers from France." Karma's face is unperturbed as he continues to stir the noodle dish.

The butter tea does its work and before long I need to use the restroom. As I tell Karma this, he shows me their bathroom, a small room without plumbing off the entrance hall. I let him know I need more than washing from a basin and he takes me outside to the back of the yard where there is a traditional Ladakhi outhouse with a dirt floor and a hole in the ground.

When I return to the house Karma shares with me how difficult it is to get running water to this community. He tells me how the local people aren't willing to match a financial offer from a German company for installing the pipes and bringing water to each individual home. The people want the Westerners to take care of the water supply completely, he tells me.

"They don't want to have to pay for the modern conveniences. They say they have done it the old way for a long time, and it works too. We still receive water in a water truck that drives up every morning and fills containers with drinking water. The homeowners pay for the water and carry it to their homes. They use outhouses instead of toilets." His normally soft voice sounds harder with frustration over the traditional thinking he struggles to change. Dolkar nods and smiles. Does she understand Karma's English?

After dinner Karma invites me to the living room and we sit on the Tibetan carpets laid on a low dais, while Dolkar stays in the kitchen with the children. The brand-new-looking Western-style couch sits empty, more a tribute to status than a change in lifestyle. Karma takes out a thick rectangular object wrapped in red and golden-yellow cloth.

"This is what I'm studying in the winter when we're snowed in." He unties the traditionally made Tibetan book, short, wide pages printed with symbols on rice paper, stacked without binding and held together by wooden covers and wrapped in cloth.

"Can you read this script?" I ask in amazement.

"Yes, but reading doesn't always mean understanding. That's why I want to speak with my teacher soon. The scripture does not answer my questions."

"What questions?" I ask.

"What to do about my relationship with Dolkar. She's not interested in spiritual matters. She wants to buy material things. I can't talk with her about the teachings."

"Spiritual pursuits haven't saved my marriage either," I say. I can't believe I'm talking with a monk about my marriage! People are the same across cultures. It comes down to connecting with someone.

"According to the scriptures, it's not acceptable to indulge in material things. I have to lead my wife and I don't know how." Karma wrinkles his brow but maintains a small smile.

"My husband agrees with the Buddhist spiritual principles of moderation and non-attachment, but spiritual principles and personal cravings haven't gone hand in hand and we are in a crisis in our marriage."

"Your husband is at home?" Karma looks puzzled.

"I have left him and my shaky marriage behind to get some answers. I hope to figure things out by trekking and exploring your

Buddhist culture. I can understand you want to get answers from a wise person." I don't know what to say to a man who has taken on his wife as a duty and is sincerely trying to make the best of it.

"I will go to India this winter to meet with my principal teacher. There isn't much work in the winter and I can get away." Karma turns over some of the book's pages.

"Does your family come with you?" I imagine Dolkar following Karma to the monastery as a dutiful wife. Will she practice the teachings, because she's married to a former monk? Will she resist? So many questions I can't answer.

"I don't know yet. If we can afford to, we'll all spend some time there. Villages and school are inaccessible in the winter, so we're all isolated at home. I want a laptop to stay connected during the long winter months." Karma closes the Tibetan scripture and starts wrapping the cloth around it. He rubs his wrinkled brow and says, "I'm worried that it goes against the teachings to have a computer for personal use."

"Seems to me, a laptop might be helpful. It depends on how you use it." I raise and turn my open hand in a gesture of relativity as I add my two cents of wisdom.

Outside it has turned dark and quiet outside. Dolkar and the children have disappeared to their room. Our conversation dwindles to thoughts and I tell Karma that I'm tired and ready to go to sleep. The dais makes an acceptable sleeping spot for the night.

As I lay waiting for sleep to take me away, I regret not being able to have a meaningful conversation with Dolkar. I like her independent demeanor and I want to know more about her career as a public health educator. I wonder if her behavior matches the description others have given me of Ladakhi women as equal partners in family and business matters. The women's status results from of a long history of family landownership in which women's work and or-ganizational abilities are needed and appreciated. I wonder if Karma has more difficulty with Dolkar's independence since they raised him in an all-male monastery. I'm all for a status of equality for Dolkar. My thoughts travel to the Tibetan refugees in India when I was there 33 years ago, and now again here in this community settled in the outskirts of Leh. I was struck by how the Tibetan refugees show the same confidence as the Ladakhis in their mannerisms, open questioning and listening with a relaxed eye.

Yawning now, the face of Dawa, my Ladakhi female host in my guesthouse in Leh, floats through my mind. At age 40 Dawa runs the guesthouse out of a typical large family home where the extended family, comprising grandparents, an unmarried aunt, children and a Nepali foster child, live and run the tourist business. Together they take care of crops, animals and a mechanic's shop. I feel a kinship with Dawa, Karma and all these intelligent, enterprising, open-minded Himalayan mountain-people. Could I live in a communal setting like I see here and get my sense of connection and belonging that way? What do the women in places like this do when their husbands betray them, when they are in a marriage without meaning? Dolkar was given a new partner when her husband died. Should I move on, now that Doyle has become a stranger?

Two days later I meet Karma's nephew, Tondup. He's young, barely out of high school. His muscular, short mountain-people stature clashes with the wide set of his slightly slanted eyes and an old man look of brown, weathered skin. An old soul in a young body? Nothing about him is neat, his hair is poorly cut, sticking out in different directions from under a baseball cap. His teeth, irregular in his wide mouth, smile in polite deference as his uncle Karma introduces him to me. He's wearing pants that seem too big, a nylon jacket, bright pink with dirty white panels, sleeves pushed up, showing his muscular arms. Will he be able to organize this twelve-day trek? I represent a summer job for him, an opportunity to see his family, income to open the door of future higher education.

"He'll do a good job of taking care of you on the trail," Karma tells me again. Does that mean that he'll keep me safe, feed me, help me understand what his world is all about? I wanted someone with more experience, someone who speaks my language better and can answer my questions. This is a boy who knows the trail as he has walked it many times back and forth from home to school during school breaks.

At the end of my retreat at the Mahabodhi monastery, I visited the school and residence of the young monks. I watched teenage boys in the school kitchen cooking rice in great quantities to feed their peers; I didn't see vegetables or savory items to complement the meal. Now that I'm being guided by a similar boy, I have little hope of varied fare while on the trail. Tondup probably knows the basics of survival too like those teenage monks, or Karma wouldn't have sent him with me.

Karma leaves us in the small trekking office where he has organized our meeting. I'm not using a trekking company. Would I be better off with an official outfit, jeeps, tents and experienced trekking guides? I don't like the feel of the tourist hype, written on signs and displayed in bright pictures on the wall; I want to avoid being part of a tourist culture that destroys the landscape, sets up a false economy. Can I be part of the cooperative businesses Helena Norberg-Hodge describes in her book *Ancient Futures*? Businesses that use native skills and products to make money for families. Bringing more tourists to support the new housing developments around Leh, cars that stir up the dust, Chinese imported goods that put a wedge between religious beliefs and human desires, none of these are my idea of a positive contribution. But, here I am, a tourist in local eyes, a spiritual seeker in mine and maybe in Karma's eyes. I'm walking a fine line between exploration and exploitation.

Tondup and I sit down at the bare table of the office and I spell out a list of foods I want. Tondup writes the items down in unrecognizable script on hand-made paper. How will I know if he forgets something, or misunderstands what I want? Rice, noodles, flour, oil, no meat. The images of fly-covered meat hanging in the open market stalls in Leh has made me careful about my protein intake. Eggs yes, peanut butter? A quizzical look tells me I have to stay with locally known foods, so lentils for daily protein, curry, vegetables? Yes, some fruit if possible, at least for the first few days. Oh, and tea of course, powdered milk, sugar, so I can have Indian style tea. Weight does not have to be a consideration—like the typical trekking outfit we will have horses that can carry our load.

"I will get all and more, Memsahib not worry," Tondup gives me his young confidence. Or is it indigenous optimism, a way to deal with the inevitability of disaster lurking around the corner?

"OK, how much money do you need to buy all this?" I pull out my travel pouch from under my clothes.

"Rs 1,500 good for start." Tondup looks thoughtfully at the list he's made. Since I'm not hiring an official trekking company, I'm not paying a standard fee. Karma had told me I would pay for the actual cost of food and transportation for the party and then add a daily fee for Tondup and the horseman on top. US$200 for food for him, myself and a horseman for twelve days isn't bad. I look at the number with relief.

There must be a per person quota floating around among the trekking organizers, since he pulled out a number so easily.

"I'd like to leave in two days. Is that possible?" My return flight to Delhi and Holland is set for two weeks from now; the trek will takeat least ten days, so the travel timeline is pushing me to get started on the trek.

"Yes, Memsahib, all will be ready. I find horseman to carry from bus stop. We need two horses. You pay Rs 200 per day?" His eyes downcast, he writes something in his indecipherable script.

"Great, yes, thank you. Where will we meet?" I'm relieved this transaction is going so easily. Good omen?

"Memsahib, come to bus station. Eight o'clock in morning. I will meet you there. Dawa can send taxi for you." Tondup lays out the plan of departure.

"Good, I'll get a tent from Dawa. She's offered to loan me one for the trek." I feel like I'm part of a family whose members all help each other.

"Yes, Dawa good woman, good karma." Tondup smiles his crooked smile.

I agree with Tondup that Dawa is building good karma. She's told me that, now that she's passed the 40-year mark in her life, it's time for her to focus on death, and put her actions in line with creating good karma for an auspicious rebirth. I'm the lucky recipient of her beliefs. My journey into the mountains can begin.

Chapter 11

It's early morning. The light is barely illuminating the gray of the shale-covered mountains as they turn mauve against the pure white of the snowcaps. The earth is poised for another day of exposure to the intensity of high-altitude sun. At the guesthouse I praise Sonam, my driver, for keeping his taxi shiny and clean, despite the constant onslaught of dust. Sonam takes the long road around the little town of Leh. I wonder if he'll charge me extra.

"Petrol expensive now," he says as if he reads my mind. "Long way we can go faster, use less." His logic baffles me.

"It's fine," I say, "the bus leaves at eight and it's only seven thirty right now."

My stomach feels full from an early breakfast at Dawa's guesthouse and it doesn't agree with the rising tension about the coming adventure. Will there be a bus? Will Tondup be at the bus station with all the supplies? After all, I only met him two days ago and entrusted him with money and a shopping list. I'm not sure if Tondup has the wherewithal to organize this expedition. Karma seemed experienced in dealing with foreigners when I met with him last week. Is his nephew as capable? I remind myself how *I* was only nineteen years old when I first set out to travel on my own, to another continent. I made it then, albeit with my share of adventures. My stomach settles a little as I surrender to what I've set in motion.

The sun just touches the top of the mountain range when we pull into the bus station. There are few buses, and the dust hasn't done its dirty work. The air smells fresh, and the light bouncing off the snow in the distance spreads a silver glow over the buildings in the back of the large bus parking area. I step out of the little taxi and grab my daypack.

"I get your bag, Memsahib." Sonam opens up the back of the little Toyota bus. I pull out the Rs 10 Dawa had told me it would cost to go by taxi. Sonam accepts without acknowledgement. Did I have it wrong? Should I give him more, or would that only promote the notion that tourists have endless supplies of money? As Sonam pulls out my pack and puts it on the ground, Tondup appears. They greet each other as family, with *Julleys*—the Ladakhi word for anything from hello to goodbye, thank you and how are you—smiles and a hug. Maybe they are family. Karma came to Dawa's guesthouse as if he was a frequent visitor. Dawa and Sonam are related and refer customers to each other. One way or other they all act like they're family.

"Memsahib, come over here, see food supply." Tondup waves his hand with two bus tickets to a platform.

"Were you able to get everything on the list?" I see the piles of supplies and it looks as if at least the food part of the trip is starting off as planned.

"Yes, Memsahib, most everything is here." Tondup shakes his unruly head of hair in the Indian *achaa* (yes) motion and points to a busy shopping street. "I still need to go to the bazaar across the street for some fruit. Do you need breakfast?" he asks with raised eyebrows.

"No, I have eaten at Dawa's already," I explain; I can feel the scrambled eggs and chapatis sitting heavy in my stomach.

Tondup says something to Sonam in the Ladakhi language. Sonam smiles at me and takes his leave. I turn my attention to life at the bus station.

Some of the platforms are occupied by homeless Indian families. They're freshly awake and going through their morning routine. Small children sit on their sleeping mats, wide eyed. Several men, fathers I presume, are washing themselves, pouring water from an aluminum pitcher over their bodies, and cleaning their teeth with small neem[28] sticks, spitting on the ground. They talk in rapid high tones to the older children, pointing at bags to move or younger children to pick up. Mothers weave themselves between caring for a crying baby, cooking chapatis and smoothing their saris around their petite forms.

"Is the bus here?" I ask.

---

28. Neem, a medicinal plant, is used as a component in some toothpaste and mouth washes (astringent), especially in the Indian subcontinent, and young twigs are used directly as crude toothbrushes in rural areas. (Courtesy of Encyclopedia Britannica)

"Not yet," Tondup answers.

Tondup appears to take delight in his new responsibilities. He shows me a long list of the purchases, all neatly written out and priced, and smiles expectantly at me. The Rs 1,500 budget has done the magic of making him into the manager-administrator of this trip, and he's wearing the image with pride.

"I will get fruit now across the street." He puts his list inside his coat and turns in the direction of the bazaar. "You can stay here, Memsahib."

"OK, I'll see you later." I pull out my camera to shoot some pictures of life in the bus station. I crouch down to aim at an Indian family. My feet, in hiking boots meant for sliding mountain shale, can navigate safely around slimy food remnants, spit and other viscous matter.

The Indian family is camped out on the hard, dusty cement. I point at my camera as a way of asking permission to intrude into the fragile privacy of their morning ritual of feeding and washing. The baby, with a runny nose, a colorful jewel of wool clothing reminiscent of a Goodwill store far away, looks at me with dark eyes out of the wrappings of the mother's flashy green sari. An unspoiled look from a life with minimal experiences, and yet, as the day starts here, it is a life so predetermined by a caste system and poverty. A day orchestrated by sunlight bouncing off the snowy Himalayan peaks, dust and noise from engines, representing the human desire for progress. A third world symphony trying to play the life I represent for them, as I point my camera and guard my new backpack wrapped in its sturdy cover. My pack is leaning against the crates of travel food, ready to take the beating from bony horses, rocks and mountain torrents.

My camera viewer now shows a boy about twelve years old with a blend of Chinese and Tibetan features. He's dressed in the maroon and yellow robe of monkhood and drags his suitcase up to the platform. It's summer break for the schools and he must be going home to his family for a visit. In my conversation with Deepak, a teacher at the Mahabodhi monastery, last week, he explained how children are considered lucky if they can be placed at a monastery school. It means one less mouth to feed for the family with often, scarce food supplies, especially in the winter months. I recall the image of a six-year-old boy at the monastery school. A little boy with a dirty face, red cheeks, and shy smile, who wanted to pose for a picture in front of the school. An older boy adjusted his Snoopy sweatshirt and pulled up his sagging pants for the occasion. They told me that he had been attending the monastery school since he was four and will not see his family until he's twelve, due to the long walking distance to his village.

Maybe, this well-fed young monk was once a little boy like that. The boy sits down next to an older man in a Ladakhi woolen wraparound coat and a Western hat from the forties. The man's face reminds me of Native American tribes across the great ocean, with the wide face, aquiline nose and dark probing eyes. The two engage in a lively conversation of which I can't understand a word. As I turn my camera in their direction, the shadow of a tall man's body falls on the viewer and changes the picture.

The man, a westerner, stands behind me on the platform. His bright blue eyes, matching his blue faded shirt, twinkle behind round-rimmed glasses. Everything about him is faded, his hair, pants, heavy mountaineering boots and pack, reminiscent of quality equipment of years gone by. The cold metal of an ice pick flashes its sharp point over his shoulder as he leans in my direction. He points at the bus a little down the platform.

"Is that the bus to Phalanji?" he asks in English with an unmistakable accent. I shake my head and answer him in Dutch:

"*Ben jij Nederlander*?" (Are you Dutch?)

Surprised, he switches to Dutch.

"*Ja, hoe weet je dat*?" (How do you know?)

"That's easy to guess. I recognize the Dutch accent."

"I can't tell that you're Dutch," he comments.

I explain I live in the States and have been away from the Netherlands for 33 years.

"How long have you been in Leh?" I ask.

"Just a couple of weeks. I've lived in India for the last nine years. I will spend the summer months in the Himalayas. What about you?"

He pulls on his shoulder straps to adjust his backpack.

"I've been here for two weeks. I'm doing a twelve-day trek to Lingshed and back."

"That's interesting! I'm going there as well. I will take the bus to Phalanji and then walk by way of Lingshed to Padulum."

"By the way, my name is Dami. And yours?" I reach out my hand.

"Wouter, *aangenaam*." Wouter uses the familiar Dutch formality of introduction and shakes my hand.

Amid all the foreign faces it's a relief to find someone who knows the Western world I've come from. Traveling alone in this part of the world is a new experience for me. I wouldn't mind sharing my thoughts with someone else besides my journal.

"The bus isn't here yet, and who knows when it will come." I raise my hands in a gesture of not knowing. "You can get your ticket at the window over there." I point to a dilapidated building at the north end of the parking lot and Wouter walks in that direction. I wait on the platform.

I look at my watch. The time of the official bus departure passes and still there's no bus. Tondup comes back with mangoes and bananas.

"Is the bus coming soon?" I ask. He sits down on the boxes, relaxes with smiling third-world resignation and answers: "Bus will come."

The momentary world of the platform is all that exists for now. Talking, feeding, exchanging, staring, and hygiene all roll into one large family affair. I sit down on a ledge and look out at the mountain peaks surrounding the Leh Valley. I will finally enter the world of dust, stone and scree that lies outside the river's edges. What has possessed me to go and test my stamina? After the losses of the last winter I've felt more displaced—more like a stranger in a strange land—in Oregon. I want to experience a more community oriented society. I want to find something new that will move my life forward, help me decide what to do with life and marriage left behind in the USA. Intuitively I know that it'll become clear what that is, as the days and hours unfold under my feet.

Wouter returns with his ticket and sits down next to me on his pack. "I hope it'll be better this time," he says.

"What do you mean?" I look at him.

"I walked last week from Phalanji to Padulum and had to turn back because of avalanches." He runs his fingers through his thinning hair and adjusts his glasses. I guess him to be in his late forties. His blue eyes look at me without expression. A blue I associate with innocence and honesty. I grew up with blue eyes. My immediate family all had blue eyes, and very few relatives in my extended family had brown eyes. When the eyes of my second child, Quinn, turned a deep brown at six weeks of age, I remember having a feeling of alienation, as I looked into the unfamiliar pools of dark light. I had a sense that I was meeting a stranger rather than an offspring. Who is this stranger named Wouter, behind the familiar eyes and voice inflection?

"I'm counting on making it. My schedule does not allow for more than one try." I realize I haven't even considered the possibility of not making it, driven as I am by the inner force that sent me here.

The throaty noise of diesel engines rolls into the platform. With a loud scratching of gears and clapping of folding doors, an old bus parks in front of me. There is a scuffle, stretching and readjusting as travelers separate themselves from the more permanent inhabitants of the platform. A driver jumps out, and suddenly I'm surrounded by men who know what to do. Arms and legs climb on top of the bus and load all the boxes, bags and packs into a travel-safe package. I imagine sharp hairpin bends, the bus swaying from side to side, and the load shifting. I let go of the worries. Thirty-five years ago on my first trip to India, I thought I could become one of the locals by traveling in local style – I resented being seen as someone who could afford more and being treated as such. Now I've accepted the predicament of privilege I find myself in. In a third-world country, I'm wealthy by comparison. I can replace lost or broken items if necessary.

Tondup produces the tickets for a seat in the front of the bus. The green vinyl seats are old, narrow, and flanked by a window through which the still fresh morning air is blowing. Our boots clunk hard on the metal floor. There's barely room for my daypack at my feet. This will not be a cushy six-hour ride.

The bus driver gets into his seat, and reaches above the dash to adjust the pictures of Tara, a wrathful looking green deity, and Krishna, the Hindus' beloved flute player. Underneath the pictures, colorful ribbons dangle around the *dorje*—a bell-bar shaped, filigreed object of Buddhist origin, symbolizing power. The driver takes off his jacket and uncovers a western-style shirt. He looks at his wristwatch and pulls some papers out of a black vinyl attaché bag. Studying the papers, he fills in a form and fastens it to a clipboard that is lying next to his seat on the wide metal console covering the bus engine. He then gets up, steps into the aisle of the bus and reaches over to a woman in a dark woolen wraparound dress who is lugging a package as she climbs the few steps of the bus entry. She hands the driver her package—a cardboard box slightly open, filled with what look like mangoes, tied together with a string—and places it under a bench that lines up with the side window of the bus opposite to his driver seat.

Why are they transporting fruit from southern India? What has happened to the local fruits, such as apricots? I remember reading about the wonderful nutritious quality of high mountain fruits, highly praised in books on nutrition. I found apricot smoothies in Leh and enjoyed them daily when I went into town. Mango must be one of the benefits of progress entering the smaller villages.

The woman says something in her native tongue and points to several younger men in the bus's doorway. The driver smiles and motions her to sit upfront in the bus, where he makes room on the seat that appears to serve as a bed at times, as it is covered with blankets. The young men, traveling with her, carefully put a bag of white rice under the bench. Rice that will be carried for days on the trail to feed the family, instead of the traditional wholesome barley grown in the region. I ask Tondup next to me: "Are these people the bus driver's family?"

"No Memsahib, no think so, we all travel long way today, bring back supplies home." Tondup smiles proudly.

Tondup dressed in his "new" nylon sports pants and a polyester quilted vest—discarded gear from some Western outfitter—wears his attire as a badge of progress. At eighteen years old he's been living away from his family for six years now, meeting foreign influences in the capital while he attended school. I wonder what he'll bring back to his family in Lingshed. Inflated self-confidence, or useful ideas for daily survival?

Once seated, the woman and her companions watch some men load steel pipe on top of the bus. The pipe will carry water to the small terraced fields and the little houses, replacing the intricate network of cooperative irrigation ditches that have watered the fields for centuries. I remember how we dug up the solid steel and put plastic pipe in when we lived on the land in northern California to bring water to our gardens. Gardens that spawned the marijuana culture. Gardens that changed peaceful country living into a dangerous commercial operation and pulled our intentional community apart. I shudder when I think how progress is changing these peaceful communities and pulling the centuries-old family structure apart.

Wouter climbs on, looks at his ticket and works his way to a seat a few rows behind me. I turn around. A sea of brown faces with shiny dark eyes fills the rows. I motion to Wouter and ask, "Do you want to sit together?" I'm assuming that he can change seats with Tondup if we want.

"No, I'm fine here," he says as he slides in next to a woman with a baby and a young child.

I turn and face forward, a bit disappointed. I guess he's not as eager as I am to get to know me. Why does he want to keep his distance? Here we are, far away from the world we grew up in, thrown together by mere fate, a perfect opportunity to share impressions and compare notes. My curiosity about this man from my native country will have to wait.

After a last look in his trip log, and a quick survey of the passengers, the bus driver starts the throaty engine. A man who looks like his assistant and ticket-collector hangs out of the door opening, and yells something to a driver in another bus. We're off, leaving the bus station with its diesel smoke and noise behind, driving westward on the only road that connects the western mountainous region of this small Himalayan country with the capital.

We exit the city through a tall archway painted with bright red, yellow and black indigenous symbols. Colorful prayer flags on top send their prayers with us in the wind as they touch the dragon figures carved in the woodwork. I see a road sign with the names of villages along this road, and notice that the distance to Khalsa, the last town before we turn off to Phalanji—the end of our bus route—is 140 kilometers. The distance is equal to the round trip I drive daily in the US to work and back in an hour-and-a-half. Here we will travel for the next six hours to get to our destination. The bus rattles, coughs and shrieks, as the driver shifts gears to get up to traveling speed.

After a while on the road, we pass a military base. It's the first of many on this route. Soldiers with white turbans guard the perimeter of the compound.

"Ladakhis get jobs here, good jobs," Tondup points out.

"Do the Ladakhis have to fight for the Indians?" I ask.

"No fighting, Memsahib, just patrolling."

"But there's fighting in Kashmir," I retort.

"Ladakhis not fight in Kashmir. Ladakhis keep out foreigners from this country."

I want to know more, but Tondup is struggling to find the English words. I smile at him, thanking him for the information of the moment. I remember how I wanted to adopt India's ways when I came to India 35 years ago, wearing silk and cotton clothing, squatting and sleeping on dirt floors, eating the local food, trying on the eastern spiritual beliefs, especially the notion of enlightenment, some ideal happy state. Aside from getting momentary glimpses of that ideal state of being, where is all that now? How enlightened am I about accepting the changes we're going through in our marriage? I certainly have not adopted the attitude of service to the husband, so ingrained in Indian marriages. Now that Doyle is focused on his own happiness and well-being and can't, or won't, meet my needs, I don't know how to deal with that. I can make assumptions as I enter this world so different from my own, a world that is reorganizing itself as it meets

Western influences, but I must witness what works and doesn't work so well and learn what I can apply as I reorganize my life.

Chapter 12

The bus leaves the city and its surrounding villages behind. The road follows a thin green strip of fields irrigated by the river flowing alongside in a narrowing valley, closed in on both sides by mountain ridges. As the road climbs the green disappears completely, and there is just the palette of the mountain terrain in grays, browns and beiges tinted with mauve.

How did people end up here in the first place? I ask myself. Who wants to carve out a life on a small ledge where there's barely any soil, and the temperatures only allow plant life to flourish above ground for five months out of the year? I'm baffled by human tenacity and wonder if the search for independence drives people farther and farther into these mountains.

Is this what drives me here now? Tenacity, not giving in to the voracious vacuum of depression that waits in the empty spaces of my life? I'm not looking for independence in these mountains. Instead, I'm searching for connection, a new view on my life.

What will I find among these people here? The faces of the people in the bus are open, expressive. Smiles come easily. In the face of the woman across the aisle I can see the excitement about taking this trip. Is she going to visit family? She's dressed in the traditional woolen dress of the region. It's a solid brown color with a wrapped bodice that shows off the colorful blouse she's wearing underneath. It reminds me of my grandmother's traditional wear when I was a child. Oma wore a different chest piece in her velvet jacket every day, while the rest of her clothing stayed the same. If it was a fancy satin piece with gold trim, I knew it was a Sunday or a holiday. A cotton one with a simple pattern showed a normal day.

The young girl dressed in a tunic and pants next to the woman sits quietly, all eyes and ears for what goes on around her. I become that child for a moment, sitting in a bus next to my grandmother while we travel to see relatives and I drink in the adventure of the moment. The experience of both newness and belonging gave me a thirst for more. Gave me the expectation that I belong to this world wherever I go.

My eyes catch the woman's and our smiles connect us across language barriers. The woman holds on to a handle on the edge of the seat in front of her, a smooth brown hand, unadorned and beautiful in its simplicity. My own hand is holding the window bar as the bus swerves around curves, trucks and an occasional jeep. No rings on my hands anymore, as the one my mother gave me broke the night she died, and my wedding band is lying in a drawer at home—alongside my disillusionment and shame—waiting for my decision about what to do with my marriage. I try to guess if she's a married woman. If the girl next to her is hers, or a relative's child. The bag and some packages at her feet give nothing away.

The bus slows down its noisy rattle. There are a few mud-brick houses along the road with flat roofs, typical for the region. I see bundles of thin poplar branches stacked on top. Poplars are about the only trees that grow around here and the teacher at Mahabodhi told me they're being cultivated to draw more moisture to these cold, arid regions. The thin branches are harvested and used as building materials, providing a support frame for the ceilings of the houses.

Two men get up and move what looks like a big gasoline container to the door, along with several cardboard boxes tied together with string. The bus attendant opens the doors. The bus stops, several young boys on the ground reach for the door as it opens, but the attendant tells them something that results in them stepping back and letting the passengers out. The woman across the aisle gets up as well and takes the child with her. She greets the bus driver as she gets out. The boys on the street have backed off under the overhang of a house. A young woman gets on the bus and stands in the aisle, as the bus moves again. There is a sudden laughter and noise. People are ducking their heads and moving away from the window. I feel a spray of water on my shoulder.

"I'm sorry, Memsahib, they don't mean to hurt you." Tondup

leans over me and pushes the window down to protect me from being a target for the boys' pranks from the street.

"Kids' play." I look back to get a glimpse of the boys' faces, but they've ducked behind a porch pillar. My eye catches Wouter's face. He sits relaxed, looking with interest at the surrounding commotion. His body taller than all the others' gives him the best view of the events. I can't tell from his expression if he's amused.

The noise of the bus as it accelerates prevents any further conversation. After some time I notice cultivated fields and houses along the road. We're coming to a little town.

"Rest stop," says Tondup, "time for eating." My bladder is more in need of a rest stop than my stomach. I'm glad to be stretching my legs, cramped as they are in the narrow space between the seats.

We all pile out. There are several restaurants next to one another along the main street. Apart from the solar panels on rooftops, the dusty, unpaved street and mud-brick houses give me the feeling that I've landed in the Middle Ages. There are a few places with vegetarian Indian food, and one with meat filled mo-mos[29] run by a Ladakhi. Tondup goes in to eat. I continue to abstain from meat for safety reasons and find a vegetarian place where I can eat. Wouter is walking down the street checking out the places. Will he want to talk to me now?

"Do you want to eat here?" I point to the nearest Indian place.

"I'll have tea," says Wouter as he produces some money. It's a step, having tea together.

"I'll have samosas with my tea." The crunchy deep-fried vegetable snacks are my favorite. We find a table and sit down to wait for our order. The shopkeeper pours the milky tea into small glasses and puts them in front of us. Wouter peels a banana he's been carrying and eats it slowly while drinking his tea. I let the brown liquid do its work of reviving me and eat the samosas.

"Are you going to carry your own pack or will you have horses on the trail?" he asks. "I'm carrying my own stuff. I'm keeping it simple."

"I have Tondup, he's my guide and cook. We're meeting with a

---

29. Mo-mo: dumpling.

horseman and two horses in Phalanji." Wouter nods while drinking his tea. "Tondup has done the shopping for the trip; he's even bringing eggs!" I add. I wonder how they will survive the bus ride and the trail on the back of a horse. "What are you going to do for food on the trail?"

"I'll buy food along the way." Wouter rubs his face with a handkerchief, wiping off dust.

Passengers are gathering in front of the teashop by our bus. It must be soon time to depart again. Tondup appears from the other side of the street.

"Time to go, Memsahib. Food OK? You finish?"

"Yes, it was good." His concern for my welfare is touching. I'm still disappointed that Karma wasn't able to accompany me on this trek. He would have been a more knowledgeable resource for me. I'm grateful though to have the introduction to local people via Tondup. Maybe Wouter will warm up to being a companion as well.

We find our seats again and the bus takes off in its now familiar noisy, swaying fashion. Soon we've left the little town behind and the road starts a gradual climb. The Indus River is now far below us as the bus moves on the narrow road to the top of the rising cliff.

The Indus is one of the *sapta sindhu*, the seven holy rivers in India. It runs its lonely course from the icy domes of the Himalayas through Pakistan and into the Arabian Sea. I had learned the river's exotic name when I was studying geography in school as a twelve-year-old. Maps fascinated me then. There were so many places to discover and it was then that my desire to see different places was born. Later I learned about the sacred qualities of the river Indus and filed it as a fact in my brain. Being raised a Protestant, "sacred" meant nothing to me in those days and I never thought to ask anyone what its deeper meaning was. I didn't think deeply about most things as I was like a container that could hold tremendous amounts of facts and regurgitate them, rather than interpret them. Two weeks ago, when my plane approached for landing in the Leh Valley, I watched the Indus unfold like a ribbon from my airplane window. Wherever this river ran, I saw small patches of green, providing life and food for people in these forbidding mountains.

I'm pulled out of my reverie, as some jeeps filled with Ladakhis and Westerners pass us unnervingly close to the edge of the road. Another way of going trekking: group tours. The bus stops. We're at a military post. The bus driver says something to Tondup. He turns to me and says, "You have to go show passport. Go out of bus."

I remember now that when I entered the country I had to let officials know where I was planning to go. This is a checkpoint to keep the country safe from unfriendly forces.

"Wouter, we need to get our passports stamped." I step over Tondup's legs and work my way toward the door. Wouter follows. In front of a little house, set back a few yards from the road, sits a guard in green fatigues and beret, gun slung over his shoulder. He gives us a form to fill out and takes our passports inside. He soon comes back with a stamp in them. I tuck the documents away in my pouch around my neck under my clothes. At least this is quick and painless.

Keeping my passport close to my body gives me a sense of safety in strange places. On my return trip from India in 1972 someone stole all my money in Kabul. My passport gave me access to the Consulate and help was soon on the way. I remember the dread Alan and I had felt when we crossed the border between Turkey and Iran on our way east and had to give our passport to strange border guards pointing guns at us. We were in the Armenian Highlands with a view of Mount Ararat, where supposedly Noah's Ark landed thousands of years ago after drifting through the flood water. No guns are pointed at me this time, but the endless mountains were all around. Were there floods here, that covered all the land? Did raging snow melts wipe out villages like the one I witnessed in Leh a week ago, when the river going through town was rising over its banks? Hardship in nature shapes people. Will the hardship of this trek shape my future?

Wouter and I climb back in the bus, and the bus takes off again into the gray landscape. The sun is bright, and the light has an intense glow, bouncing off all the rock corners. I look at the Ladakhis who are without sunglasses and wonder about their eyes. A road crew of men and women stand leaning on shovels and picks. They look out over scarfs tied around their faces, which just leave their eyes uncovered. The dust and intense sun are constant enemies.

The bus creaks as the driver shifts into low gear, inching up the road. The road is narrow and I wonder how anyone will pass. Just as I think that, a bus from the opposite direction is coming into sight. Our driver swings sharply to the left of the road and parks on a rocky ledge, at least 1,500 feet above the river. I ask Tondup if I can get out and take some pictures. Tondup says something to the attendant and the doors open. I step out onto the two-foot-wide rocky edge and peer down into the abyss. The Indus is a wide band of red mud down below, carving its way from east to west in the sheer, steep rock that form the mountains. To my right I see another river coming from the south and joining the Indus.

"What river is that?" I ask Tondup who's stepped out of the bus as well.

"That is Zanskar, comes from Zanskar country." The gray band of this river is as wide as the Indus, and where they meet, there is a line, as if painted by someone, marking gray from red. The Zanskar must be deeper or faster flowing to mark the red Indus so precisely. It's a mystery that there isn't a mix of the two colors at least for a while as they flow together. It makes me think of human lives flowing together.

I ask myself if this is what happens when two people meet. The line of distinction between them is there when they meet, but once they join, does one of them get absorbed and lose his or her definition? Have I lost my definition in my relationship with Doyle? I tend to think not. I'm an emancipated, free-thinking woman. But why do I feel so untethered, as he's getting involved with another woman? As he's choosing to live away from me, in his own house, his own river, so to speak.

The river that flows on here is still called the Indus, but she does not look like the Indus that started high in the mountains. She's now the color of the Zanskar. Why not call it the Zanskar, I muse? This must be the issue of who takes whose name at the time of marriage. I never took Doyle's last name when we married. I had gone through the name change once for my first marriage and then reverted to my maiden name afterward. I could not give up my identity twice. Calling the confluent rivers the Indus may have something to do with the fact that the Indus comes from higher up in the mountains, closer to the "abode of the gods". I look at Tondup and wish I could ask him, but the language and educational barrier leaves this question hanging in the air, unspoken. I have no choice but to let the mystery do its work on the ever-hungry rational part of my brain. From here on the Indus slowly winds its way as a gray flow to lower elevations, where she'll change color repeatedly. Will the color of my identity change as I move through life?

The bus from the opposite direction has passed, and so have a few more trucks loaded with rock and road-building materials. Were those men and women with scarves around their faces waiting for the trucks? Their eyes haunt me as we travel on. Guilt for my privileged life rises in me. The Buddhist view of karma is not a satisfying answer.

As the bus travels on I notice the tension I feel caused by a new watchfulness. Questions such as, *Are my documents tucked away safely? Is my drinking water accessible? Do I have my sunglasses, sunscreen handy?*, float around my brain. There is no-one but me to care about me.

When a marriage ends a safety net is pulled away. There is no-one to automatically come into action when you are stranded, when something breaks, when you hurt yourself. The agreement to be there for each other in good and bad times is broken. Will this be how my life will be from now on, will I be traveling through life alone? Will anyone notice if I don't come home at night, if my car breaks down, my plane is delayed? Will I be like my sister who died many years ago of a brain hemorrhage, alone in her bed? It took 48 hours before someone wondered where she was.

There are Indian military posts along the few highways and the bus passes one of these compounds with its barracks and barred windows, Indian style. People in civilian clothes and in uniform are walking around the compound. Guards are at their posts. There are trucks parked. Boxes stacked around warehouses. No troops doing drills, no tanks doing maneuvers, nothing indicates military action.

It seems more like a military camp-out. This scene does not do justice to the stories about terrorists hiding in remote mountains preparing for attacks on the Western world that have filled the media for the last few years. The military posts in Ladakh seem a more Indian-colonial approach to providing employment—at least to my politically naive view. I have mixed feelings about this: on one hand I feel manipulated by the media, and on the other hand I'm relieved that all is so calm. If there is nothing to fight about why even have such operations here? Why impose a structure of war on a society that has been long independent and taken care of itself without an army? Ladakh has long been linked with China through ancient trade routes such as the Silk Road which exchanged goods and cultural treasures to the benefit of both countries.

Even here, this far away from home, I can't get away from the mistakes of my ancestors and current leaders. Will my presence here make people like Tondup and Karma want more of what I want to run away from in my daily life? Will it change how they approach their life and raise their children?

The bus enters a small town and my mind turns to what there is to see. The street narrows, there are small shops and little restaurants along the main street. Locals in Western and traditional clothing are open for business: shopping, cleaning, repairing.

"What town is this?" I ask Tondup. My map of the country is tucked away in my backpack and I reach for it.

"Khalsa. I went to school here when younger." Tondup looks out and waves to a familiar face. This must be a regional center, as there is market ware everywhere.

"Lunch time," he adds, "you have money?"

I nod, remembering that he must hang on to some of the money I gave him, to negotiate pack horses for our trip.

The bus finds a narrow parking space between two trees over a gully that transports water and waste during rainstorms. The passengers pile out. Tondup points at a little restaurant across the street.

"We eat there." More telling than asking me, he crosses the street.

I look for Wouter, whom I notice walking up to a small stand selling bananas and mangoes. I decide to eat first and then catch up with him.

Inside the little restaurant, Tondup is already shaking hands with the owner and ordering his meal.

"You want dhal, rice and chapatis?" He motions for me to sit down.

There are some formica-covered tables and wooden chairs all around. The walls are plain, covered with painted panels, decorated with a few posters touting Chinese vacation destinations, with lakes, mountains and temples. The kitchen is accessible through a swinging door. When it opens I see gray concrete walls, old commercial equipment, and a sweaty looking cook with hair hanging in his face reaching over big pots, steaming on a range. Soot and baked-on grease complete the picture of this mostly male-run Indian restaurant kitchen. I try not to think about the hygiene involved in food preparation and serving. Hot, cooked and spicy will have to do the trick of protecting my vulnerable gut. I accept Tondup's offer of the basic menu, as the safer option. Tea arrives soon after we sit down.

"Tell me about school," I turn to Tondup. "How old were you when you went here? Was it a government school?"

"Yes, government school. I live at school, when I was twelve to age fifteen."

"You left your village when you were twelve, all by yourself?"

"More children went, we go together. Walk to Phalanji, take bus to Khalsa."

"How often did you get to go home?" I understand the ruggedness of the independent spirit I'm seeing in the locals here, an acceptance of the facts, no room for sentiment and whining. Progress dictates the changes.

"Go home in summer, vacation starts about now, three weeks, go home. Then again for harvest at end of summer."

"Do you stay in school all winter?" I imagine the intense cold, the simple buildings that house the students, and the hardship they have to suffer to gain their basic education. From seeing some of the school work Karma's stepson was doing when I visited, I know that students get a basically British education, left over from British colonial times in India, an education focused on reading, writing, math and science, in preparation for a more advanced education at the university. The practical things of life have to be learned through living and often get lost when students go away to school. Dawa's son was home for the summer from Chandigar, where he was studying to be a teacher. It seems to me his parents could use his help to run the family guesthouse business and mechanic shop. Instead, he rode around on his motorcycle with his friends while his aunt and grandparents did the work on the farm, his mother ran the guesthouse with the help of a foster girl from Nepal and his father worked in his mechanic's shop. Are Dawa and Chandar contributing to the local cultural changes by not expecting their son to participate in the family business as generations have done before them?

"Yes, school all winter. Winter long time." Tondup flashes his smile, a mixture of awkwardness and polite subservience. I wonder how long it will take before barriers between us will break down. Will hardship on the trail do it?

The dhal and rice *thali* arrives. The smell of spices from the dhal mixes with the sweet fragrance of the rice. I notice my hunger.

"You like Indian food?" I ask, wondering when this food has entered his diet.

"Indian food good, I like mo-mos, meat and vegetables better." Tondup scoops another big bite from his chapati and chews it rapidly.

"Ladakhis no eat spicy food, just barley, meat and vegetables."

I have tasted the Ladakhi kitchen fare in my guesthouse in Leh. It was adapted to the western palate by adding more vegetables, but it was tasty, wholesome and simple. I liken the simple forthrightness of these people to their daily fare.

"I look forward to your cooking on the trail."

"I learned to cook in school, food will be good." He says it with assurance. The polite deference from this young man allows me the new status of revered elder which is so easily given here, a step up from the eye rolling and, *"Oh, Mom! You're too old for this!"* comments from my young adult daughters. I finish my meal and decide to find my Dutchman and strike up a conversation with him.

I find Wouter a little ways up the street where the street widens. He's sitting on a stone bench eating fruit.

"Enjoying your lunch?"

"Oh, yes, fruit is my staple and I won't see much of it, when we enter the mountains." Wouter moves his bag and makes a space for me to sit.

"Tondup is treating me so nicely. He ordered Indian food because he knows I'm not eating meat. I brought mangoes for the trail, but I'm tired of bananas, it's all you see here this time of year. Bananas and mangoes."

"I try to eat light, it's good for my spiritual practice." Wouter stares down the street absentmindedly.

"What is your practice?" I ask. Maybe I can compare his experiences with mine.

"I've lived in India in Sathya Sai Baba's ashram. Do you know who he is?" Images of a dark-skinned man with a big Afro hairdo float through my mind.

"I think so. I've seen pictures of him. Never met him though. My guru search ended a long time ago, after I met Neem Karoli Baba."

* * *

I remember how I connected to Neem Karoli on the bus in Afghanistan reading *Be Here Now*[30] and then my miraculous encounter in Delhi with Ram Dass. Alan and I arrived in Delhi after a long train ride through Pakistan and Rajasthan. It was our first introduction to India. We wound our way out of the train station through the thick flow of human bodies in saris, lunghis[31], and very few western shirts and pants. We had an address for a cheap, but clean hotel.

We had negotiated the Rs 5 fare (50 US cents) with a bicycle rickshaw driver to take us to the hotel. The muscles of the rickshaw driver's brown legs bulged as he pushed and pulled our weight to get up to speed. I felt guilty that I let another human carry me when I

30. Ram Dass. 1971—*Be Here Now!* Lama Foundation.
31. Lungi/lunghi: a skirt-like garment made of a single length of fabric worn by men.

had perfectly healthy legs myself. The rickshaw, as if extracting an elephant out of sticky mud, moved slowly through the chaos of colors, beeping horns, taxis and foot traffic, and turned a corner into a small alley where it stopped at our hotel. We could have easily walked here! The Rs 5 became a donation to a man's struggle for survival in a sea of people.

The hotel manager showed us to the top floor of the hotel. Our room opened up to a rooftop terrace. The temperature was balmy, a wonderful change after the dry, cold mornings in Kabul. I didn't have to brace myself against the elements even though it was almost November. The years of weathering November storms, peddling my bike against rain and wind in Holland, had become a faraway memory. An ease filled my body. I liked the new climate.

We stepped out of our simply furnished room with two beds and a webbed suitcase holder that had seen better days, and sat down on the terrace in comfortable, colonial-style rattan chairs. Comfort, warmth, a view of an endless sea of flat, slate and white colored roofs. Golden spires raised their spiritual heads above the sea of rooftops, red clay colored statues of gods and demigods, animals of elevated status, mingled on temples, barely visible through the waves of electrical wires jumping from rooftop to rooftop. The two-month overland trip was over, we had arrived in Delhi!

The rooftop door of the hotel room next to us opened, and it pulled me out of the feeling of warm comfort and arrival reverie. Somehow familiar piercing eyes of a bearded westerner in Indian clothes caught my attention. He walked out onto the roof terrace, smiled, and folded his hands against his white-robed chest in the Namaste gesture which meant, "May God be with you," and sat down.

"Hi," I greeted him. "I'm Nellie, and this is Alan." I waved my hand in Alan's direction. "I'm from Holland. And you are?"

"Ram Dass, how are you?"

I remember my shock. No, this couldn't be. Was I dreaming? Of course! It really was him, the graying beard, the balding head with curly hair around his skull, gentle mouth and piercing dark eyes. I had just closed the *Be Here Now* book with a picture of his face in it. I must have walked into the good fortune of my life! Meeting the author of my "in the sky" guru dream. I felt sparkly inside. Maybe the Beatles knew something when they'd created the "Lucy in the sky with diamonds" song and I got to be the girl with the kaleidoscope eyes, seeing magic everywhere. How would I get a touch of Ram Dass's magic? What should I say? All I could come up with was, "I'm well, considering I just arrived in Delhi on an overnight train ride from Peshawar."

"Yeah that was a long train ride," Alan chimed in. I didn't want to talk about travel routes, I wanted to ask him about life and spiritual practice. Being Here Now loomed big. Could I? I hesitated and asked my not so *Be Here Now* question.

"Where are you going? How long are you staying in Delhi?"

"I'm only in town to take care of some paperwork and then I'm going back to Nainital where I'm staying with my guru." Ram Dass shared the details of his life as if it was anybody's normal business. This man had written a book, he was famous, he had found answers to great questions, had a guru. I wanted what he had found.

"I read about Neem Karoli in your book," I said, "an amazing story."

"Yeah, we almost missed the bus in Afghanistan because of the book," Alan added, "Nel was determined not to lose it in the desert." Ram Dass nodded, his dark eyebrows shading his blue eyes. "Mahara-ji reaches people in strange ways sometimes. If you pay attention, you might find out what he wants to tell you. I have so much to learn from him. He sees right through me and tests me every day," he answered.

"I hope to find someone who can teach me," I said. Would Ram Dass tell me what my next step in India would be?

"You'll know when you meet your teacher. Be open," Ram Dass directed me.

As I had pondered this nondescript road map for my travels in India, and while thinking of my next "diamond Lucy" question, Alan shifted the conversation to practical things, asking questions about avoiding bedbugs and "Delhi-belly".

I felt jealous of Ram Dass. He had a guru and knew his direction

143

in life. I didn't know if I would find a guru.

* * *

I look at Wouter who's eating his fruit lunch. A lunch dictated by a spiritual practice, he says. So much has happened since that first meeting with Ram Dass. Thirty-four years later I'm back in India—still with questions about the guru tradition. My search for a guru and all my spiritual practice has taken a long winding road. I don't have anyone telling me how to live—and I'm not looking for someone to tell me, either.

"Is Sai Baba your guru?" I ask.

"Yes, I've devoted myself to him for the last ten years."

Does devotion mean the man really is his guru? I wonder about this strange connection, so accepted in these parts, and so foreign to the West.

"So what are you doing here then?" I ask.

"Sai Baba told me to go to the Himalayas for a while."

"To do what?" My practicality is oozing out.

"I don't know. It will become clear somehow."

I have to admit to myself that I don't really know what I'm doing in these parts either. "Yeah, I know what you mean." This could become interesting, the two of us walking in the same direction, not knowing what we're doing here. "Do you want to trek together?" Two will know more than one, I think.

"Yes, that makes sense. At least we can start out together and see how our pacing is," Wouter says as he looks in his food bag. I take Wouter's gesture to keep a back door open as giving me freedom to back out at any time. "I'll see about buying more supplies in Phalanji." He finishes his last banana and gets up. "For now, I'm going to buy something at that little market." He points at a small general market across the street.

"I will find a restroom somewhere." I walk toward a teashop next to the market, weaving my way around people, food carts, and small taxis parked while their chauffeurs stand around talking. At the tea-shop I'm directed to a facility behind the teashop. Relieved, it's a clean and Indian style bathroom, which I find most hygienic.

Inside the whitewashed walls the bright light that comes through a skylight bounces back. Have I been here before? In this little white-washed cubicle I think how much one place is like another. I could be anywhere in a Mediterranean country, anywhere in a Middle Eastern country along this latitude in the world. How is it, that particular light can transport us to other places in our minds? Is this what they mean, when they say time and place didn't exist? Somebody must have experienced this before me to write or talk about it.

Wouter is standing on the narrow sidewalk when I come out of the restroom alley.

"It's a decent place," I say.

"It's almost time to get on the bus, but I'll make a visit." Wouter walks into the alley.

I find the bus and join other passengers as they board. Tondup is already in his seat.

"Last stretch to Phalanji, no more chai stops." He smiles and moves over so I can get past him on the green vinyl seat.

"I'm ready to go on, let's go find those mountains." I nudge him jokingly. Wouter climbs on board, just as the driver starts up the choking engine.

Chapter 13

14,000 FT, PHALANGI

Soon after leaving Khalsa, the bus turns off the main highway and heads south. The road narrows and the mountains close in to form a gorge. Stone, more stone and rushing water form a wild river that takes anything that falls in down into a twirling, forceful dervish dance. Its force awes me.

When I was a young girl living on an island, my brother and I would walk the double row of posts that formed breakers for the forces of the sea. The posts were short, buried in the sand where they met the beach, but grew to eight-foot-tall as they moved farther into the sea with basalt blocks between them. My small feet fit the posts, my toes grabbing the edges, barnacles boring into my flesh, arms out wide for balance. Our game was to see who could walk farther without falling off, big black basalt blocks grinning from the depth as the waves broke on them and retreated. What was better, to fall off in the black gurgling water or hit the basalt? It was a game of dare that let me taste the edges of comfort.

On stormy days when the tide came in, the water between the posts was dark, forceful and unforgiving. It would thunder against the basalt and suck with slurping sound everything with it as the waves retreated. On such a day, I watched my father go out, the strong swimmer that he was, to save a foolish man caught by surprise by a swift tide.

This river here, pushed between mountain walls, is an unforgiving powerful force that has only one mission, to move everything in its path. Maybe my life is only that, a simple act of nature just following the force, pushing me along as I travel in these parts, taking myself out to the edge of my comfort zone. Maybe I'm here to walk the metaphorical posts as far as possible.

The mountains enclose us now totally. We can almost touch the walls of the gorge through the open windows as the bus turns the curvy corners of the road. The bus crosses the wild river over a narrow metal bridge. On the side of the road stands a westerner, wearing a western shirt and pants with a wool Ladakhi overcoat. He motions for the bus to stop.

"Where did he come from?" I ask Tondup.

"There is a small road going to village that way." He points to the west. My curiosity piqued, I check the man out. He looks like he's in his fifties, with rugged features, lean, average height, blondish hair mixed with gray. He speaks to the ticket collector in what sounds like Ladakhi. He carries only a small daypack and does not look like a westerner going on a trek. He sits down in a seat one row behind me across the aisle. I turn to him and ask in English, "Do you live around here?" For that is what I assume.

"I've been in a village west of here for two months now." He answers in English with a French accent.

"Vous êtes Français?" I ask.

"Non, Canadien," he answers without asking my nationality.

He switches to English and says: "I'm getting supplies in the next town." He raises his bag on his lap in a gesture of shopping. I nod in understanding. My French is limited enough that I don't want to try a conversation in his native language. The Canadian doesn't seem to want to ask me anything as he looks ahead.

We're coming to a widening in the gorge. A small fertile valley with fields and gardens suspends the feeling of being in the heart of impenetrable mountains. Houses and shops cluster along a dirt street; machinery is set up in small yards. The bus stops, men and women with bags and packages are waiting to get on. This road into nowhere must serve as a supply line. The Canadian gets up, nods a greeting and gets off the bus. I'm sorry to see him go. Now I'll have to satisfy my curiosity about what he's doing here with my own tale. Rugged and lean as he looks, I imagine that he came here to explore the mountains. The altitude and peaceful life that pervades here probably mesmerized him. People measure time by the change of day and night, by meetings with people on the trail, moving about to provide the daily fare for themselves and their families. He could've met someone and entered a family, just like Karma received me.

I've considered Karma's welcome to me as doing a friend a favor. Now I'm thinking his hospitality may have come from an altogether different place. It's part of a lifestyle, a religion. Ladakhis are open, forthcoming with their thoughts. Even if they don't speak a language I understand, they have a way of looking at me that invites. There's room in their life to let me in. *Julley! Julley!* is a jubilant greeting that sings like bells whereever I go.

To settle in somewhere here and leave all the mess of life at home behind, is quietly becoming attractive. I turn to Wouter and see that he's holding on his lap the child who was squeezed between the mother and the window. Letting your child sit on the lap of a stranger you met a few hours ago would not happen in the West these days. In this environment it makes perfect sense. Could I make a life here?

As the bus bumps along on a narrowing and bumpy rock road the sun moves across the fields with the warm golden glow of afternoon, touching the blooming mustard and exploding the crop into millions of hopeful torches that nourish both man and soil. I look at my watch and see that it's three o'clock, the time we're supposed to arrive in Phalanji.

"Almost there, Memsahib." Tondup must've seen me looking.

"Not bad timing for a mountain route," I concede.

"We will meet horseman and set up tents," Tondup says, but it may be more to boost his confidence in being able to manage this trek than to inform me.

The valley ends in a narrow strip of green. The side of a mountain blocks any further view. A small village forms the end of the road: Phalanji, the end of the bus route.

Everyone gets out of the bus, and the unloading begins. A group of nuns, in robes of red and orange, open a door to what looks like a storage cellar, hoist burlap sacks on their shoulders and put them inside. Strong, stocky women, none looking older than mid-thirties. Their robes are a joyful contrast to the drab and dirt of the mountainsides which dominate the landscape. Drying along the narrow road are tan colored bricks, stacked, waiting to be used. Some men are working on building a new house. I look around and don't see a monastery where these nuns might live.

"Do these nuns live around here?" I ask Tondup, who's busy bringing down the boxes of supplies from the top of the bus. I take my pack and lift it on my back.

"Nuns go back to Lingshed with supplies. Food stored here for other people too." So this is the mountain cache that supplies remote villages. I wonder if these are nuns I'll visit with in the Lingshed nunnery. Wouter is catching up with me, his pack on his back.

"Campground a little further down, where we can set up camp." He points ahead.

"A real campground?" I have difficulty imagining facilities that can bear the title of "campground."

"It's a designated place, where there's running water," Wouter says, as he walks ahead and I follow, curious about my accommodation for the night.

The dirt road forks as we approach a bridge over a river of gray mud. A little path leads past an outhouse to a flat spot along the river, shaded by trees. There is a hand pump at the far end of the area where some girls are washing clothes. Tondup catches up with us and says: "We camp here tonight, wait for horseman." He puts down the gear he's carried from the bus. I take the tent, lent to me by Dawa, my guesthouse host in Leh, and start setting it up. Wouter unpacks his tent. The noise from the mud river is overpowering. I wonder how well I'll be able to sleep with this roar in my ears.

Tondup sets up a tarpaulin as a tent and attaches an overhang under which he creates a kitchen. He pumps up the kerosene stove and starts boiling water for tea. I'm pleased with the light, roomy tent I'll be able to call my own for the next twelve days. The yellow and orange material filters a warm light inside. I lay out my few books and journal in anticipation of a moment of reflection and journaling with a cup of tea.

When I step out of the tent, the sun is sinking behind the

mountain wall across the river, and the late afternoon shadows of the trees are creating ghostly patterns on this patch of dirt. There's no grass, and where the river touches the bank, muddy clay emerges.

"Tea almost ready, Memsahib," Tondup announces.

"Can I invite Wouter?" I ask, since we haven't talked about how to include Wouter in our travels, if at all.

"Yes, Memsahib, he your guest. I go find out about horseman soon." Tondup's eyes shift quickly.

I stop at Wouter's tent. "We're having tea and cookies. Would you like some?"

"Oh yes, that sounds good, shall I bring my cup?"

"Probably a good idea, I don't know how many cups we have."

I walk on to check out the pump and wash up a bit. A few swings of the pump handle produce a cold, fresh stream of water. As I stand there wondering how I'll wash and pump at the same time, a young Ladakhi man steps forward and motions to the pump. I nod and accept his gesture of help. With a few swift movements he keeps the water flowing, and I can splash and cool myself off. It's been a long, dusty ride, and it feels good to wash off the grime. I smile gratefully at him, and he smiles back.

Back at my tent, I sit down on my sleeping pad in the tent opening. I call out to Wouter: "Tea is served!"

Wouter comes over and folds his torso into the small tent opening. Tondup pours tea with verve and smiles.

"Well, here we are, Tondup, the adventure can begin," I say kiddingly.

"Oh, Memsahib, no adventure, all is taken care of, I go see about horseman now." Tondup straightens up, swinging the tea kettle, and walks back to his kitchen, shoulders straight, head held high.

"He's so concerned about pleasing me, I'm glad I have him on this trip," I turn to Wouter who is inhaling the aroma of his tea.

"I can't afford horsemen or guides. I'm living off my savings and want to stretch my time in India as long as possible. I need to go and find some food for the trek and for dinner in the village." Wouter bites into another cookie.

"It's really quite cheap to hire them. I haven't even considered doing without. I did that in my twenties. It was OK then, but now that I travel alone, it's good to have support." I think back to my trek to Mount Everest. It seems so long ago that Alan and I ventured out with rucksacks, tent and cooking supplies.

"I've always done it this way. I guess it's become a habit," Wouter rises nimbly for someone with such long legs, "thanks for the tea. I'll see you in a while."

I stare at the swollen mud river flowing by in front of my tent. Will it become clear again on a quiet day later in the summer?

I pick up my journal and make my first entry for the trek. It feels good to put my thoughts and observations into words on paper, even though much abbreviated. It gives me a sense of anchoring the many new experiences I'm having, so I can revisit them later and maybe make more meaning.

After finishing my tea and writing in my journal I take my daypack with my valuables, zip up my tent and follow Wouter and Tondup to the village to have a look around. Village is really too generous a word for Phalanji. "Hamlet" might be more appropriate. The only store that sells anything is a house with a little storefront window and counter facing the street. A few shelves on the wall behind the counter hold some food and household items. To the side of the little room is a patio where plastic chairs and tables are set out. The house is a square building with a flat roof that reminds me of similar, simple adobe structures in the Mexican-American border states. Economic progress is hard to detect here. The important factors are climate, what's available locally, and the hard work each family can muster up. Wouter is standing outside on the patio.

"Did you find any provisions here?" I ask.

"The women who run this shop are making some mo-mos for me." He points to the house. "I'm getting enough for a couple of meals, but there are no supplies for food on the trail."

As I look around in the display area, I see sodas, some packages of noodles, some candy, and incense, but not much that could form the ingredients for a wholesome meal.

"How did you do this last week when you went out on the trail?" I ask.

"I brought food from Leh that lasted me for the three days I was out on the trail," Wouter answers.

"Will there be food available farther on?" I wonder.

My thoughts go back to my trek to Mount Everest thirty-three years ago, when we tried to feed ourselves with food along the way. Meals comprised white rice, cooked greens and the traditional bowl of dhal. We were ecstatic when we found eggs or when other trekkers gave us some higher energy trail food. In the three weeks on that trek I lost twenty-five pounds.

I remember the little *gompa*, a one-lama monastery at 10,000 feet altitude, where we spent the night. The lama lived, meditated and slept in one small, smoke stained room. His meditation area doubled as a sleeping area, and I always wondered if he was one of those accomplished ones who slept sitting up, practicing 24-hour awareness. The meal he cooked for us had tasty greens in it. The greens turned out to be fiddlehead ferns. My insides had a strong reaction and the next day on the trail I spent more time in the bushes than walking.

Wouter responds with a pensive look. "I hope so. If not, would I be able to eat with you? I'll pay you for it."

I wonder if there will be enough to go around. Wouter showed up in my life, unprepared for his trek. Do I want to join forces by sharing my supplies? I could take a chance and see how we get along. I tell him, "I'd like to let you eat with us when you run out, but I'll have to check with Tondup to see if he thinks we have enough for all of us to last to Lingshed. Tondup has family there, and maybe we can restock."

A shy, smiling young woman emerges from the building and motions Wouter to a small table. "Food, ready soon," she says.

"You want to join me for some mo-mos?" Wouter walks over to a table, sits down and motions for me to take another chair.

"Sure, I'll try one. Don't know that I've had them before."

The young woman returns with a plate of shell-shaped noodles, about the size of Chinese won-tons. After placing them in front of

Wouter, she puts down some silverware. Wouter motions for some for me also. She smiles and takes some from behind a little counter and lays it down by my place. Wouter moves the plate between us and takes his first bite. We're the only guests in this patio restaurant. A few children are wandering by and staring at us. They giggle and run along when I look at them and say, *"Julley!"* I take a bite.

The mo-mos are filled with spinach and resemble Italian ravioli in flavor.

"These are good," I grant. "I'll hold off though because Tondup will cook for me."

"I will get another order for tomorrow's meal," says Wouter as he eats heartily. "I usually find what I need, when I travel," he states confidently.

"I like the idea of living with what the road offers, we did that when we hiked to Mount Everest, but the food wasn't always very nutritious. So now I plan more. I don't feel like testing how little food I can get by on, when there's a lot of physical exertion ahead." I remember family trips with Doyle. He would sit in the car waiting for me as I ran back into the house remembering another thing we must take along for the road. "Let's go," he would say, "I have money and a credit card. We'll find what we need along the way." When the kids got bored or hungry in the backseat, I always had something I could pull out of my bag to entertain and feed them. Washcloths and water to wipe them when food got smeared all over were also good to have down the road. When I think what might be ahead on this trek, I'm glad I'm using a guide and have plenty of food. Hiking at this altitude will be enough of a struggle that I need not add worry about food foraging. Besides, I like the luxury of my cup of chai with cookies in the afternoon.

"I trust that Sai Baba will take care of me." Wouter shares his surrender to his guru, and I feel a jealousy running through me when I look at his face, showing conviction and ease. Does this man have something I've been looking for figured out? Time will tell if we trek together. For now, I will leave him to collect his mo-mos for the days ahead. "I'm going back and see what Tondup has concocted for me." I get up and step out from the patio.

As I walk the short street, I stop at the granary, or cache. The door is standing half open and the nuns are sitting on the steps in front, chatting and shaking the flour off their clothes. There's a sign on a post next to the cache that states in English, *Phalanji Women's Cooperative*. This is one of the projects I learned about in Leh. Foreign workers are helping indigenous women to organize and develop small businesses for economic and cultural improvement. I'm encouraged to see the results out here. Independent womanhood is not an anomaly here.

When I pass the "Hotel" a young Western couple is lounging in front of a tent. I stop and ask, "Have you been on the trail from here to Lingshed?" The couple look at me, sit up and say, "No, we haven't gone the whole way. We've only hiked out for two days." The young man takes his backpack and moves it behind his back to lean on. "It was very doable but there are some narrow crossings along the river. There's no snow as far as we went." The young woman shakes her blond hair in agreement.

"Were you able to buy food on the way, or did you bring your own?" I shift my weight and adjust my daypack.

"We brought food from Leh and have our own cook stove. There doesn't seem to be much available in the villages." The young man wraps his arms around his knees, while the young woman pulls a baggie of food out of the tent. "We're just about to cook our dinner," she says.

"A man I met on the bus was planning to buy food on the way," I explain to them. "I've enough for an army, it looks like, but I don't know how much my guide and horseman eat. We will use two horses to carry it all."

"Next time, we might want to use horses," the young man adds.

"Next time." Words that have fueled my travels. I didn't go back to Nepal. Didn't go back to India. I had felt the longing to be around Mahara-ji and let him direct my life. What would've happened if I had followed the longing and gone back? Would I be sitting in an ashram like Wouter did? Why didn't I follow that longing

to experience that all-encompassing love Maraha-ji exuded so pro-
fusely? Did I not believe it to be real? Was the Dutch down-to-
earth mentality overriding the heart? I followed Alan to the west of
America for the promise of that all-encompassing love in relationship with a partner. Then another partner. Now here I am, without
a partner, another failed marriage, trekking in the same mountains,
looking again to find what will fuel my life.

"For how long are you in Ladakh?" I ask.

"We have six months in Asia, and four months have passed
already, but we haven't been that long in Ladakh. We'll go back to
Leh, recover and restock. We still want to go out and trek for a while."
The young woman pulls her blond hair back into a ponytail. My six-
week journey is feeling minuscule and much too short.

"I must go, my dinner will be ready," I say, "have a good trip,
goodbye."

Tondup is busy cooking rice and a sauce, when I get to the tents.

"Have you seen the horseman yet?" I ask.

"Oh, Memsahib, horseman not here yet, we wait and see tomorrow." Tondup's voice trails.

I sense some discomfort with the lack of unfolding of his plans.
It now occurs to me that it's possible the horseman who is supposed to
come from Lingshed, might not show up. What will we do if there is
no horseman?

"Food ready, Memsahib," Tondup gives the pot a stir.

"I'll get my bowl," I answer.

"Oh no, Memsahib, go sit down by tent, I will serve." Tondup
is in his role of cook-servant now. I sit down by my tent and watch
another small group as they set up camp. Tondup serves me and the
food is tasty, curry over rice. Wouter ambles into view with a boxful
of mo-mos in his hand.

"I was able to get some boiled eggs as well," he
announces triumphantly.

"Good, that will feed you tomorrow." I go over to the kitchen
with my empty dish.

"Tondup, Wouter has little food for the trail. Can we share? Is

155

there enough?" I cock my head wondering if Tondup understands.

"Memsahib can share, more food in Lingshed." Tondup looks at the supplies stacked in his shelter and shakes his head confidently.

My assumptions about his connections in Lingshed are confirmed. I turn to Wouter. "Wouter, you can eat meals with us when you run out, we'll work out the cost."

"That's good to know, I'll do my best to find more and make this batch last." Wouter rubs his hand over his head. "Thanks for including me in your journey."

By now dusk is setting in and the evening colors are disappearing rapidly from the rocky slope on the other side of the muddy creek. I feel thrown out into the elements. The rough campsite and the darkness make me want safety, security. My tent is my only shelter now, and the yellow and orange colors invite me to enter and make it home. I do a minimal hygiene routine by the pump. In my tent I surround myself with my few possessions to ward off the feeling of emptiness that creeps in, even though I'm surrounded by small groups of people. The incessant sound of the rushing water gives a chill to the air and lulls me into a dreamy state as I warm myself in my sleeping bag.

* * *

I think of myself back in Oregon, the last time Doyle and I were camping out on the coast. I relive how we were holed up in our van. It was very dark and the camping spot we found late at night didn't have any amenities. I hadn't spent the night with Doyle since our separation nine months earlier. This camping trip was an attempt to explore mending our differences. The fog had rolled in from the ocean and created a chill even though it was spring. I huddled under the sleeping bag that covered both of us next to this man who had become a stranger to me in such a short time.

I was wearing all the warm clothes I'd brought and wasn't sure how physically close I wanted to be. I listened to the sound of his movements in the bed. It all felt so familiar, and yet I no longer knew how he felt about me. I waited for him to say something to break the distance between us, but he was busy making himself comfortable and said nothing. The wind rattled the antenna on the van, the trees around the van were moving in the wind. The van was our safe haven from the elements tonight. Could we feel safe with each other? When he finally settled down, we just lay there next to each other, our clothes touching. Doyle's breathing soon got heavier and the sleeping medication he was taking nightly took him away. I looked out into the deep darkness and didn't know then how to make the connection that had been lost.

* * *

The darkness outside my tent here holds the unknown. Tomorrow I'll start exploring. Will I find a solution to the connection I've lost with Doyle?

Chapter 14

Sleeping on a high-tech mini-pad does not make for morning lingering in bed. It's the end of June, and sunrise comes early, even here among the high peaks. The fresh light dances through the poplar leaves and joins the sound of the muddy river in a spritely good morning song.

Tondup has been awake for a while by the time I emerge from my tent. He's huddled in his "kitchen" while the kerosene cook stove is heating water for tea. He rubs his hands and wraps them around his slight body. He's wearing his vest, cap and sweater on this summer morning. The sun has not yet touched the morning chill rising out of the creek.

"Good morning, Memsahib, you sleep OK?" Tondup produces his crooked smile.

"Yes, I slept, I'm a little stiff, but that'll go away when I walk."

"I go look for horseman. If horseman not here, I go look for other way." Tondup looks down avoiding my eyes.

"Alright, I hope we get to take off today. You know I only have two weeks before my plane leaves for Delhi again. I really would like to make it to Lingshed." When I planned the trek I hadn't thought of the possibility of not making it to my destination. Anything can happen between this moment and ten days from now. Will my plan work out? I straighten up, pull back my slumping shoulders and look around the campground where more tents have been set up since last night. I will not worry about it, it doesn't do any good; I will trust that everything will work out for the best.

Wouter emerges from his little blue tent, stretches and takes in the morning situation.

"Share tea?" Tondup sends a questioning glance in Wouter's direction.

"Yes, we'll share tea," I answer.

Tondup serves tea and then leaves, announcing that he will find pack animals. I let the tea swish through my body and brain.

"Do you think he'll find pack animals at a last-minute notice?" I ask Wouter.

"Hard to say. People are always willing to make a buck. Hard cash is in short supply. Then again, the locals seem to have a different sense of economic priority than we do in the West."

"What do you mean?" I ask, raising my eyebrows.

"Family issues always take priority, and they will not show up for work when they're needed at home," Wouter explains.

"I wish we could be a little more sensible in that way in the West," I reply, realizing that it might impact my travel. I might as well get used to the possibility of delay.

I finish my tea and pay a visit to the camp "facilities". It takes some bravery to enter the little house with a hole in the ground. It's dark inside, and the smell of dirt and dust mixes with the stomach-turning smell of excrement.

When I emerge from the dark little building, there are some horses and donkeys braying and scraping their hooves at the entrance to the campground. Tondup walks up and announces: "No horseman, but I found donkeyman. He will carry to Photaksar. We meet horseman on the way."

"Good job, Tondup, how much we have to pay?"

"Donkeys cost less, 100 rupees a day. But we need three donkeys." He announces our first kink in the budget. I nod, accepting the inevitable.

"Memsahib not angry?" Tondup searches my face.

"Oh no, we get to go today; that's all that matters." I give him a smile and thumbs up.

Tondup visibly relaxes and sends a beaming smile. "We have breakfast, pack and leave."

Excited by the prospect of walking in the crisp air, I return to the tent site. Wouter is sitting on a log by the creek. "We'll be going today. Tondup found a donkeyman and three donkeys to carry our load," I tell him.

Tondup gets busy with breakfast and soon scrambled eggs and chapatis satisfy my hunger. I offer Wouter some, but he sticks to his eggs and mo-mos.

While I'm eating, Tondup waves a man in our direction. "This is donkeyman, Longsup, we will pack up and load donkeys."

I nod and smile, taking in the man's appearance. He's a tawny, rugged man of short stature wearing a dirty baseball cap and a shirt the color of road dust. In his hand he holds a stick. He nods, raises his hands in the familiar gesture, palms together, and says: *"Julley!"*

"Julley," Wouter and I reply. The conversation ends here for lack of a shared language.

Tondup motions Longsup to sit, and offers him tea. Longsup squats, and accepts the yak-butter, salty version Tondup has made for himself. When I'm finished with breakfast, I take down my tent and pack my daypack. Tondup hands me a box with lunch—chapatis with tahini and cucumber—to carry in my daypack.

"Memsahib walk ahead, we will catch up." He moves his head toward the mountains.

I look at Wouter, who's pulling the last straps tight on his pack.

"Are you ready to start walking?" I ask.

"Yes, almost." He ties a handkerchief around his neck and swings the pack on his back.

I have my hat hanging on my back and am wearing a long-sleeved UV shirt to protect me from the intense high-altitude sun rays that are warming the site. I make one last trip to the pump to fill my water bottle and cap it with the purifier. A nervous excitement buzzes through me. I'm eager to enter this roadless cap of the world. What will it be like? Can I climb at this altitude? Will we have enough time to get to Lingshed?

Wouter and I take the dirt road that passes by the campground and walk around the mountainous stone walls that form a barrier to our view to the east. During the first half hour of walking, a river courses down on the right side of the road, supplying water for planting projects along the banks. Spindly trees are clinging to the barren soil. Irrigation appears to be manual, by the look of pipes and hoses near the plantings. It seems an act of hopeless persistence to reforest these rocky slopes.

"Do you know the way we need to go?" I ask Wouter.

"Yes, there's only one way to go. When this road ends, the trail starts." He points in a southern direction and I see how the road crosses a bridge, turns and becomes narrower as it winds its way up on the other side of the river.

"Is it a hard climb today?" I ask. My mind is hungry for facts. Having some mental preparation for difficult things ahead makes it easier to pace myself.

An image of a long, long, never-ending bike path flashes through my mind. I was six years old and my family and I were biking to a vacation home on an island. After biking to the ferry and ferrying across, the seemingly endless flat road stretched ahead of me. My young legs were tired, and nobody seemed to notice. Emotion fueled by tiredness turned into a stubborn refusal to go on. I stopped, laid down my bicycle on the roadside and sat, head down, with a cabbage field in front of me. I peered over my arms, wrapped around my knees to see if my parents noticed that I'd stopped. My father looked back, but didn't stop. He called out, "Keep going, you can do it!" In that moment, I hated him and his tough expectations. I stared at the cabbage field and told myself I wouldn't do it. After a few minutes I gave up in this struggle of wills, got up, picked up the bicycle and started peddling again. My legs were stronger than my mind and I caught up with the others, eventually. Did they even slow down for me?

I don't see an endless road stretched out in front of me here. This is an unknown, invisible path. I have little preparation except the strength in my legs and a dotted line on a map. Wouter's voice brings me back to my question about the climb today.

"No, it's easy, just find your pace and keep walking." Wouter adjusts his pack a little higher.

"How much hiking have you done?" I'm ready for conversation as I find my pace.

"I did a lot of climbing in Switzerland, when I was still living in Holland. My father, brother and I used to go every summer and climb the peaks." Wouter adjusts his pace to match mine as we walk next to each other on the road.

"I was at the Jungfrau with my husband and children fifteen years ago, but we went up by train. We walked around in the snow. Were you there?" I asked.

"No, but I climbed the Eiger one summer." Wouter moved his glasses up his nose.

"I could see the Eiger from the Jungfrau, it looked difficult." I remember its pointy peak rising across the valley from the Jungfrau. At the time I didn't think of climbing mountains, I was too caught up with raising children and exposing them to new experiences.

"Yes, the Eiger was difficult. We made it our goal to ascend one mountain each year. That's how my father shared his manliness with us, his sons." Wouter's voice trailed off as he took himself back in time.

"Do you miss your family?" I ask, wondering what his relationship with his family is now.

"No, I'm not like them, and it's uncomfortable to be with them." Wouter's eyes narrow in a half squint.

"But you shared all that climbing."

"Yes, but I've changed. I have broken away since I met Sai Baba. I don't want to prove myself through big accomplishments, physical or financial. My family is financially successful and I'm the failure in their eyes." Wouter says it without shame.

"You must be somewhat successful financially, if you can afford to live without working for this many years in India." I press on with my questions, while feeling my legs loosen and finding my walking pace.

"I was in the past. I made a bundle of money when I quit my job, and I'm living off that." Wouter smiles and rubs his stubbly chin. I guess shaving isn't part of the daily routine on the trail.

"What kind of work were you doing?"

"I worked for the government, in accounting."

"So did my father, he worked in The Hague for the government as an accountant."

"I found out that there'd been some embezzlement by superiors. I

162

wanted to quit working, and they offered me a handsome sum if I kept it silent. And so I did." Wouter looks at me with a small turn of his head. He must expect a reaction.

"You took the money and let them off the hook?" The influence of my ethical father oozes out in my emphatic tone.

"Yes, it would've been a big stink you know, if I had told. Can you imagine the discomfort of continuing on after being a whistleblower?" Wouter was matter of fact.

"Hmm, how does an act like that fit into your spiritual practice?" I snort and raise my hands questioningly.

"I had already found Sai Baba through some friends. I was getting strong messages to follow and join a group of his devotees. Getting the pay-off seemed like a gift from Sai Baba, to come out here." Wouter stops and takes out his water bottle.

Dumbfounded by Wouter's use of logic to justify his actions I walk ahead while Wouter stops to drink. I recall another conversation when Doyle argued he couldn't end the relationship with his project partner because the project had to keep going. He didn't acknowledge the affair he was having; he didn't tell me about the money he had invested, our money. He let the means justify his actions. The hope that I mattered had crumbled.

I wonder about the serendipity of meeting Wouter. This is day one together, and he's presented me with ethical issues similar to what I was dealing with at home. Is there another way of looking at infidelity with Doyle, or in Wouter's case does the goal of leading a spiritual life justify the means? My work in the justice system of the last few years has already taught me that justice is relative. Ethics don't determine justice, the law does. In being silent Wouter didn't break the law, but is accepting a bribe illegal? Will this man teach me something I need to understand about my life? I don't have an answer and shift my attention to where we are and scan the road. I see that we're approaching the bridge. I look back and wait for Wouter who's following me. I don't see Tondup or the donkeyman yet and we've been walking for an hour.

"Do you think we should wait for Tondup and the donkeyman?"

I ask Wouter.

"No, they'll catch up when we get on the trail. They're much faster on that terrain than we."

The sun is now hitting the road, and the temperature is pleasantly warm, with a cool breeze rising from the turbulent waters below. Wouter stops next to me on the bridge and I can smell his manly musty smell in the warm air. We look up at the narrowing opening from which the river tumbles down.

"We'll walk in a gorge from here on." Wouter points in the direction. "It's beautiful, very rugged."

The road narrows as we walk on, but still has the signs of being a road. Picks and short hoes are lying next to some sifting trays. No sign of a road crew at work.

"Does a crew come around with machinery to work on the road?" I ask Wouter.

"No heavy equipment, mostly pick and shovel work and if need be dynamite. It'll take them probably ten years to complete this road-bed all the way to Lingshed," Wouter answers.

"Ten years?" I can hardly believe it.

"Yes, they only work in the three summer months. It's a lot of chiseling of rock by hand and then some jack-hammering to loosen bigger pieces of rock."

"Are the road crews local?"

"No, they hire people from Nepal, the poorest of the poor, who'll work for little money and sleep right on site." So this is where the parents of Dawa's Nepalese foster girl may work to earn a living. I can see that this is no place for a young girl to hang out, so earning her keep at Dawa's guesthouse isn't such a bad solution. At least Dawa treats the girl well.

We're passing an overhang in the rock and I can see a cave-like space underneath where cooking gear and bedding is lying around. I remember the men and women along the bus route leaning on their picks and shovels, silent refugees of a faltering society elsewhere.

"This seems more like prison work." I have images of prison workers chained together working on railroads.

"Not much crime in these mountains, so no prisoners. Not yet anyway. These are prisoners of poverty."

As I walk behind Wouter, I can hear the snapping of a stick and the whistle from the donkeyman coming around the bend in the road. Tondup and Longsup are quickly catching up with us. The donkeys tread with their dainty hooves steadfast on the uneven rocky path and just an occasional swat keeps them moving steadily.

"Memsahib walking good?" Tondup asks.

"Yes, it's good to be walking." I'm not experiencing any breathing difficulty so far.

"Trail will be harder, just walk slowly, we wait for you," Tondup advises as they pass us up. "Keep donkeys going."

I nod and maintain my pace. The trail narrows, and we're entering a gorge between two rock walls towering three hundred feet high on both sides. The opening is carved out by the river and there's just a narrow rock path on the side. I find myself in a tunnel, the trail is beckoning, enticing with corners, caves and cloud patterns. What musty secrets live here?

The deafening roar of water and wind take over my thinking. I let myself become absorbed by the sound and feel at one with the trail, at one with the mountains and a path carved out in it, a mark of the life people live around here. I feel at one with the cave along the trail; feel the emptiness of not knowing, the emptiness of not having a clear direction inside me. I feel as if I can be a cave, cold water dripping down inside me, forming a puddle of fear. I identify with the lonely, flowerless plant clinging, chewing rock and spitting out the remnants that file down my teeth until I can't chew any more. And I cling. I cling while the wind blows, with an ancient will to live and survive, breathing one breath after another. I'm walking in the gorge and the rushing water below me is staring coldly at me—stirring briskly the fear of death in my heart. Will I slide in, or will I cling and edge my way on?

Wouter looks back and yells something over the roar of the water, while pointing at a swinging bridge leading to a narrow trail on the other side of the river. Does he mean we have to cross here? Water is spraying up as the river thunders around a bend. The trail is wet and curves under a rock overhang. I follow Wouter and cross the swaying bridge hanging on to a steel cable. Ducking under the overhang we move ahead. How did the donkeys do here? I wonder. Soon we find that rocks are blocking the trail. Obviously this is not the way the donkeys went.

"They must have re-routed the trail," Wouter announces, "we'll have to go back and try the other side."

We turn and walk the short distance back to the bridge and enter the deafening roar of the river in the bend of the gorge again. We follow the path on the other side, which curves around and suddenly opens up to a wider section of trail and a wider section in the gorge. I walk and breathe the water-infused fresh air while sunshine touches the path from straight above. My life is in Nature's hand. Each step, each breath is my commitment to living. The narrows are only a moment in time.

The walls of the gorge, ominous when I walked through them, separate into two tall, sloping mountain ranges on either side of a widening valley and the river is flowing ever wildly in between. The water is supplying small plots of land, which are dark green with barley. These communal gardens lay just outside the village of Hanupati and are surrounded by low stone walls, topped by an intricately woven network of prickly branches, effective in keeping animals out. The prickly branches are from sea buckthorn, a Himalayan berry that provides a delicious fruit high in vitamin C. Hanupati isn't more than a hamlet, a few houses clustered along a trail in a valley that rises to a mountain ridge that we'll climb tomorrow. There's no store, no restaurant in the village to supply Wouter with food. We set up camp just a little east of the village on a cleared area called a campground. No sign of fresh running water, no sign of bathroom facilities. Tondup gets water out of the roaring glacial river for cooking. Even though I believe the water from up high in the mountains to be clean, I use a filter to drink it. Wouter drinks the water without filtering.

While Wouter and I are having our afternoon tea, I look back at the gorge we came through earlier, and think about how the narrow opening makes the strong flow of the river coming down from above so turbulent. The gorge makes me think of how my marriage has gone through a process of narrowing. How the pain after the accident and the malfunctioning of Doyle's body clamped down on the vitality of our love for each other and created a turbulence that rocked our relationship and absorbed his open, adventurous spirit. I sigh and as sadness rises in my throat, I wash it down with my tea. Wouter is silently drinking his. Good, at least we can sit in silence. I continue with my thinking. Doyle's battle with his disease took priority and my love had turned into caregiving, while trying to figure out where I stand with myself, and what kind of relationship we can still have. Does Doyle still love me? Will he come back to me in a way that lets me feel that love? I pull my sweatshirt tighter around me as a chill wind blows through the exposed camp. I'm here to sort out if I still belong with him, but what if he doesn't want to belong with me? I swish and swallow more tea. Wouter gets up and says:

"I'm going to lie down in my tent for a while. Thanks for the tea."

"You're welcome," I say, relieved he knows when to make himself scarce. I'm not in the mood for talking. I look out at the high mountain range across the river from me. The fear I felt of being swallowed up by the turbulent water when I hiked through the gorge, was a similar fear I had about being swallowed up by Doyle's illness and his desperate attempts not to drown in disability.[32] I hadn't wanted to acknowledge my fear as the disease clamped down on our relationship. I ignored my feelings and focused on the day-to-day survival. I put down my teacup and wrap up the left-over cookies in the bag. What will happen if I let the betrayal, the absorption in work, the impulsive buying sprees become the daggers into my heart? Will I drown in a flood of emotions? I turn my gaze toward the mountain range we'll be climbing tomorrow. Just as I don't know what lies on the other side of tomorrow's pass, I don't know what lies ahead in my marriage. I didn't get swept away in the gorge. I can hike on and hope for new insights in my life.

---

32. I hadn't known about the side-effects of the medication he was taking; I also didn't know then that Doyle was increasing medication to improve his physical functioning: he was getting a medication high.

Chapter 15

The next morning the sky is partially cloudy, a change from the hot sunny day before. It will make the ascent to the 15,000 feet Sir-sir-La pass a little easier. It's time to pack up the tents, eat breakfast, and pack a lunch for my daypack.

Wouter, who didn't find any food along the trail yesterday, finishes the last of his food supply for breakfast. Without saying anything Tondup is cooking enough for all, including Wouter. Wouter keeps saying he'll find some supplies in the next village. We'll see. Photaksar is our next stop.

From our camp spot I can see women and men already at work, moving about, weeding and preparing soil for more planting. The short growing season requires intensive planting to provide enough food for summer and winter. No-one seems to hurry, even though there must be some sense of urgency to get the planting done in time. The sheer mountain walls dwarf the people busy with their daily tasks. A herd of mountain goats with their shepherd is dotted among the sparse vegetation. The contrast between man and landscape stirs a memory of a conversation of long ago.

* * *

I was twenty years old, staying in The Hague at the home of a lover who was older and seemingly wiser than me. I told him what I had learned in that evening's philosophy class: according to the theory of relativism, a point is only a point because of the space around it. Jan laughed at my serious face. He pulled out a book by Nietzsche (*Joyful Wisdom* also known as *Gay Science*) and said: "You know, there is really nothing to hang all this up on. You will learn that there is just this, you and me, the dark and light, the cold winter and warm summer."

"There has to be more than that," I retorted, "all this has to come from somewhere and connect somehow."

"Good luck finding it," he answered as he put his arms around me.

I pushed him away. I hated his wisdom and didn't want to be tempted by his love advances.

* * *

As I wander all day in the shadows of these giants, answers about life form in my bones and tissues. I walk and experience the answers with every step as my breathing adjusts to the emptiness. I know that all things connect. I have no fear this morning. I'm ready for another day of walking and being.

"Let's go," Wouter pulls me out of my reverie, "this morning we're climbing and we better get a head start if we want to keep up with the donkeys. They keep moving even if it's up the slopes."

"It doesn't look all that far, how long will it take?" I ask, more out of habit than concern.

"A couple of hours at least, distances are deceiving on the incline." Wouter pushes his glasses up his nose.

"Last week I wasn't able to get over Sir-sir-La, the snow was too deep. This time it looks like we can make it." He starts up the path.

"We're going ahead," I call out to Tondup. My voice echoes over the constant rushing of the water against the walls of stone.

"OK, Memsahib, go slowly, slowly." Tondup's caring words for my hiking success are becoming my mantra.

The footsteps that have gone before us mark the path, a walkway formed between rocks and clumps of vegetation. For how many generations have people walked in these parts? Walking up and down the passes with no other goal than to find and transport food and supplies for daily living. After twenty minutes we come to the river and a small wooden bridge. Once on the other side, the path hugs the slope of the mountains, smooth in their uniformity from overgrazed vegetation. It's colder today, and I'm wearing a sweatshirt to keep warm. We walk along quietly, Wouter is ahead of me, our paces are similar. I take in the wide-open mountain ranges, rising up to touch the clouds that are moving in the cerulean blue sky.

Cerulean blue, where did I learn the name of that color? I'm back in a watercolor painting class listening to the artist-instructor, hearing him say, "Form is only form because of the negative space around it." Where have I heard that before? "Look at the space if you want to find the form you want to paint," he continued, "and, while you're at it, know that you won't make a good painting for a long time. It takes two thousand bad paintings before you'll get it right. So why don't you get busy making your mistakes." Freed up by his comments I dipped my brush and let the watery blue touch the paper.

I cringe thinking of my teacher's words about how long it will take to find true expression. Do his words also translate to living and getting it right? If I focus on the space around me, will I find true expression of self?

Wouter walks in front of me with balanced gait, he seems at home in this environment.

"Hey, Wouter, did you live in Amsterdam all your life?" I want to know more about this stranger.

"My family did; I went to school there but lived on the moors of the Veluwe[33] later on."

"I can hear your wonderful Amsterdam accent. People from Amsterdam are a nationality of their own. I had my first long-term relationship was with a man from Amsterdam. I went to the university there. I met my first husband, an American who was avoiding Vietnam, there."

"When did you leave?" Wouter did not volunteer more about himself and kept on walking.

"I left in 1973, uncertain that I would stay in the States, but I did. I found freedom of living in the country. I found community, had a child. First marriage, second marriage, kids." Out here in the open it all seemed so insignificant. "Are you married?" I'm still curious.

"No, never have been. I've never stayed in a relationship long-term." Wouter turns his head. He also turns his body at an angle on the path so that we can walk closer and continues, "I don't know what it is, women do not stick around. When I turned 35, I decided I wasn't

33. Veluwe: an area of Holland famous for its scenic beauty.

cut out for marriage. Then I met Sai Baba."

"You don't miss the close interaction of a long-term relationship?"

"I have friends, and now that I feel connected with Sai Baba, I don't feel alone." Wouter blinks and gives a shy shrug.

I'm a little envious that he's so completely surrendered to his guru. I didn't hang on to that kind of connection with Mahara-ji. It seems that it's more a decision of giving the guru the power than the guru having it. I never gave up my life to hang out with Mahara-ji. He never asked me either even though I wanted it at the time. It seemed a way out of the confusion of all the questions about what to do with life. Surrender to a being who tells you what to do? Now I'm glad Mahara-ji never did that to me. He never told me to stay, he wouldn't intervene to extend my visa, so I had to go back to the West to figure life out for myself. Gratitude for the early flow of events in my life floods through me. Putting my feet down right behind Wouter as he climbs in, I say:

"I'm taking some time away from my life at home. I'm not sure if my marriage will last." Wouter, bent under the weight of his pack, moves his head in acknowledgement. I don't know if it's the wide-open space or my need for a sounding board, but I continue speaking my thoughts out loud:

"I'm back to the rudimentary question of whether a meaningful long-term relationship is possible. Ultimately, it seems, we're alone in this world despite our attempts at being in relationships." My breathing slows as I climb and talk at the same time. Wouter says:

"I don't worry about what is and isn't possible; I have my relationship with Sai Baba and it will last as long as I devote myself to him."

"That must be like traveling. I don't feel alone when I'm traveling. I don't know if it's the distraction of new experiences or the unspoken promise of new connections." I plant my trekking-pole in the coarse rock on the path and pull myself forward. The path is slowly rising and my breathing is more labored. "How are you doing with the weight on your back?" I ask Wouter.

"It's fine so far, I'm used to it."

"Just because you're used to it, does that make it feel OK? You could say that about being alone too, but you haven't yet." Now I'm testing him.

"You're right, aloneness is not what I seek in life, or maybe I was taught not to seek it. No-one else in my family is alone. My brother and sister are both married."

"So, you've justified your aloneness for your family by being with your guru?" I stop to zip up my sweatshirt more. The wind picks up, the temperature is dropping and more clouds are in the sky.

"I don't think it matters to them, they don't accept my life in India as a valid way of living life, and I remain the odd one in the family." Wouter's matter-of-fact statement doesn't reveal how he feels.

As I look back down the trail, I can see the small pack of animals and the figures of Tondup and Longsup a little past the river crossing moving steadily in our direction.

"In my twenties I was the odd one out in my family," I comment as I step it up behind Wouter. The others will catch up soon enough, and I continue my one-sided conversation. "The late sixties in Amsterdam helped me drop out of the established ways of doing things, and then I brought back a different lifestyle from my travels in India."

"How's that?" asks Wouter as he turns his head.

"At least it looked like that from the outside. I was a vegetarian, insisted on taking shoes off at the door, I'd sit cross-legged on my parents' couch when I visited." I grimace, thinking of how uncomfortable I made my parents with my new habits. "I always somehow went back to my family and hoped for some acknowledgement, if not actual approval. I don't think you can get away from that."

* * *

I'm thinking back to the struggle between feeling and thinking I always felt with my parents. I remember us sitting in my parents' living room. After dinner my mother would serve coffee and my father would start his usual conversation about politics.

"The socialists have lost against the liberals again. People just

want things for themselves and think these guys will give it to them."
My father was disappointed at the changing trend.

"Well, you have to give people a chance to express their feelings," my mother piped in.

"What do you know? Your party can't make up their mind.
They're willing to bend their principles to please the Bible talkers," he
had jabbed at my mother.

Red-faced she drank her coffee. I couldn't stand his disdain and
jumped in: "Pa, you can't continue to put down the religious parties.
They also have a right to be."

"You can't base political actions on the Bible. There are no facts in
faith," he answered.

I didn't know what to say. I had my own struggles with the
religious views they had exposed me to. My mother's quiet but hurt
demeanor went right to my own feelings of budding feminism. Why
didn't she have a chance to educate herself and learn to stand up to
him? I wanted to show my father that women could think!

* * *

I tell Wouter: "My parents slowly accepted my odd ways. It helped
that I had created a family with children."

After a few moments of paying attention to the terrain, which
was growing rockier, Wouter responds, "I write to my parents and
stay in contact, but I'm not trying to explain my life to them."

"What do you write to them about? Your life at the ashram?" I
can't imagine his parents understanding it. "Oh, I write about acquiring property and I write about health issues. I have bought a little
house near the ashram." Wouter emphasizes "acquiring" as if he's in
the real estate business.

"What health issues?" I look back to see where Tondup and
Longsup are. They're still a ways behind, turning the animals around
the switchbacks. I'm feeling the altitude and slowly put one foot in
front of the other. Wouter continues, "I've had digestive trouble for a
while. I was sick for a time in the first couple of years of my stay. I've
learned to eat carefully."

"That's a standard illness when you stay in India for a long time," I say. "I was lucky during the year I was in India, but my boyfriend ended up in the hospital." I remember the overcrowded hospital in Goa with the limited medical services. "That's why I avoid meat during this trip. I don't want to risk eating spoiled meat."

"Sai Baba directs us to eat mostly fruit and vegetables. I find that it's better for developing sensitivity to higher vibrations." Wouter follows the trail that now goes up the steeper slope to the pass. The village is hardly visible behind us. Tondup and Longsup have almost caught up with us.

"Talking about being healthy, these guys seem to be able to keep going while living on basic food without much variation." I think of *tsampa*, the roasted barley flour they eat for breakfast with butter tea, that's their fuel for the whole day. "They hardly ate at lunch yesterday."

"They have smaller bodies and different metabolisms. Don't forget that they don't get very old around here either, so they wear themselves out early," Wouter suggests. I must admit he has a point.

"Is it from wearing themselves out, or from diseases that they die earlier?" Slowly I lift my leg for another step up the incline, leaning on my poles for support. My legs feel heavy. "There isn't much medical care out here in the mountains as far as I can see and my friend Karma in Leh has confirmed this. He travels into the mountains for an organization that encourages the traditional *Amsi* style of healing. It's a healing with herbs, and works well as a preventative, but cannot stand up to serious infections or diseases that we control in the West through a combination of surgery and medication."

"Interesting, healing with herbs in the mountains, I might be able to use that," Wouter muses. He too is now going slower.

"Is your digestion still a problem then?" I ask.

"I'm better, but I'm careful. Eating fruits and vegetables a lot is easy on the digestion." So that's why he's been eating bananas at every food stand... I can't understand how he can climb and carry a pack on such a light diet. My appetite has been hardy so far, despite the high altitude, which lowers the appetite. My stomach is growling now. Time for an energy bar. I stop and pull one out of my pack. "Do you want some?" I ask munching away.

"No, we're almost at the top. I'll wait till I get to the top." Wouter keeps on walking.

I need the rest, and a stretch for a moment to look around. I've been getting too involved in talking. The openness of the landscape makes itself felt now. No more mountain ranges forming a wall. I'm almost at the crest and I can see ranges of mountains stretching out layer after layer into an endless sky. It feels like I'm almost on top of the world, and this notion sends a chill through me. This is a place for taking off in flight and soaring; it feels like a spirit place where the body can be left behind. I feel tears in my heart, tears of longing. Longing to be free, free from connections that inevitably cause pain. Free from desires for comforts and safety. Free to just *be*. What would it be like to have no more work, no more just one foot in front of the other, no more breathing?

I think of Neem Karoli Baba, Mahara-ji as devotees call him, and his life. It was a simple ashram life, wrapped in a blanket for the cold and a lungi in the heat. He owned no houses, or property. His devotees cared for him and he seemed to just hang around in his body to be able to help others let go of attachments to their own bodies, relationships, life. I'm walking here to let go of notions and expectations that don't work for me anymore; I'm walking to get to the edges of my energy stretched so thin that I can no longer feel the grasping for those transient things.

I put my pack back on, grab my trekking poles and start up again. I want to get to the top before Tondup gets there.

The sky has become gray, there are some light snow flurries blowing in my face. Wouter is waving from the pass. He has his camera pointed in my direction. These last hundred feet are my ascent into acceptance. I still have a body, I can't deny that; it's breathing, walking, and seeing, and I have a heart that feels. I'm trekking into the realm of living with *what is*, the rocks, the path, and the sky.

"How high are we?" I call out to Wouter. Just a few more switchbacks and I'm at the top of the pass.

"15,200 feet, from what the map says." Wouter blows his nose and his handkerchief flaps in the wind.

"Wow, not much of a place!" I look around. There are rocks stacked together to form a small *mani* wall,[34] the traditional Buddhist prayer wall. Prayer flags represent eternity and change, a constant reminder of the impermanence of things.

"I want to make a video of this moment. Are you willing to film me as I walk to the top?" Wouter is holding out the camera.

"How do I do it?"

"It's easy, just push this button, look in the viewer and follow me."

"All right, I can manage that. Why do you want to film this part?"

"I want to show my family that I actually walked here."

"So, it's important then that they know you as you are now?" I remind him of what he had told me earlier and feel like I caught him in his own web of reasoning. Is he willing to change his perceptions of his relationship with his own family, I wonder?

"It's the only live thing I can share with them. I have no plans for returning to Holland soon," Wouter says.

"You'll be the hero on his journey. You'll be holding the place of magic and adventure for them, while they're living the ordinary, responsible life." I point the camera while Wouter walks for his scene of the ascent.

"I suppose that's one way of looking at it. I just thought it would be fun to use the video feature on my camera. I can't do it very much, because it uses up too much battery power." Wouter's practical view shatters my hero imagery.

When Wouter and I are both waiting at the top, I say, "Let's wait here for Tondup and Longsup." I look in the direction of the valley we came from. To my other side, down the slope, is another valley with a new view. A river runs through that valley as well and in the distance a village appears to be hanging on a cliff.

"Memsahib tired?" Tondup's voice carries ahead of him over the sounds of the donkeys' loads and hoofs as he and Longsup approach the pass.

"A little, but now it'll be downhill, so that's good." I'm looking

---

34. *Mani* wall: a wall decorated with prayer-engraved stones.

forward to easier breathing.

"We walk on, have lunch in Photaksar." Tondup points toward the hanging village. The river that comes out of the mountains to the south of the pass carves a deep gorge that disappears in the distance of what look like impenetrable mountains. The few tall houses that form the village are perched on a narrow ledge overlooking the gorge. To get to the village, we have to come down an open slope, which transitions into meadows and agricultural land on both sides of the river.

"Are we going to stay in Photaksar?" I ask Tondup.

"No, Memsahib, we take trail over there." Tondup points to the right and south side of the river. "We camp out higher up." My eyes move to the slopes on the other side of the valley to the snow far away. That must be the highest pass on this trek.

Tondup follows Longsup and the donkeys, which are already on their way down to greener slopes and some fodder.

"Will you take my picture here?" I ask Wouter.

"Sure, why don't you walk up and I'll film you. You can do that with your camera too."

"OK, just a bit then, I don't have all that many batteries with me either." I like the idea of some live footage. The still pictures I have at home of climbing Kala Patar 18,000 feet high on the Mount Everest Glacier are just that, static, a frozen moment. They don't capture the feelings of awe I had when I climbed. So I walk back a little on the trail and come waving at the camera and make my *this is a fantastic moment in my life* speech as I approach.

It is downhill from here on. The path is rocky, and it takes concentration to traverse the narrow, tight switchbacks. I'm flooded with good feelings, the aftermath of exertion and accomplishment. The rocks on the path jump out in a jigsaw puzzle of shapes, waiting for a hand to place them. I step on them and listen to the soft crushing as they sink into their sandy environment.

Songs are bubbling up, and I'm humming and soon singing out loud into the wide openness. The song forms a rhythm for walking, a repetition of thought that settles into the very fibers of my being. I'm happy—I am in my soul-being, a child of the universe living out her dreams.

Chapter 16

We've set up camp after a day of hard walking. I'm relaxing in my tent. Wouter is in his. This first climb has left a heaviness in my limbs, all I want to do is lie down. It may be from the exertion or from the altitude or both, but I take my altitude remedy just in case. I'm a novice in these rugged mountains. They stare down at me from high across the ravine that holds the river deep down below. The day which had turned summerlike around lunch time, has given way to cloudy cold with rain flurries, and my small tent seems so vulnerable next to these staunch veterans who have years of experience in dealing with desolation, wind, and temperature fluctuations. Small as they may be, though, my tent and sleeping bag keep me warm. I can survive the night which is coming fast.

A few yards away from my tent, I can see that Tondup is producing a meal under the tarp strung between his lean-to tent and some rocks. I'm hungry and a warm meal sounds good right now. I don't know if it's the exercise or the cold temperatures, or both, that make me hear my stomach growl. The sound of my stomach is almost as loud as the water running outside my tent. The sound of water is a constant backdrop, the heartbeat of this country. Not a gentle gurgle or a quiet flow, but a rushing, pounding stream made strong by elevation and melting snow. Strength that evokes will.

Thoughts rumble around in my head. I'm tired of having to will myself to go on with the life I'm in. I want to feel a balance of my strength and my softer vulnerable self. In Leh I had looked for a painting of white Tara, the benign feminine principle, to remind me to focus more on this softer energy. I couldn't find one that expressed the benignity I'm looking for. Now that I'm here in these mountains it seems that I've entered the realm of green Tara, the wrathful feminine principle that provides the transition to inner change. As if we're on her green skin, we are camping on green plants clustered on this mountain slope,

green tufts with an astringent tawny fiber, forming fodder for the few
animals that graze and live up here. Dark clouds rise out of the deep
crevices of her skin. Over this open expanse loom giant rock formations in purple and gray, forming a high wall for the trail that leads in
the direction of Senge-La, the highest point on this trek. I've seen it
in the far distance, snowy and touched by clouds. No wonder people
think there are other realms when they live in an otherworldly place
like this. My emotions seem to parallel the landscape and the weather.
I feel exposed, vulnerable, and taken care of at the same time. I can't
hide in this landscape, it's so vast and open that I bump into myself
constantly.

I think about how Wouter appeared on my path, how he tells me
about the things ahead. He's satisfying both my curious mind and my
worry mind. I'm not totally surrendering to the unknown—not yet.
Wouter is an unknown, but familiar enough that I can make assumptions that fit the realities as I've known them. He smiles warmly; he
talks about life in a way that is familiar, and he provides protection
and guidance. I provide him with food and company. We're a team
thrown together by the forces of the universe, by chance. Our intent
brought us together. It was a simple intent to walk five days in the
same direction. We walk, eat, and sleep as the cycle of light and dark
dictates. Now that we're camped out we can indulge our individuality.
What to do with the time? Wouter is in his own tent. I don't know
what he does, nor what he thinks.

And so here I am, just me with myself, my words bouncing
around in my mind. I'm one of the millions of creatures who sleep
alone and wake up alone. I delineate myself by the smallness of my
mind. I'm on a path, walking and breathing the path. I'm becoming
the realm I'm in, this vast realm at the top of the world.

I don't know if we'll continue our trek tomorrow as the donkeyman has gone home in Photaksar. Tondup has come back from the
village and told me he found another donkeyman willing to carry the
load for us. We now depend on this unknown village man for our
transportation. Will the money, that has power in the other world, the
world outside these mountains, be a strong enough attraction to make

him keep his word? I have no wool, medicine, or food to help them survive around here. I have some trekking equipment. Wouter has his pick-ax, a desirable tool, a sign of manly prowess with which he can scale the forbidden looking slopes. We're small creatures in this landscape and I'm discovering the code of living here. These are the parts of the earth that have erupted out of the depths. These are the parts that have withstood harsh conditions, like an old woman who has survived, a crone who carries the wear and tear as ripe beauty. Tara has us in her grip.

Maybe the locals know that better than I do. They've lived with this notion so much longer and they've learned that a greater power is outside of them. It can work for them, or against them. The locals appease Tara with juniper smoke, the incense of these mountains. Today when a local traveler gave me a little branch I left it by the side of the path. In my ignorance I wasted a spiritual gift. Now would be a good time to offer it to the ancient ones across the abyss, and ask them to protect me, to change the course of the storm that is looking over the shoulder of the mountain range above me. I've walked inside the heart of Tara, the Wrathful One, and I can feel the shaking of her rage.

Am I angry about the avalanche of events of the last ten years that buried my life as I knew it? The day's walking has kept me ahead of the moraines, the debris, of the breakdown. I have to keep walking to find my way out. I cannot ask questions or look back. I have to stay ahead. Is Wouter walking away from something? Sai Baba told him to go explore the Himalayas, an exploration of living, instead of sitting and waiting. Wouter doesn't know it, but I think he's being weaned off the constant flow of spiritual food at the ashram. He may not think so but he's also walking in the realm of the Wrathful One and it will transform his life.

Just as I'm thinking all this, Wouter's head peeks into my tent.

"You want company?" he asks. Speaking of the devil, maybe it's time to get to know him better and leave my self-involved, whirling thoughts alone.

"Yes, sure."

I make room by moving my books and journal and clearing a

little space on my sleeping pad that is doubling as a high mountain couch. "Sit down, tea will be served soon," I tell him. "Do you have your cup?" Wouter points at his cup hanging on his belt.

Just then Tondup is ambling up the slope with the teapot and cookies. This ritual at the end of a day of physical exertion is fast becoming a delightful addiction. The sweet milky substance that stimulates the brain produces thoughts that have been waiting in the back of muscle movement.

"How long are you going to stay in India?" I ask, as Wouter is looking at the map of the region he spread out.

"I have bought my little house," he answers. "I plan on staying."

"Can you stay the rest of your life?" My voice trails as an old fantasy of living in an ashram and devoting my life to spiritual pursuits clutters my brain.

"If I live frugally, I can manage another nine years. Then I'll have to go back to Holland and find something to do that makes money."

I frown as I contemplate this inverted retirement picture. "I gave up living in an ashram in my twenties. I revisit the idea at times, but less and less. Mostly when I'm depressed and want to escape life as it is. I guess I've learned to deal better with my emotions as I've gotten older. I'm not saying that you must be depressed to live in an ashram." I scramble to undo any negative insinuation. "Tell me more about your life; what's your daily routine at the ashram?"

"Oh, let's see," Wouter hesitates as he eats another cookie, "I get up in the morning, bathe and go find some breakfast in the local eating places nearby. I live close to the ashram, but not inside the actual compound. I usually meet up with some other devotees and we spend some time eating, talking, while we wait for the morning darshan. Then we go to the ashram and chant and sometimes Sai Baba comes out and talks to people. Sometimes we just do the chanting."

My thoughts go back to my brief time at Mahara-ji's ashram in Kanchi and I recognize the routine. "Do you actually talk with Sai Baba?" I ask curiously, wondering what the scope and size of the place is.

"Oh, no, he's talked to me directly maybe three times in the last thirteen years."

Visions of other large ashrams I visited when I was in India in my twenties now come to mind, and I remember the large crowds, the groupie atmosphere, the sense of a world of its own that occupied those places.

"So basically, you just live in a place with people who all wait for a glimpse or a moment with the master?" I realize that my comment already contains a judgment, as I've never had the patience to fill my life with someone else's energy.

Wouter looks at me puzzled. "I'm with him all the time. He has access to me and directs me without direct physical presence."

The total surrender in his expression makes me realize that I have not understood the concept of following a master in the same way Wouter has. The possibility of such a path becomes real to me as I find myself immersed in the forces of these mountains and experience the omnipresence of what I might call the "spiritual realm". I look out through the tent opening and watch the clouds thicken behind the walls of slate and granite that rise up straight from the depth of the river gorge below the slope of our mountain meadow. Flurries of moisture blow by, interspersed with warm rays of occasional sunshine. It's summer after all, and the sun's intensity keeps raising the temperatures that want to dip and intimidate us.

I'm amazed that I'm here. I'm the ant lugging a piece of twig to her mountainous home under the watchful eye of a bigger creature. One step, one swipe, and my existence will end as I know it. The benevolence that has graced my explorations is at the core of the workings of this realm.

Wouter is not just an innocent fool. He's taking a daring step on the path of living in the larger realm. He's switched the set on the stage he entered at birth. A sense of timelessness arises as when the scenery is changed in a play. The actor is still the same. There is the same delight in living, in aliveness, the same joy when rainbows color the sky, when the dawn rises and splashes an ochre and gray display in the visual field. But by switching the sets, events on the stage become more permeable and as an observer I develop a broader understanding of what's happening in the play.

By being here, I too have chosen a different set against which my life is playing itself out. Will I be able to observe and understand what's happening in my life because of this? Will I become an angel without wings—connected to something bigger than me? The Hindu Vedanta scriptures say *I am That*, the unnamable, the stuff that pulses, vibrates and finds its innumerable forms.

I look over at Wouter who is thoroughly enjoying his tea, and I newly appreciate the gift he represents on this journey.

"So what do you do the rest of the day, after getting darshan?" I ask.

"Oh, I take care of daily business, laundry, shopping, post office. I read, or nap, depending on the season, and go back for darshan in the afternoon. Actually, about right now, is when we gather again, for singing and a talk by one of the Indian long-time devotees. There is some discussion about how to live the spiritual life. I follow Sai Baba's directions for living." Wouter looks up from his cup of tea, grins and points at himself and then at me. "This is our darshan time in the afternoon. We're talking about living."

Directions for living, words I heard in my earlier life in India. At the time I was so goal-oriented, in the mode of going from here to there, that I took such words in as if they were a tourist guide. I look at the tourist guide that is now lying on my sleeping bag, a useless piece of instruction in the arms of these mountain gods. After just three days on this trek the words take on a different meaning. I'm no longer looking for directions on how to live, I'm looking for what living is.

"So today doesn't differ from your ashram life, except for the details of chanting and hanging out with other devotees?" I feel excitement rising inside me as I'm getting a glimmer of how the pieces of life's puzzle are fitting together.

"I guess you could say that, I'd never thought about it that way. I'm just doing life as it presents itself to me. I trust that Sai Baba knows what's good for me."

"How do you get the trust that Sai Baba knows what's good for you?" I test him.

"I feel at peace when I do what he says. It's much simpler than you think." Wouter smiles his blue-eyed smile.

Outside the tent opening Tondup's wide grin, in a face dirtied by soot from the kerosene stove, peeks over the rock wall that shelters his cooking area.

"Dinner, ready!" he shouts. His voice disassembles in the vast openness of the valley.

I'm ready for something more substantial than tea, cookies and conversation about the spiritual life. I want to shift the expansive mind to a focus on food, notice the palate and the slow satisfied feeling of a full stomach at the end of a day in the open air. Tondup brings over the simple one pot meal of noodles and curried vegetables and serves us. He looks up expectantly and waits for approval of his cooking skills. Tondup's deferring to me as his mistress reminds me of my dog's complete devotion, her inborn need to check the territory and its inhabitants.

"It's delicious," I say thoughtfully chewing my first bite. This is the signal for Tondup to have his own meal and eat the enormous quantity he can put away at the end of a day and wash it all down with butter chai. As he sits in his open kitchen area, he looks forlorn, left to the mercy of the elements. Yet he's strong as the hardy plants that hang onto the rocky mountain slopes. He doesn't seem to be conscious of himself as a vulnerable entity. I envy his connection with his environment, which gives him freedom from fear. Fear of the unknown is the price I pay for growing up sheltered. I've spent a lot of hours working during my life to maintain that level of being sheltered; to have the ease and comfort that goes with it.

"It will be a long night," Wouter says as he finishes his food. The dark clouds are helping nightfall along. "I'm going to read until dark." He unfolds his legs and moves his body out through the small tent opening.

I take my dishes and follow. I walk over to the stream that is bubbling through the rocks and green tufts. The water is ice-cold. My fingers become numb as I scrub my bowl with a bit of gravel. I stand up and stretch myself out to get rid of the stiffness of sitting crouched in my tent and see the first stars between the clouds in the big sky. This place is mine to be for now.

The sound of bird-chirps cuts through the icy air and pulls me out of my sleep-wrapped unconsciousness. I get up, layer all my warm clothes and go exploring. When I emerge from my tent no-one is around. Gray clouds are racing across the sky. It'll be awhile before there's any packing for the day to do, since we have to wait for the new donkeyman to show. Wouter has told me that there are big marmots in the area, but the activity of our group has kept them at bay.

I walk up the trail and the vivid green of grasses near the stream makes way for gray-green lichen-covered rocks, gravel, and brown and olive green grasses struggling to gain some height. Lack of rain and overgrazing has created this moonscape. There is not a bush or tree in sight. I'm the only visible living creature moving around at this moment. The world busy with survival, procreation and progress seems so far away. Green Tara is probably laughing and has her many arms hovering over me, ready to tear me to pieces when... Yes, when? Is there a reason for misfortune, death and decay? I feel a sudden release of tension inside me, as the ludicrousness of human striving for safety and security, in this environment especially, strikes me as the image of a three-year-old standing in the middle of a crowded freeway clutching a teddy bear for safety.

There is a brown scurrying I catch in the corner of my eye. Dark twinkling eyes turn in my direction. I stand still and the animal, a marmot, sits up on hind legs, and shows its two-foot height. It's perfectly camouflaged in brown-green color and now I see others sticking their heads out of holes in the ground. When they sense that it's safe, they emerge and sit with their rounded rear ends majestically tall on the uneven ground, heads up, looking around their kingdom. I point my camera. My arm movement makes them withdraw their bodies into their holes and the image on my viewer becomes less than interesting. I better be still and become part of the landscape for a while. This is how I can experience what's going on, not through the pictures I'll be viewing later.

I wonder what they come out of their holes for. It's a sparse vegetarian diet and I can imagine that during the long winter months under the snow there will be no plant life at all. I soon lose interest in the movement of brown and green. Apart from yaks, I haven't seen large animals or birds that might feed on these creatures. Few enemies mean less need for procreation to keep the species going. I wished these rules applied more to humans as well.

The marmots reappear now that I'm quiet. Their quick moves blend with moments of absolute repose as they scurry and scan, scan and scurry. My journey is like that, movement and rest on a piece of this earth. I'm like a marmot with no more or less importance than the perpetuation of life. My life seems to be nothing more than the shadow that life throws, an endless wave of energy pulsing with greater and lesser surges. I keep thinking the greater surges will give me insight into the meaning of it all. I can only reflect and know that such great surges come and go, and be ready to accept them when they come. What change will today, this day here in the mountains of the Himalayas, bring for me? Will I be stuck here, or will I move on? Will the weather warm me, or create cold and wetness? These are questions I can't answer. I can create many more questions about this day, but they're useless mind wanderings right now. I have shelter and food, and all's well. The marmot has its hole and fodder.

My body is getting stiff in the morning cold. My mind is getting bored with my contemplations. I stretch. The marmots duck into their holes. I turn and find my way back to camp. Wouter has emerged from his tent.

"Hey, good morning, did you sleep OK?"

"Hmm, yes, good dreams," he answers with a smile.

"What did you dream about?"

"I was back at the ashram, there was darshan going on, everyone was chanting." Wouter looks out at the valley across the gorge.

"Ah, celestial music in your dreams," I joke, but see the poignancy of the experience as the misty morning light shrouds the looming granite in the landscape. Tara is wearing her silver crown and for the moment the power of her grip seems light.

"It's a gift from Sai Baba to come to me in my dreams and fill me with his light." Wouter is serious about his interpretations.

I think about the time in my life when I dreamed about Mahara-ji and would wake with longing and feelings of joy about the connectedness that cut across earthly distance and unearthly realms. Now I'm not sure that it was really Mahara-ji who came to me in my dreams. Just as I'm not sure right now who it is that Wouter really embodies. Is he an apparition, a form Mahara-ji took on to teach me something? Will he vanish when I have no need for the embodiment of the guru anymore? My father and mother never came to me in my dreams after they died, or when they were alive and far away from me for that matter. They didn't have answers for me about the things I was looking for in life. I sensed that Mahara-ji knew things I was looking for, and I wanted his answers. The connection I made with him came from my need. Is that always the case? Does every person who shows up in my life come from a need I carry deep inside me?

"I'm glad you're feeling good." I'll give him that much. "I will see if Tondup is cooking something up for breakfast." My hunger is leading the way and I walk toward our open-air kitchen.

The sun is shining on the little droplets of morning dew, creating a sparkle on the rocks and lean-to. Tondup's head comes out from under the tarp, his smile is the sparkle on his soot-smeared face.

"Good morning, breakfast is cooking," he announces. "Tea is ready." I offer to carry the teapot to my tent. He lets me, since he has to attend to all kitchen matters by himself this morning.

"We take time and wait for donkeyman." He exudes confidence.

"Shall I pack after breakfast?" Hope for a normal procedure of the day seeps through in my voice.

"We wait, then pack," Tondup answers. "Not very far today to Senge-La, enough time to get there."

Senge-La has looked not very far for the last two days now. I know it's no use to ask for exact times and distances. In this place, calculations are in days not in hourly increments. I breathe in the spaciousness that comes with that notion. Here with this time frame, governed by the sun and moon, my mind is free to connect with all that is around me, the natural and the supernatural. The real and the unreal. It's easy to give Tara form and let her interact with my experiences. Not only is it easier to do here, it's also satisfying. Maybe that's why some have called the mountains the abode of the gods.

I take the teapot to the tent and call Wouter over for a cup.

"So, this is farther than you made it last week, isn't it?" I ask.

"Yes, as far as I know we go over one more pass, before we head up the valley to Senge-La." He seems to have studied the map.

"How high is this first pass we have to go over?" I'm not looking forward to another day of gasping for air, moving my heavy limbs up an incline. Why did I think hiking at altitude would be easy?

"It's nothing; do you see the trail there as it goes up to that hill? That is the top of Bumitse-la. We basically have already done the bulk of the climbing yesterday afternoon by camping here. Bumitse-la is just on the way up to Senge-La, which will be a 1,200 foot climb tomorrow. We will not go down much after Bumitse pass." Wouter spouts his mountain knowledge. I'm glad he knows because I haven't memorized elevations. With my limited experience of mountain climbing I have no feel for what elevation gains mean. I'll be learning as I go, and trust Tondup to make good climbing decisions for me.

The sun is now burning away Tara's crown and the formidable rock walls across the ravine are showing their faces again, dark against the light blue sky and the sparkling green of the slope we're camped on. The little river that crosses this meadow is gurgling happily nearby.

"I'm ready for breakfast. It looks like Tondup is coming this way with the grub." I point in the direction of our kitchen.

Tondup's body appears above the little dugout he camped in for the night, out of the wind. He motions us in his direction.

"Breakfast must be ready." I rise up from my crouched position. "Are you coming?" I look back at Wouter, who's still sipping his tea.

"Yes, I'd like to share your breakfast. I have nothing left in my supplies – I've run out. I want to pay you though."

"We'll work it out. I wish you would just accept where we're at. You have come this far, and it's obvious that there is no food for sale. If you really don't want to rely on me for food, you should have planned differently. I've invited you to share my food. There's enough." I can feel the irritation rising in me over his ambiguous approach.

Wouter looks up at me. His muscular hands fumble with his cup, as he says, "Oh, OK, I accept."

I think about Wouter's hesitancy to accept my food supplies. We have come together in these vast mountains. Two pools of resources thrown together for unknown reasons, but able to survive better together than alone. My hospitality is merely the practical approach to living.

Wouter appears to be less into sharing. Even though he tells me he lives in an ashram, he hasn't lost the *don't ask for handouts* habit of his root culture. Roots I'm all too familiar with. I remember my mother busy in the kitchen. It was her birthday, a cold day in January. The living room was full of guests, family who made the two-hour train ride from the islands to the city. Coffee, pastries and the usual *glaasje*, pre-dinner drinks, had been served, but evening was approaching and it wasn't clear how long they were staying. My mother muttered: "Why couldn't they let me know ahead of time they wanted to come for the day? I could've prepared a meal." She rummaged in her pantry for some packages of soup she could add to the meal she'd prepared for the family.

Fourteen years old and irreverent, I said: "Why can't you let 'em take care of themselves?"

"I wouldn't hear the end of that for years," my mother replied.

"Well, it's your birthday, doesn't that count for something?" I asked.

"They are my guests," she said.

I shook my head and left the kitchen full of the heavy energy of such family expectations.

Wouter's behavior reminds me of my aunts and uncles who say they don't want to burden anyone but sit around expecting to be fed, as family tradition dictates. It's a cultural behavior I never adopted. I prefer the open, warm-hearted American-style hospitality I've experienced. I don't see any hidden agendas and favors which you have to pay back. In my experience, American hospitality seems to have been born out of long trips through rough country to reach new land and opportunity. I sense this same hospitality in the people who live here in the mountains, in their open smiles, and their willingness to share what little they have.

It's not obligation or an outworn code that compels me to feed Wouter. It's a sense of community that ties into the connectedness of everything and everyone on this planet, that moves me to do this. I have a choice, I can see Tara as threatening, and wrathful, or I can see her in all her glory, wearing the crown of strength and power. There's no division, there are only two sides of the same coin. Every day on this trek, every step I take, takes me closer to absorbing this mystery. I can't quite fit Wouter's unequivocal acceptance of everything that comes to him as his guru's care for him with his hesitance in accepting the food I offer him on the trail. Is his hesitance a cultural habit left over from the old country? Is my fierce independence a similar cultural remnant?

After breakfast, while waiting for the donkeyman to show up, I write in my journal. I study the map of Ladakh a bit, to be able to describe our location. The map is very general. Until now, I've let myself be guided without having a detailed picture of the trail. I trust that Tondup knows where we're going. The map doesn't tell me much more, except that we are on the trail that eventually leads to Lingshed.

The sound of bells breaks my concentration. I look up out of my tent and see a young man and two donkeys crossing the little stream. The young man walks toward Tondup's kitchen. The donkeyman is here. Even though I want to surrender to whatever the trail brings, I feel my innards relax knowing that our trip can go on as planned.

Chapter 17

Our donkeyman is young, rosy-cheeked, despite his dark complexion. I sense a healthy amount of adolescent shyness and embarrassment as I introduce myself to him. He nods, smiles and looks at Tondup for a translation of what I'm saying. His name is Tsering, a name as common in this country as John in America. I thank him for coming with us and rub the donkeys behind their ears, hoping to appease the animal spirits for the day. The donkeys stand docile, their brown ruffed up coats dusty and showing bare patches of wear. I cringe thinking how the load that will ride on their backs will only make these patches worse. The frame that is placed on the saddle blanket is rough wood and will shift and rub as the donkeys sway with their dainty steps. Feeling sorry for animals is a luxury their owners cannot afford.

While Tondup and Tsering pack up the load, Wouter and I strike out ahead in the direction of our goal for the day, the base of Senge-la, the Lion Pass. I know the beginning of the trail from my morning wanderings and the walking is easy and quiet. A herd of miniature yaks comes down the slope followed by a herder. Our *Julleys* ring out and I feel a part of the local traffic. I watch the herd spread out on the lower side of the trail toward the river that roars below. Small dots of man and beast in the landscape, vulnerable at the breast of the imposing rock walls.

After an easy twenty-minute walk, I'm approaching a large wide pile of rock that divides the trail into two paths, a *mani* wall marking a high point. This must be Bumitse-la, 14,000 ft up. It hasn't even felt like a climb to get to this pass. There are no prayer flags to mark the spot. The wall is unusual in its size, about fifteen feet long, six feet wide and four feet high. I wonder if something happened here that created this size wall. Is someone buried here? There is no-one to ask, so I make up a story in my head about villagers gathering to ask for special protection from the howling winds and snowstorms that can intimidate any traveler going toward Senge-La. Will I meet up with these forces? The stones on the outside of the wall are carved with the familiar symbols of *Om Mani Padme Hum*.

"Let's wait here for the others to catch up." I turn to Wouter who's been following at a little distance. I lean against the wall. The stones feel warm and solid. I want to add my stone and look around for a colorful one in the landscape. I find a red colored one and place it in a niche.

Tondup comes around the bend and calls out, "Bumitse-la!"

"Yes, I figured. Is it OK to take pictures of this wall?" I call back.

He nods, and Tsering shoos the donkeys on up the path ahead. I take a picture of the three men who surround my daily wanderings—three men, like limbs of Tara, keeping me safe and on the path—men I trust on this journey to look after me. Am I a fool to trust these men? I trusted Doyle, thought I knew him well, and now I don't recognize him as the man I trusted. Even the ones we deem trustworthy can change. I can only trust the moment. I feel an easing of tension in my chest as I'm living the fact I'm not in control. These vast mountains and high passes are my reminders. The deep tearing, that occurred when Doyle betrayed our marriage, is losing its acute searing pain out here.

We walk on, each one of us at our own pace, I'm in the rear. The landscape is now sprinkled with wildflowers along the path, yellow ones, blue and white. There is a plant that looks like a miniature rhu-barb plant. If I'd been trekking with Karma, he would've been able to tell me about the plants, as he studies *Amchi*, the ancient form of healing with plants.

As I walk, I remember the time in my life when I lived in the countryside, off the grid, just as we are here on this trip. I was mak-ing herbal tinctures and poultices to heal everyday illnesses. Living in the country had sufficiently slowed me down to pay attention to nature's gifts. I felt the grace of the natural world, as I learned about its offerings and gave it a spiritual significance. The frustration of liv-ing in isolation and the lack of resources for a growing family made us move to Ashland. This small town nestled in the mountains, with access to the natural world, education and cultural events, allowed me to leave country living behind. I thought I could have the best of both, the spiritual and the worldly, but now, walking in these mountains, I wonder if it's ever possible to get both. While doing the hard work of breathing and carrying I'm experiencing the core of my being. In the constant presence of nature's vast power I'm easily drawn to contemplate the spiritual aspect of things. Tondup and Tsering, steeped as they are in this enormous natural world, appear to be living with an understanding of the spiritual realm, exuding faith in the nature of things, but for how long? I may rob them of their spiritual innocence, as I bring the seduction of the material world with me. Walking here in gear that deals well with weather and a harsh environment beats prayer any day.

Just as I'm thinking about my feet and the need for a rest, Tondup, who's been ahead of me with the donkeys, calls out and points at something as he rounds a bend in the trail. I keep on walking to see what it is. Around the bend I see a river coming down the mountainous ridge to our right and crossing our path. This must be the river crossing I've read about in the guidebook. A river crossing that can be dangerous, cold and wet according to the book.

The river foams as it tumbles over rocks down the slope. It's about thirty feet wide, and winds around little willow bushes. When I get to the edge of the river, Tsering is already walking along it to find a crossing for the donkeys. Tondup, who has been scouting the depth of the river, is jumping from rock to rock to come back in my direction.

"Not too deep, Memsahib, we can get across, no problem." He exudes confidence.

"OK, I'll find a way. I poke my trekking poles in the gravelly river bottom to find my footing. The bottom is rocky, too, and I can't poke the poles in solid ground for balance. I work my way across, stepping from rock to rock, without relying too much on the poles. Soon I'm in a deeper part of the river and the water is swift, the rocks slippery. I might slide and get seriously wet. I don't like such cold. I'm hesitating, wondering how to go further. Wouter is already on dry ground in the middle, with wet boots. Shall I take off my boots here while standing on the rock and keep them dry? I decide to do so, despite the cold water and slippery rocks.

The gravel and rocks hurt the soles of my feet. I remember a shallow crossing on a backpacking trip in the Marble Mountains in California. To stay dry, and too lazy to take my shoes off, I'd jumped, self-assured with my thirty-five pound pack, from rock to rock, slipped and tore a tendon. We were two miles from the end of the trail. My friend had to carry both our loads in shifts, while I dragged myself along the trail. I can still feel the shame for the stupidity that ended up burdening my younger, more agile friend.

I don't want to tear anything right now, I'll take the discomfort of the gravel. The ice-cold water numbs my feet as I put them in the stream and the water rises above my knees. How much deeper will it get? With the pictures from the guidebook of trekkers wading neck high through this river in my mind, I use my poles in an attempt to have some sense of where solid ground is. My camera, I just cannot afford to get it wet! How will I use my poles *and* put my daypack above my head if it gets deeper?

"Keep moving, don't think about it too much." Wouter's voice and helping hand pull me up onto a larger, flat rock.

Pfff! I'm through the deepest part it seems. When I turn around Tondup is jumping from rock to rock, a smile from ear to ear as if he's carried by a force I can't see. I shiver, even though the effort of river crossing has warmed me. I don't trust my body like Tondup trusts his. I feel like a loser, because of fear, and I don't know how to access the magic powers of the river to carry me across.

With just the shallower water to wade through, I'm wetter than the others by the time I make it to the other side. A little, white-washed, stone *stupa*[35] sits at the top of the bank. What's a sacred relic, buried in plaster, doing here for me? Tondup sits himself down to rest against its sun-warmed walls, pulls his cap over his eyes and gives himself over to sleep. I sit down with Wouter on some rocks and pull out lunch for both of us. This time there's a hard-boiled egg with the

---

35. *Stupa*: a Buddhist shrine, usually a dome.

chapatis and cucumber.

"I hate feeling so helpless," I blurt out.

"What do you mean? You don't look helpless to me," Wouter replies.

"I can't jump from rock to rock, like you and Tondup did. I'm afraid to fall and get my camera wet. I've fallen in a river crossing before and tore my knee up." I tell him about my mishap a few years ago.

"I think you're wise to be careful. You're far from medical help here," Wouter tries to assuage my fears.

"I guess it's this old family thing of wanting to keep up with the men, my father and brother. My father could only be tough, he did not know how to appreciate different capacities, and so I felt inferior or weak when I couldn't keep up with his standards. It was the same intellectually. He only knew reason, and capacity for feeling and intuition were the realm of females and below the acceptable grade." I feel the tension in my diaphragm increase as I feel the familiar hopelessness. I sigh and let go. No father here to get approval from. I'm living by my own standards. I hand Wouter his lunch.

"Yeah, my family's practicality outdid me. It's the only standard they measure by."

"Is that why you have made such a complete shift to living an ashram life?" I ask.

"I see it as following my heart." Wouter smiles.

"Well, there wasn't much room for the heart in government bookkeeping, was there?" I say.

"You can say that, especially with the corruption that was going on." Wouter shifts his body against the *stupa* wall.

We finish our lunch in silence. Even though Wouter's reasons for leaving family and family standards behind to find his own answers are like mine, his spiritual aspirations feel more alien to me as the days go on. Despite our cultural connection and his friendliness, I don't feel any closer to him. With my stomach full and feet warm again, a nap against the warm stones is inviting. Tondup and Tsering are still asleep. I settle down on a side of the *stupa* and let sleep and the holy shrine do its work.

We wake a little later, feeling the cold air as clouds hide the sun. Tondup jumps up and shakes his body. Tsering whistles to his donkeys, who are grazing at the river's edge. A few more hours of walking lie ahead of us before we reach the base of Senge-La.

"Are we going to cross over the pass today?" I ask Tondup.

"No, we have to wait on this side, Memsahib—be patient."

"Wait for what?" I'm curious.

"Snow too soft in the afternoon, donkeys can't get up." Again, Tondup lets me know what for him is a natural ongoing connection between man and beast. As he jumped easily over the swift flowing water earlier, Tondup moves like a magician between animal, people and nature. His life, and mine now too, depends on this magic, this ability to sense and know the world of man, beast and nature.

"Does the snow stay all summer?" I ask.

"Snow comes, snow goes—more rain now in the summer months. Monsoon now come to Himalayas. Weather change, everything change." I receive his report about climate change and think about my contribution in daily life to this phenomenon. Is it bad that there is more rain in this region? Maybe there will be more trees and vegetation for animals, more possibility for living here. Then again, less snowpack[36] will surely change everything down the line. Images of the brown and red Indus River of a few days ago with the green settlements on her banks float through my mind. If snow crystals are no longer feeding the Indus, will it change her spiritual quality in the eyes of believers?

"Just short walk to camp now." Tondup tightens his daypack. I strap mine on as well and start walking. I'm the last one in line again. Wouter has already gone ahead without waiting or asking. I shrug internally, trying not to let my expectations of our trail relationship get in the way. I guess I wish for some caring from him. Tsering has caught up with the donkeys, and Tondup's pace soon leaves me behind.

I set a leisurely pace, not interested in trying to catch up with the men. Knowing that there will be no more hard climbs for the day,

36. Snowpack: a mass of snow rendered hard and compacted by its own weight.

I can manage by myself. This is my walk on the path, my communion with sky, snowy mountain ranges and awe-inspiring vistas. The grandeur of this place doesn't diminish the fact that I got myself here. I think back on all the journeys I've undertaken in search of something bigger, something unknown. I'm the toddler that wandered across the bridge to an unknown neighborhood to look for frogs in the moat. The little girl that walked up the dunes to see the other side. The ten-year-old who pressed her forehead against the train window to see the world flying by as she traveled by herself to her grandmother's house. The eighteen-year-old who flew on an airplane, as the first one in the family, to see another continent.

My curiosity has driven me. My legs have carried me. Wherever I've found myself there has been another place to go, a new world to discover. No fear, no physical limitations have held me back. I'm a living, breathing element, at home in this world. Will I do this for the rest of my life, move from one interesting place to another, meet one wise person after another? Look under rocks for new insights about living, ask people about their quest for answers to mine? Will I ever find a satisfying answer?

I think back to the time I spent with Goenka, another time of looking for answers. Goenka had said: "You'll know when you no longer have the question." I was stumped then. Thirty-four years later and I still have the question, renewed in its fervor because my life as I've known it is falling apart.

Here's a trail with sand, rocks, beautiful plants and sunshine to delight my soul. Is there more to life than this? This moment of being alive in the body, smelling the air, touching the ground, seeing the sights to be seen? Here, walking alone, I'm a friend of this environment and no-one can make this experience more complete. I can feel my lungs expand as I drink down this notion into my mind. My mind is the lung. My mind is the foot in the boot, warm and snug, on the ground.

The path meanders around white rocks and alpine plants. Flowers yellow, blue and white let me think I'm in a park, neatly landscaped to delight visitors. All the hard work I have done in my backyard at home seems presumptuous and petty when the big gardens of the world have their designs to inspire and nourish me if I visit and open my eyes.

Little rivulets cross the path that leads me to the upper sloping side of the valley floor. There are some low rock walls and a stone building. As I come around the building, Tsering and Tondup are walking around a flat area scoping out a campsite. A little closer to the creek which runs through the landscape, forming erratic bends and carvings as it hollows out the creek bed, Wouter is already setting up his tent.

"Are we staying here tonight?" I ask Tondup the obvious.

"Yes, camp, rest, cook." Tondup smiles as he leans against the warm stones forming a circle around a little hollow. He playfully throws a clot of dirt in the direction of the donkeys that have been unburdened from their load. The donkeys bray, jump with awkward legs. Tondup and Tsering laugh, their voices sharp against the ice-blue sky.

With the afternoon sun still warm at three o'clock this is my chance to do some laundry and bathe. I eye the creek that comes down from the snowy pass. The wide-open landscape has provided little privacy for bathing in the last five days, neither has the cold been inviting for a dip in the streams. Without talking to Wouter who's now in his tent, I set up my tent a short distance from his on the bluff near the ever-sounding water.

I organize my pack inside the tent, sort through the few clothes I brought and decide what can be washed and possibly dried in the short time of sunshine left today. Socks and a few pieces of underwear are all I dare to get wet in this capricious weather. Who knows, it may snow again later!

When I emerge from the tent to walk to the river, a pair of yaks, males apparently, are charging at each other close by. Their snorting and head butting give me the chills, they're so close to me, and their show of power makes them seem bigger in the open landscape. The *domos*, females of the herd, are quietly grazing a few yards away. So far I've considered these animals to be like cows of the Himalayas, docile and servile, not a wild beast which might be a threat. It's been so rare that I have met animals in their own habitat, and I really am not prepared for the rush of adrenaline I feel coursing through me. What if they come this way, trample through my tent? Chase me, as I run?

With the hair rising on my neck, I quietly move away from the spot. The snorting comes to a crescendo, there's a thumping of shoulders as they make contact, and then suddenly, as unexpected as it all started, they wander toward the females. My breath caught in my throat, I stop and realize how insignificant I am, a spectator in the theater of nature, a marmot scurrying for safety. I descend from the bluff down to the creek and find a spot where I'm invisible to the men. It's time to strip, feel the sun and the cold, icy water on my skin. The delight of gooseflesh and blood flowing as my skin contracts to keep warm, is a welcome contrast to the stale feeling of body odor in warm clothing of the last few days. A rub down with the little travel towel sets me aglow and takes me back to the days on the beach in Holland, getting rubbed down hard by my father after a cold swim, jumping up and down, cringing under his strong hands, followed by sandwiches for the hollow feeling in my stomach.

I finish my creek visit by doing the laundry. A quick rubbing and swirling of cloth in a gurgling pool, water from the main part of the stream slowed down by rock formations. I look up at the snowy incline where the stream originates, water jumping, laughing in the light reflections as it's freed from its more solid form by the sun. Water drops and rivulets escaping in all directions like children from a school building finding their way down the main street as they leave the playground. The water first forms a thin shiny sheet that covers the earth and slowly starts the inevitable erosion of the softer materials and carves out its path down the mountain. I have stood on glaciers belonging to high mountains, the Rhône at the beginning of my overland trip to India, and Mount Everest near the end of that trip. Glaciers that melted into rivulets, slowly forming powerful rivers. I witnessed the beginnings, the moment of conception in the endless cycle of warm and cold. The core of life, the rhythm of creation. I stand still. As much as this natural landscape frees my thoughts and increases my awareness, it isn't enough to answer my bigger question. Snow doesn't ask questions, it just melts when the temperature rises. Tondup doesn't ask what life is all about. He lives in the world given to him. Wouter asks his guru and hopes to get an answer by doing what the man tells him to do. Even after days in this no man's land I'm not ready to accept that this is all there is. I still long for another person who completes my thoughts and feelings, so I can be in the world more wholeheartedly. A world that will give me a reason to be.

I climb the bluff; the yaks have wandered far away from our campsite. Wouter is sitting outside his tent on a rock. Tondup and Tsering have fired up the kerosene stove. I hang my laundry on my tent wires and hope that the no longer warm sun can still do its work.

"Chai ready?" I call out to Wouter. No sandwiches here, cookies and tea will have to fill the hollow pit in my stomach.

"Yes, I think tea is coming." Wouter looks sullen.

"What are you doing with your afternoon off?" I ask.

"Just sitting here, I have no energy."

"Isn't this a wonderful place to be?" My recent view of creation is spilling over.

"I suppose. Rest and sunshine feel good." Wouter doesn't sound as convinced as I am.

"I will explore that side of the valley after tea." I point toward a crevice in the rocks that form the valley wall leading up to the pass. "Have you seen those rock formations?"

"I'll just hang out and have tea." Wouter picks up his book.

Undaunted by Wouter's lack of interest in my plans, I walk over to the kitchen area. Tondup and Tsering are sitting in the dugout they created by stacking more rocks as a windbreak around the natural hollow area where they made camp.

"Is it going to be windy?" I assume they have the read on the weather with their close relation to the mountain gods, Tara included.

"Wind lives here at night." Tondup wraps his vest a little tighter as if to warn me about what's coming.

"Does it blow hard? Is my tent safe over there?" I point at the glowing orange and yellow form that sits on top of the bluff, as if modeling for an outdoor company catalogue.

"Yes, this not winter wind" Tondup assures me, while tossing some tea leaves into the pot on the sputtering stove, as if to show the wind won't even blow these away. Then offers his all occasion comfort remedy.

"You want chai? Chai ready."

"Yes, thank you, I'll take it over to Wouter." I reach out for the pot and the box of cookies.

Wouter joins me as I sit down in the opening of my tent with the tea accoutrements. I pull out my journal and start writing about the day. After pouring each of us a cup, Wouter sits silently while drinking his tea.

"What is the elevation here?" I look up from my journal and check with him to get my facts straight.

"4,400 metres," Wouter answers.

I do a quick times three in my head to to find the US equivalent: 14,400 ft, not quite what I thought, maybe it's more than times three.

"I thought Senge-La was almost 16,000 feet high. It doesn't look like an 1,800 feet climb from here to get up there."

"I don't know what the elevation is in feet, but you'll be surprised, when you start up that slope."

I'll have to leave it to the guys here, they all know more, or at least conduct themselves as if they do. My inability to gauge distances and measurements in concrete numbers is making me the inferior species of the moment. All I know is that we're at high altitude. I finish the details of the day in my journal, and my tea in the cup. Wouter stares out of the tent opening, not engaging in conversation. What's the matter with him today? Did I touch a sensitive nerve? Well, if I did, I can't think of what's going on with him and I will not dig into his wall of silence. Time for something else.

"I'm going to explore the rocks. Do you want more tea, or can I take the pot back to Tondup?" I ask.

"No thanks." Wouter still gives me no opening.

I tighten the laces on my boots so I can walk around safely and pick up the teakettle. I make my stop at the dugout where Tondup and Tsering are stretched out against the rocks, enjoying butter chai, their salty version of tea. They've created a cover for their bedding with a red-checkered plastic sheet. The food bags are stacked under it.

"Does anybody stay over there in that little house?" I point at the deserted stone building with rock wall compound.

"That place for travelers. When bad weather, animals go in compound," Tondup explains. Not much different from mountain folks' behavior in other Alpine places in the world.

"Have you stayed there before?" I ask Tondup. Tsering is looking at me smiling, but I don't believe he understands what I ask.

"Yes, during snowy time, walking home from school," Tondup answers.

"Was it cold, or did you make a fire?" I wonder how he did all that as a teenager.

"We make fire. Take turns sleeping, keep fire going." Tondup gives me a peek into the tough life of mountain children in this region. No wonder he can give me that sense of trust, having survived so many rough trips already. What would I do without his mountain expertise here? Wouter tries to rely on himself and his guru's guidance and look where that's gotten him. I prefer to put my stakes on Tondup.

"I'm going to see what it's like." I wander in the direction of the stone hut. There are many rocks with the familiar *Om mani padme hum* carving in the compound wall. People must spend considerable time here to carve these symbols. I wonder if they get stuck in snowstorms and create their prayers for survival in this way. Maybe this religious custom is also a way to keep the mind from wandering into fear and worry, as the hands keep busy with the carving work.

I walk across the rock-strewn landscape. Rocks of all sizes, from small pebbles to boulders, are scattered around. It's as if the mountain wall opened up and emptied herself. I see a five-foot opening in the rock wall, showing a winding walkway between twenty-foot high stone walls, in shades of gray, black and red. I enter and step into the rock world. I'm no longer connected with the wide-open space of the valley floor where the river connects me with the waters that lead to the ocean. This path is going in, into the mountain. There's no sign of plant life. The sun does not shine in here. Will this path take me inside the earth? J.R.R. Tolkien would have had a feast day with this landscape. Is this the portal to another realm, a world of gods and ghosts? Breathless, I hurry on, as if hurry can ward off the fear of getting lost, that crops up in the back of my head. The air is still. The sound of the river doesn't reach here. I stand, touch the stone wall, cool against my palm. In my mind I can hear the winter gale whistling around the corners, blowing up the rock dust, blinding any living thing. In my mind I can see the snow piled high, filling every crevice like a coat of fur around its slender pillars. This is no place where human or animal life can survive. This is a spirit place, a place of deep quiet, where knowledge is whispered to become the future of the world. Just as the ocean floor holds its secrets, this place is the core in this sea of mountain ridges where knowledge is stored.

I close my eyes and register the sensations in my body. My face is warm from a day of high altitude sun, my breath is almost suspended, my arms tingle with energy, my legs are heavy with the unknown. I'm disconnected from everyone I've known, I have walked away from the familiar and entered the earth. I'm surrounded by the essential energy that supports life. Earth in its earliest inception, with nothing but the winds, the cold and the heat to mold its forms.

Dying must be like this. Disconnecting from the familiar, the known, and being surrounded by the essence of life. Energy that will take on form, again, and again. This is the place where there are no *why* questions, this is the place of just *being*.

A deep movement in my diaphragm fills my lungs and brings me back to rock, air and temperature. It's cooling down, and when I look up at the sky, the blue is fading. How long have I been here? Will I find my way back? I need to find the others again. I turn and wind my way between the gray walls. The walls that have given me a glimpse into the greater connections of life and matter, now seem to close in on me. I'm not ready to die here, I want to see the open valley again. Every corner of stone pushes me forward to another corner. They all look alike. Where's the opening out of here? My shoulders tighten, my breathing speeds up as I hurry.

Then, around another corner, there is the mouth of the crevice. I sigh with relief at seeing the sloping valley. The sun is still in the sky; the yaks are still grazing. I hear the sonorous music of the animal bells as a group of animals and people approach the upper side of the creek. The red and yellow colors indicate the arrival of a monastic order. We will not camp alone tonight.

Chapter 18
ALTITUDE 14,500 FT

The ice crackles in spider-web formation as my rubber-soled boots put their weight down. I jump from stone to stone to avoid the icy water that rushes under the ice to the bigger stream and loudly expresses its force, gathered from the melting snow up above. I look up at the climb ahead and see the first sun rays skirting the towering peaks and hit the blue snowbanks that loom cold on their slopes still untouched by summer's warmth. July in the Ladakhi Himalayas is just a brief warming respite from months of frozen stone and howling winds. Even now that the snow has receded enough to allow passage over Senge-La, our climbing terrain is still composed of snow and ice on the northern slope leading up to the pass. I'm glad I won't have to scale the mountain giants around me and can make my way through a mere foot of snow. The distance to the pass appears to be just a short walk, but by now I know that distances are hard to guess from just looking. I've seen this trail laid out ahead of me for the last two days now, a benign ribbon stretched out along the constantly rising valley floor as it follows the river.

Wouter tells me we have a climb of about 1,200 feet ahead of us, and it'll probably take a few hours if we're lucky. He is determined to make it to Padum, a village beyond Lingshed—yet another week of walking farther in these mountains. Remembering the retching sound I heard coming from his tent last night I ask him how he's feeling.

"I didn't sleep much," he says without his usual upbeat tone of voice. "After dinner my stomach did a somersault, and my head pounded all night."

"You didn't eat breakfast," I noted. "Do you want a homeopathic altitude remedy? I took it when I arrived in Leh and when I started on this trek, but it's hard to say how I would have felt without it." My confidence in my approach to the dreaded altitude state is waning, but it's all I have to offer for now.

"It's too late for that now, I have to get to a lower altitude to feel better." He hoists his forty-pound pack onto his back. I make one more attempt to penetrate his stoic wall of self-sufficiency and offer help.

"Do you want to put your pack on a donkey?" I hesitate, not sure that it's even a possibility, as the donkeys are loaded down already as it is.

"I'll make it. I'll just go slowly. Don't wait for me." His expression is unreadable in the shadow of his hat.

Wouter's withdrawal reminds me of Doyle's withdrawal from me. I'm in these mountains because I can't reach Doyle behind his wall of Parkinson's. I feel a familiar tension rising in my chest, a wobbly sensation as if I'm on my toes and reaching out with my arms without being able to hold on. I don't want Wouter to unsettle me. Why do I even want him to take what I offer? Why do I reach out to him to do this trip together? Habit of inclusiveness? Fear of being on my own? I have no answer but will find out what my feelings are as I walk alone today and let Wouter take care of himself. All I can do now is explore the freedom I have and didn't want.

"OK, do what you want. We can wait for each other at the top." I adjust my daypack and check the laces on my boots. I don't want to be like Wouter with his stoic stance. With his complete surrender to his guru Wouter turns each event into either a teaching or a gift, never a self-made choice with consequences. I'm not sure if it covers up an inability to live with the lonely realities of his life, or if he's exuding an equanimity that sprouts from a spiritual connection. Even though I'd like to point all this out to him, I withhold any comment as he starts up the path to find his pace. I look back and see Tondup and the donkeyman packing up the camp. They call out to me: "You walk ahead, Memsahib, slowly, slowly, we'll catch up." I know they'll pass me, just as they have over these last few days.

I walk in the direction of the snow and adjust my pace. I let my breathing find an even rhythm that I can maintain for a while. The cold, thin air is forcing my body to go slow and do what it can; my will and my habit of wanting to be in control have to step aside. The climb ahead isn't a task I can put it to and muscle my way through. With every step I listen as my lungs grasp the air and my chest muscles adjust for needed oxygen. Thoughts are fleeting, they are brief moments of noticing things, sketches for a larger body of thought to come.

Except for the early morning buzz of the jetliner connecting this remote desert of stone with Delhi, I haven't heard mechanical activity in the sky or on the ground for the last five days. I remember that today is the 4th of July in the States—Independence Day. Of course, there are no jets flying over to announce the beginning of a parade here. There's only the peaceable sound of bells as the herds of donkeys and small mountain horses loaded with supplies are being driven onto the trail by my guide, my donkeyman and the teenage nuns and monks who spent the night at the compound.

Soon I'm surrounded by animals and red and yellow robes clacking and whistling. It's as if the intent of the young minds pulls the animals through their resistance and their desire for the little nibbles of green that poke through the dwindling patches of crusty earth. Up, up, the push is on before the sun melts the snow and it becomes impossible to move the animals to the ridge. Hooves are slipping, loads shifting, there is upbeat chatter among the novices as they shake off the night's cold with their activity. I don't see any boots on their feet. I see sneakers and some leather shoes, matched with socks, vests, jackets and hats that saw the racks of the Goodwill stores in the West decades ago. The head Lama is easy to spot because of his traditional fur-lined yellow hat,[37] his body is wrapped in the thick wool garb of the region.

He brings up the rear with some heavily loaded, skidding horses. I fall in line behind him and am grateful for the slow pace of the animals. This allows me to keep going without having to experience the lonely lag that normally occurs when my guide and pack animals find their pace. We pass Wouter, who silently falls in line a few steps behind me.

I think about meeting Wouter at the onset of the trek. It surprised me to meet a fellow countryman and I looked at our connection

---

37. Gelugpa Order is the Buddhist Order of the Yellow Hats

as an unexpected gift. Maybe it was just a coincidence, but I want to see it as a protective move from the universe. I wonder if Mahara-ji is playing tricks with my mind. Can a dead guru have a hold on my mind? Having Wouter around has been stirring up my old constructs about living a spiritual life. What is my practice? Should it be devotion to Mahara-ji or rigorous mental training through the practice of Vipassana meditation, or both? Here in this powerful natural environment the validity of following a guru and having a meditation practice seem to melt together into a simple practice of focusing on walking and breathing, while the glorious vistas of mountain ranges melt my ego and sense of importance.

Aside from uprooting my spiritual constructs, Wouter's presence has brought back the familiar; he's a reminder of family and home country, interacting with him forms a layer of comfort between the unknown of the hired crew and me. Can I really get away and experience myself alone in the reality of this barren elemental landscape? Will I find answers for my dilemma about my marriage? The shortness of breath I experience, the hard work my lungs do as they expand against my ribcage, step after step with relief only on an occasional downhill slope, feels like I'm breathing to the bone. The hard work of breathing minimizes thoughts and emotions about what's happening in my life back in the States. Emotions are a luxury in this place, something you can indulge in when the day's work is done and you're not too tired to feel. Tondup's evenhandedness and his calm demeanor isn't cultural or spiritual, but an outcome of living with daily hardship. By having had Wouter as a trekking partner, I've looked to another person for answers to my questions about living.

I remember our conversation of a day ago. I'd told Wouter about Mahara-ji and how I had considered him as my guru after he had given me an empowerment initiation.

"He changed your life, didn't he?" Wouter asked eagerly.

"I wanted to have that experience of bliss and connectedness again," I said, remembering all the hours of meditation I had sat through to train my mind to replicate what had happened.

"I know my guru enters my mind when he looks at me. I can

feel the energy lift me. I know he's with me when I think of him."
Wouter's voice softened in a moment of devotion.

"I'm not sure anymore, it depends on how I want to interpret the
events in my life," I answered.

As I lift my leg to step up into the snowy treads made by the novice monks in front of me, I wonder if that's truly so. Am I in charge
of how I see the world, or is there a universal consciousness I can tap
into? Sometimes when I look at Wouter, I do a double-take and it's as
if I see Mahara-ji. Wouter has the same round head and twinkle in
his eyes when he shows his excitement about the magical things in
his life. Do realities cross over when my inner consciousness meets
with the energy of this big universe, and do the two merge? I don't
know any more. The mountains just look on, and life as I've known it
becomes very small. All I know right now is these endless hard rocks,
sparse vegetation, snow and immense skies.

The trail has completely disappeared in the snow and, zigzagging
to find a footing, we scramble up the incline and make a trail of our
own. The trail ribbon we've seen for several days up to the saddle
is now showing its straight-faced whiteness without letting on where
we might crack a smile and find our way in. I'm in a crowd of snorts,
whinnying, whistling life that has never seen the pleasure of snow
with toboggans or skis. Here play comes as work. With a relaxed optimism the novices work their way to the top as if it's the tenth time
they're going to come down this hill for another great ride.

For me, pleasure comes after an hour of extracting my boots from
the knee-deep snow, placing them into the next step made by the people in front of me, sinking down as I shift my weight and pull out the
other leg and boot, breath screeching in my lungs, step by step, up
and up. We finally arrive on Senge-La, aptly called The Lion Pass, as
I'm sure the winds roar in a leonine fashion here in winter and maybe
even in summer at times. Rows and rows of colorful prayer flags, some
tattered, some new, fly in the wind above the *mani* wall that graces
the saddle of this high ridge. I've reached the highest point of this
trek. Tondup and Tsering are waiting for me, smiling, and I smile back
at them, letting out a sigh of relief and accomplishment. I can catch my

breath a little. I sit down on a rock and I break out a food bar from my pack, which they eagerly share. Tondup does have an appetite after all when he climbs, I'm glad to know. He's not this super-athlete who can go all day on mountain air alone.

Looking back toward Bhumitse-La I see the snow-ax swinging slowly in Wouter's hand as he hooks it into the snow above him and takes his last dragging steps up to the saddle. He faintly smiles when I congratulate him.

"Do you want a bite of this food bar?" I ask.

He shakes his head and says: "I have to get down lower." He takes a drink of water and goes off in the direction of some far-away patches of green.

I stand deflated and watch him walk away. Wouter isn't sharing. He's a man on his own journey.

Sitting on the ridge saddle with the prayer flags blowing gaily in the wind I can see in all directions. All around me are the snow-covered peaks that will never surrender their whiteness, below me are the valleys and patches of green tucked between 3,000 feet high sheer rock walls. Layers of walls that undulate in different shades of gray, sand and brown. The rock walls scare me with their solidity and impenetrable lines; the green patches in the distance give me the relief that life is possible around here. I celebrate this moment of ease after the snowy hike and snap pictures with a smiling Tondup, for whom this place is home. Tondup pulls out a prayer flag and shows me how to add our token of impermanence to the stone *mani* wall covered with scarves and prayer flags from those who passed before us. I like this ritual, a simple marking of a moment in these vast mountains, a joining in with others who've passed before us and left their mark, giving it up to the harsh elements that will blow the thin cloth apart thread by thread, after we move on step by step along the trail.

I point at a green mountainside in the distance: "Is that Lingshed?" I ask Tondup.

"No, Memsahib, it's just a village on the way; we will make decision there how far to go today." Tondup is the planner for this trip. He knows how to be in this place, he knows the distance and circumstances on the trail. An old stubbornness of getting what I want rises inside me as Tondup mentions the possibility of not reaching the goal today and I'm ready to tackle the next leg of the journey.

"Let's go then!" I call out.

"We will, but let others pass." Tondup turns his head toward another group of novices who just now arrive after pushing their animals up through the snow to the pass. They don't take time to sit and think. They drive the animals down the mountain in a colorful cloud of red and yellow clothing to find some green pasture, where they'll make the ever-needed energy source, butter chai.

Our small group follows and soon my stubborn feelings are turning into movement and I'm enjoying a moderately level hike. The trail down is easy, Tondup, Tsering and the donkeys are moving ahead of me, leaving me alone with my mind. I miss the explorations I've had in my daily conversations with Wouter. Walking alone, my mind exhausts itself by producing thoughts that then seem to hover and abort themselves as there's no one to speak them to. Is this what happens when you lose a life partner? The craziness of a one-sided conversation running through the mind looking for a place to connect? When I write in my journal, my thoughts become complete. Instead of watching a parade in my hometown celebrating freedom on the 4th of July, I'm watching the parade of my mind. Freedom here comes in being able to walk, breathe, think and overcome the taunting of the elements. Further down Wouter is sitting by the side of the trail, resting and breathing a little easier.

"Ready for food?" I ask. It seems the only thing I know to offer to his closed demeanor.

"No, I'm fine, just need rest." He shakes out his handkerchief, wipes his forehead and stares off in the distance at row after row of gray-brown mountain ranges. I can't revitalize him and my powerlessness feels familiar. *Men, Dutch men, my father—they're all the same*, I think, as his wall of unexpressed emotion prevents any warmth of connecting. This opportunity for feeling our shared humanity is smothered in his dogged perseverance. I swallow a snippy comment, adjust my hat against the sun and follow the tiny specks in the distance that

I know are my guide and donkeys.

The sunlight at high altitude is intense and penetrating my weaker exposed flesh. By the time I reach our lunch stop, I've developed a case of "bubble" lips, sun blisters adorning my lips. I should have tied my handkerchief around my face in this fierce light. Along the trail in the middle of nowhere there's a small tent-store and teashop. *What's a store doing here*? I wonder. Is there enough trail traffic? Must be, or maybe we're getting close to other villages. Now that we've made it past Senge-la, it looks like we'll be able to make it to Lingshed. If not today, we should get there tomorrow. I move the plastic sheeting that forms the door into the teashop and enter to get some needed shade. As I unsnap my backpack and stand in the milky light coming through the plastic cover of the teashop tent, I feel an elated strength that adds to the growing trust that is my challenge on this trip of unknowns.

Tondup smiles a broad smile as he offers a carpeted seat in the lunch tent. He takes my pack and brushes the seat for me; you'd think he'd just found a first-class restaurant.

"Chai?" he offers.

"Mmm, yes!" I can already taste the milky sweetness, the only remnant of decadence left among the food we've been packing in.

"Chocolate?" he asks again, as if we're in the local supermarket. And indeed we are. It's an amazing array of packaged goods, ramen noodles, brown and red lentils, packages of tea, incense, colorful boxes of unknowns and even some toys; little tops and wooden airplanes are lining the back wall of the tent cave. China is doing its job of exporting cheap trinkets here in the high mountains. A little boy with a dirty face above a colorful shirt stares at every move I make. There's an opening in the back of the tent cave that leads to what must be living quarters. Is there a mother around, I wonder?

To find some sign of "civilization" on this endless stretch of trail, where sky and rock determine my feelings of the day, makes me think of what I've left behind: a family, a failing relationship. Wouter's presence, a person I can converse with in my language, threw a veil over the experience of being alone in this desert of stone. Today, with Wouter walking at his own slow pace, there have been just the rocks, the sky and this person called "I". And none of them are talking.

The owner of the shop brings the chai. Tondup gets up and takes a bar of chocolate from the back wall and breaks it into pieces on the make-shift table. The child comes closer and when I offer a piece, the owner, apparently the father, nods and then sends the boy to the back of the tent. I take my lunchbox out of my pack and find the daily fare Tondup has prepared for me: chapatis rolled up with sesame butter. No more cucumbers or other fresh produce as we had at the beginning of the trek. I find a hard-boiled egg that I crack on my forehead as my father taught me and start peeling it. Protein for endurance.

The tent flap cracks open as Wouter, bent over to fit his tall frame through the opening, drags his body in and sets his pack down with a sigh.

"Chai, chocolate?" he asks with surprise, as he looks at our lunch table.

"Ramen also, if you like." I point at the store shelves, still trying to convince him that food means energy. He ignores my comment, orders chai and chocolate, and leaves the noodles to Tondup and the donkeyman. Well, what Wouter does isn't my business, I try to convince myself.

"I'm not going all the way to Lingshed today," Wouter says as he sips his tea. Here he is doing his own thing again. Doesn't even ask what I want to do. The heat of the sun on the plastic tent enhances the smoldering I feel inside me.

"I'd like to get to Lingshed if I can and have more time in the village." I wait to see if he'll ask me to stay with him.

"Go if you can make it. I'll eat now and find a place to rest soon for the night."

Does he really want to do this last part of our trip alone? A mixture of relief and disappointment runs through me as I say the words. Why did I join up with him, anyway? We're so different. Was it to find out more about myself? Stupid me, connecting with someone who turns out to choose himself.

As Wouter eats, I unfold the paper the chocolate was wrapped in. I don't recognize the script on the paper. Where did this come from?

From my travels I know that Indians, Nepalis and, so far, Ladakhis rarely eat chocolate. The mystery chocolate melts into delicious creaminess on my tongue. I dig my money pouch out of my pack and find the few rupees for the snacks and ramen. The teashop owner stands by, smiling with a broken-toothed smile, bowing and mumbling words that mean something friendly and grateful for the business we provide. Tondup and Tsering smile and don't ask questions about what Wouter and I discussed. They have their stomachs full and that's what seems to count for them. Wouter, energized a bit, gets up and walks out ahead of our group on the trail that is still descending.

Outside Tondup and Tsering tighten up the loads on the donkeys. Their body movements are quiet and relaxed, the movements of people who don't know what hurry means. They joke about something in their language, a language I don't understand, as Tsering tickles the donkey behind her ear. They laugh and give the beast a firm pat on the rear and send her on her way. The consistency in their actions is somehow related, woven in with their approach to everyday life life, giving them the stamina they bring to surviving in this terrain. I want to ask if they think about how far it still is, if they're bored with the routine of daily trekking, but I know they'll just look at me with the smiling tolerance that they show me every day. They don't clock their hours; they are here, living this life with whatever it may bring.

I follow the steep switchbacks slowly down the slope, barren and sunny. The emptiness of the space makes my mind wander to the people celebrating the 4th of July on the other side of the world. I watch the images in my mind: the whole hot, garish custom of people dressed up in costumes in a parade. The expressions of individuality, making their statements as residents of a free nation. Tondup has stopped to talk to a man with a herd of goats coming from the other direction. Community in the mountains here is not just a one-day-a-year affair, but a constant one, as these sturdy, poor mountain people call out their *Julleys* and share effort and resources. Their camaraderie shines in their faces as they welcome each other, bearing news from the next village.

I think of how in the west we pay the price of connectedness by speeding in our cars—the four-day distance I'm walking here takes a mere 45 minutes on a freeway. Just as the green patches that spring up around the gathering streams in the valleys provide basic sustenance for those who live here, so does human connection bloom between humans in the vast space of rock and sky, like the rare wildflowers on the trail. Finding and creating enough space in daily living to allow human contact to take root and bloom will be my challenge on my return to the States.

Brown, smooth, rounded mountain sides now dominate the view from the trail. No rock is visible, just soil – dotted with little tufts of green that cling to the surface and remind me of the marram grass plantings in the dunes in my native country, to keep them from shifting into the sea. Some invisible hand must keep these mountains from eroding into the ravines below and exposing its rocky undershirt. Will trees grow here 50 years from now? The locals say the weather is changing and there is more rainfall in the summer. Could these giants soften and be covered with green in time?

For now, it's rock, slate and soil under my feet. As I approach the bottom of this canyon, the challenge of crossing rushing water and rocks with my 58-year-old compromised balancing ability is ahead of me now. The river is tumbling down with hard, slurping noises as it flows over the rocks, dragging down anything loose. I shudder, I don't want to slip and be in its grip. On the other side of the river Tondup and Tsering are finishing their crossing with the donkeys. Wouter is 50 yards ahead on the trail, not looking back. Can't he wait for me! He knows I'm nervous about crossing rushing water.

I take my boots and socks off, tie the boots together and hang them around my neck. My feet steeled against the icy cold, I wade across, bracing myself with my poles. The stones cut into my soft feet; I slide a bit, grip and lean heavily on my poles. I'm risking breaking my poles if I put too much of my weight on them. I can't do without them on the trail. I carefully place my now numb feet between the bigger rocks to avoid sliding and grit my way across, while the water makes sucking and slurping sounds as it swirls around my knees. Tondup's voice calls out, "Hand pole, Memsahib, I pull you." His encouragement helps me take another step, and now I'm close enough to hand him the other end of my pole for balance. Tondup waits for me with mountain-man caution and pulls me up the side. He doesn't know how frightened I am.

As I put my socks and shoes on again, Tondup's calm and patient expression gives me thought. Born at sea level as I was, the mountains aren't in my blood, and I'll never be one of the mountain people—I will never measure up. Weighted with the feeling of inadequacy I carry on up the trail.

Wouter is sitting on some stones along the narrow trail. He's leaning against the incline of the mountainside, his dusty blue pack open. His stuff is strewn around on the rocks.

"I will stay here tonight," he announces.

Nothing in me wants to join him in this nameless place, a stop between villages, the river roaring just below. A river where I surrendered my fear. All I want now is to see if I can master the last climb to Lingshed.

"I want to see if I can make it to Lingshed." I kick the rocks on the path with my boot and stir up the dust. "I'll stay if you want my company, though." I leave the decision up to Wouter.

He picks up his sleeping pad and moves it around. His water bottle rolls onto the path. His round glasses mirror in the light as he briefly glances at me: "There is no need, I have my tent, water, and I've eaten enough for today." His voice trails off as he looks out over the wide-open river canyon.

"That's not what I'm asking you. I asked if you want my company," my voice tone is rising as I continue. "Here we are, five days walking from the motorized world, and you are drawing a circle around you in the sand of self-sufficiency. I understand that you feel you'll be OK, but that's not what this journey is about. This is a journey of discovery, discovery of new ways of interacting and being with others. At least, it is for me. From our conversations, I thought you were exploring these things as well." I feel the familiar tugging in my throat as I name my ongoing need for connection.

Wouter blocks the low-lying sunlight with his hand, as he looks uncertainly at me and answers, "I'm just traveling, discovering what my guru has in mind for me."

"Don't you get it?" Impatience with him puts an edge to my words. "Whatever you can make of it, is what he wants you to discover. You've been sitting around his ashram for thirteen years now, waiting for a sign, a word from him. Isn't it time you make your own life? This is it, Wouter! All the ingredients for living with others are right here, people who care, who will support you, and have a common goal; you can do with it what you want. It's up to you."

The relief of knowing that I'm at least making my own decisions washes over me. I can hear Mahara-ji's *Jao!* loudly inside me: *Go live your life! Don't stay here and look for guidance from me. The guidance is inside you.* Wouter's ongoing attempts to be acceptable to his family in Holland have surprised me. Selling out his principles when working for the government put him in a different ethical category for me. Telling me he accepted that he wouldn't have a long-term relationship with a partner, made me wonder where the fight was in him. His passive acceptance of circumstances leaves him a life too narrow for me.

Suddenly I feel free. I don't have to stay with him to make a connection. I can follow my own needs as I figure out the new paradigm given to me by the big changes in my life. I've been afraid of the new life that's in front of me. A life without a partner, or at least a partner who no longer behaves as a partner, a life with a family strewn in all directions. I need to climb out of my fear. The fear of my aloneness.

Wouter is silent, he looks down at the trail in front of him. He doesn't seem to have any words. I look up the trail where I can see Tondup and Tsering waiting. They are my support, my connection to where I want to go. I don't need to hang on to a man who doesn't want to travel with me.

"I'm going to catch up with Tondup. I'll see you tomorrow in Lingshed." I know that our meeting tomorrow will be a cursory one. Our trip together ends here.

I'm finally letting myself journey alone.

The sun is moving westward, and it reflects the light in yellow from the brown mountainside. A small village along the trail will be the decision point to stay the night here or move on. Tondup doesn't ask about Wouter. When we arrive at the village, it's still early enough that Tondup decides we can do the three hours more to reach our final destination. I don't stop him.

I set my mind in gear for the next uphill stretch. I don't want to have to rest until I get to the top. Step, breathe, step. Freed from trying to accommodate Wouter, an energy is loose in me, and it pushes me up and up. When I get to what looks like the top, this spot is just another marker to yet another higher point. Another peak and climb awaits me. I keep going, letting the rhythm of body and breath push me on.

Eventually I have to rest. The endlessness of things is stripping the inner unrest out of my body, and I'm left with just the working of lungs and muscle. What a way to know myself here at 14,000 feet— raw earth meeting raw human stripped of fancy thoughts, feelings and expectations. I'm life embodied, no more, no less. I understand the saying about working oneself to the bone, as each breath, each step is work. I'm propelled by my aliveness. Hard breathing and putting one foot in front of the other is replacing my hardship of loss.

I came here to get perspective on my life. I'm learning that there is joy in a breath, calmness in a mind stripped from its thoughts and feelings in the sparsely oxygenated air, strength in a step. The simplicity of everyday hardship living is a focus on survival, a detachment from what cannot be had. I feel my bones as I strain to get enough air into my lungs. I feel my bones as I lift my leg for another step up the mountain. I feel my bones as I lay down on rocky ground at night. In the everyday mountain hardship I discover joy, strength, and aliveness. I'm living to the bone.[38]

I feel a sense of freedom I haven't known until now, freedom from emotion, freedom from my expectation of what I can or cannot do. Who will I know myself to be when I'm finished?

I know I'll finish. The determination is in my dirty, scuffed up boots as they continue to carry me to the top of the mountain. There,

38. "to the bone" all the way through, or very badly: "I was frozen/chilled to the bone after waiting so long for the bus". Courtesy of Cambridge Dictionary .

through another line of prayer flags, I see the smile of Tondup waiting for me to catch up—Lingshed lies below on the other side, green and inviting. I smile back, stand for a moment to take in the view of this valley, where my mission will be complete. No more climbing—just downhill now—and my tired muscles pick up speed in the excitement expressed by Tondup who runs ahead. For him this place is home and family. His laugh embraces my earlier feelings of not belonging and gives me the freedom to find a home in this village. Arriving in Lingshed is a coming home to myself in this strange land. A day of such celebration in my adopted country in the New World of America, has become a personal day to remember.

Chapter 19

That evening, after coming down from the last climb, I'm sitting on a blanket in a courtyard on the perimeter wall of the Lingshed monastery. Tondup's uncle lives in the small rooms which open up into this courtyard. The courtyard is no bigger than an oversized balcony with a stone wall overlooking the fields of the valley. Narrow stone spiral stairs go down to a dirt path around the monastery and lead to the village and valley. A monastery, dating back to 1200 CE, hundreds of years old. I think back to the powerful monasteries of Europe—is there a difference, I wonder? They're similar in that they're perched above, or often separated from, the land from which they derive their income. They're similar in structure, similar in their control of a peasant population, but they're born from a different religion and society. As in the time of the Middle Ages in Europe where the church kept a tight control, providing the careful preservation of souls in exchange for monetary worldly riches that allowed the church's acquisition of land and power, this monastery on a mountain ledge presides over the village and its population and provides spiritual guidance in exchange for monetary donations.

I've set my tent up on a narrow ledge of dirt next to the path that circles around the monastery. Although I can't see it from my spot on the blanket where I'm sitting, my eyes can just see over the stone wall to where Tondup and his uncle Sonam Nyam Gal are making dinner on our travel cook-stove. Sonam smiles beatifically every time our eyes catch each other. He waves his hand in an invitation to show me his sleeping and kitchen quarters with low ceilings, which hold the basics, such as a sleeping pad with blankets, a roughhewn wooden side table with a few items on it. The kitchen space holds firewood, a few pots and some food supplies. I imagine winter; the courtyard filled with snow, deep cold penetrating everywhere. How does this man, who looks at least eighty years old, stay warm? I'm reminded of another man whom I met when I was hiking with Alan: this man was a Sherpa, living alone, in a high, barren place, the Himalayas in Nepal.

* * *

I remember how, after hiking all day on the Mount Everest glacier, the icy cold had penetrated my limbs. Endless blackened channels of crusty snow and ice had forced me to pay attention to where I put my feet. My gaze downward, altitude headache throbbing, pack pulling against me, I was hauling myself up the mountain against the forces of gravity. Alan, a step or two ahead, was my guide on this adventure. Where would our camp be in this endless terrain of ice and snow? Step, breathe, step. Voices sounded and as we looked ahead, a Western couple was coming our way. Soon we were face to face and made the usual inquiries. "Where are you from?" and "Where are you going?" The couple let us know that they were heading down to Namche-bazaar. They told us that there was a hut with a Sherpa living in it not far up, a place to spend the night for us.

At the end of the day, as we were wrapped warmly in our sleeping bags in the smoke-filled hut, the Sherpa cooked potatoes for us with yak butter. My body melted with the comfort of the warm, buttery smooth texture of the potatoes, the best meal I had enjoyed in a long time. The Sherpa, dressed in pants made of yak skin, and a western style wool-lined leather jacket, smiled a broken-toothed smile from under his ski hat. Host turned angel, he was making a living off our scarcity on the roof of the world. I couldn't imagine what the winter would be like there, considering how cold it was even in June.

* * *

As I turn my attention to my current host and his circumstances, I remind myself that, at least in summer, the sun comes out and warms the balcony. Still, the harsh circumstances he faces, lifelong circumstances, give a new perspective to the problems I'm dealing with in my own life. I've been able to follow my dreams and aspirations in western life; and it's only now, after years of working and raising a family, that my dreams have been shattered. Do the people who live here settle into the limitations of their life early on? Do they give up their aspirations, can they even afford to have aspirations?

As we enjoy the curry and chapatis, I ask Tondup about his future plans. "Will you teach in Lingshed when you finish school?"

"I don't know. Schools in Leh better salaries." He looks at his food and tears another piece of chapati for dipping. "I come back to see family and bring them things," he adds.

"Do you have a girl you like in Leh, or here?" I ask.

"Hmm, not sure, Memsahib." He smiles shyly. "Studies first." He finishes his food, starts cleaning up the dinner remnants and packs up our supplies.

"Will find more food for us. Go see my mother now." A dedicated trekking manager, he doesn't let family interfere with business. Eighteen and operating on his own in these mountains, he's building his future.

Later alone in my tent, I'm thinking about the temporary bond I have with Tondup. A bond of loyalty based on what? Cultural values, money, or just humanity? As I'm getting to know him, he's becoming more than a guide whom I pay to get me to where I want to go. I'm developing a fondness for his smile, his dedication to my wellbeing and his entrepreneurial spirit. As his first trekking client, what is my responsibility to him? I don't want to ruin his unspoiled uprightness by asking too much of his kindness or by taking advantage of his dedication. As I roll over to go to sleep, I think of the days ahead when I will be traveling with only Tondup and a horseman. I'll have a chance to appreciate him, without Wouter as a distraction.

The next morning after waking, I climb the stairs to Sonam Nyam Gal's balcony for morning tea or breakfast. Sonam is up and about and there is no sign of Tondup. Sonam motions me and I follow him into the monastery. Sonam wears his monk's garb, dusty red robes and a leather, fur-lined hat with ear flaps for the cold. He has no goosedown jacket but maybe a sweater under his robes in the cold of winter.

The hall is dark, lit only with butter lamps, and the swinging reflections of the copper teapots the boy novices carry around, as they keep each chanting monk's cup filled with butter tea. The sound of the chanting lulls me into a meditative state. I sit down at the entry to the hall since they don't allow women in this male-dominated sanctuary. No sign of a hearth or furnace. Heating must be minimal, even in the cold. There are no trees or other sources of fuel easily available. Dung and gathered sticks feed the small stoves in the living spaces. Sonam is considered lucky to live under the protection of the monastery. He'll have food and hot tea all winter long, as long as he does his duties: pujas in the morning and evening, long hours of chanting and meditating and circumambulations around the monastery during the day to move the large prayer wheels on the prayer wall. All this is a necessary part of the "good works" a monastery performs. The monks of the monastery maintain the sense of spiritual promise the villagers need to sustain their religious beliefs. Prayer in exchange for food and shelter.

As I sit and listen to the drone of the chanting, I remember another monastery in Nepal on my trek to Mount Everest in 1972.

* * *

Alan and I had crossed a roaring river and entered an Alpine valley dominated by the stone walls of the monastery on one side of the river and a Swiss cheese factory [39] on the other. After buying some cheese we asked for lodging in the monastery, the B&B of the region. A welcoming monk showed us around a hall where the deep shadows of the late afternoon sun were gliding over the walls draped with thangkas, Tibetan Buddhist paintings on cloth. Some thangkas were draped with their silk coverings, some exposed the images of Buddhas, demons and mystical marvels. The monk explained that they displayed only certain thangkas at certain times according to the prescribed practices for contemplation. It reminded me of the practice of celebration of saints in the Catholic Church.

"I'm looking to buy a thangka. Are any of these for sale?" I asked,

39. A cheese factory making Alpine-style hard cheese from Himalayan yak milk got its start long ago, through the work of Swiss dairy specialist Werner Schulthess, supported by the United Nations. It was badly damaged by the earthquakes of 2015, but the Swiss government is contributing to the rebuilding of this originally successful project.

in awe of the large collection of art hanging here two weeks' walking from any paved road.

"Yes, I'll show you." The monk took us into a back room and pulled out a thangka painting that hadn't yet been mounted. Deep warm colors jumped off the canvas, as I took in a painting of the 36 Buddhas: so many Buddhas who attained enlightenment; it would take me a long time to contemplate what attaining Buddhahood meant. The deal was sealed swiftly, the price ridiculously low compared to garishly colored modern thangkas I'd seen being sold at tourist prices in Kathmandu.

The friendly atmosphere and simplicity of living in a monastery were enticing. I dreamed that night of living in the valley and practicing meditation, while subsisting on local grains and Alpine-style cheese, so that I could work in the Alpine-style cheese factory. The following day I walked on with a small nugget of the produce in my pack.

* * *

As I look around the meditation hall of the Lingshed monastery, I notice a thangka of the 36 Buddhas, identical to the one I brought back from Nepal, which has been hanging in my home in the States. I chose family life over monastery, worldly love over nirvana, and I'm glad of that. My breathing deepens as the rhythmic chanting goes on; my body relaxes. I don't have a desire to practice and attain nirvana in a monastery setting any longer. Even though I'm in a mess in my marriage, I would not have wanted to live without my deep relationship with Doyle to teach me about life, love and connectedness in a worldly way.

As a reminder of worldly needs, my stomach growls with hunger. I leave the monks to their spiritual pursuits, get up and after putting some rupees in the donation box near the entry to the hall, I walk out of the innards of the monastery to Sonam's compound, hoping to find Tondup and some food. As I climb the narrow flight of stairs to Sonam's balcony, a small door opens at the top of the stairs and Wouter emerges.

"You've arrived already!" I stop, look up and lean against the wall of the stairwell.

"Yes, I got an early start. I'll stay here for a few days to recuperate." He steps down on the narrow stone steps.

"Oh, I'm going to look around Lingshed today and prepare for the return trip." I take a step up, pressing against the wall to make room for Wouter to pass, while he bends his body to fit around the narrow curve of the stairwell on the other side. As he passes me his arm rubs my shoulder and I smell the earthy smell of dusty cotton on his shirt.

"Maybe I'll see you around." He turns his head with a quick scrunch of his shoulder and steps down.

"Yes, see you later." I stop and look down as he walks down the steps. Is this all I get, I wonder—he won't have tea with me or set up some proper goodbye? Although I offered to share my food supply in Photaksar, he offered to pay. Will he come around to make good on his offer? I shrug and climb the last few steps of the stairs, I don't care anymore and I don't want to ask.

I turn right at the top of the stairs and enter Sonam's compound, where Tondup is already busy making breakfast.

"Good morning! Did you see your family?" I ask.

"Yes." All smiles.

As Tondup serves breakfast, a girl with rosy cheeks and dark, starry eyes arrives. The blue color of her jacket brings out the freshness of her face. She laughs and talks rapidly in local vernacular. Tondup smiles a lot and introduces her as a "cousin". I'm not so sure she's just a cousin to him. We make plans to visit the nunnery, the health clinic and possibly the school. Tondup tells me he'll spend time with his family again later that day. He doesn't invite me to meet the rest of his family. I'm disappointed but I remind myself to be sensitive to local *mores*, as this may not fit in with Ladakhi customs.

After breakfast I go to my tent to pick up the pictures I took of my friends Carol and Peter back home, to share with the nuns. I want to see the building that gave me an excuse to make this journey, five days' walking into desolate mountains. I'll see how women have been given an opportunity to rise out of poverty. Tondup will walk me over there. The nunnery is visible from the main monastery. It's a long rectangular mud-brick building, set on a strip of land, a terrace on the mountainside. It looks as though limited funding restricted any ornamentation to the plain building style. As we walk on the path toward the nunnery a light drizzle is obscuring the far view out over the Lingshed Valley. The path is a narrow, muddy trail along the side of the mountain.

We arrive at what looks like a cleaned-up construction site, with the new building sitting on a ledge overlooking the valley. At least the women have the same gorgeous view as the monastery, high up above the village. The flat area is much smaller though, and I can't imagine large groups of visitors entering this site. Tondup knocks and a nun opens the door. Tondup explains my mission and the woman's face lights up as she welcomes me in. Tondup is taking his leave and tells me the nun will show me around and serve me lunch afterward.

I follow the nun, who appears to be ageless, not young, not wrinkled nor old. She leads me around the back of the nunnery and we enter the far end of the building. The nun shows me into the ceremonial hall, a long rectangular room with windows on one of the long sides and thangkas hanging three rows thick on the opposite wall. At the far end of the room sits the statue of Buddha, with an altar in front. The colors are bright, red, gold and yellow, contrasting with the soft opaque light that's coming in through the windows.

As we enter, the nun points at a visitor book and a collection box. I know what's expected of visitors and I put some rupees in the box. I look around and then take some time to just sit and feel the atmosphere. The thangka paintings show sensitivity and skill; they give a rich vibration to the hall. This is a place for women to do their spiritual practice and learn about the Buddhist teachings. I remember a story about the women at the time of the Buddha. The women wanted to practice just like the monks – all men. It was quite a to-do before they were given permission. Since then the Buddhist hierarchy has kept women practitioners separate from men and has given them less power in the running of Buddhist organizations. Yes, women differ from men but I can't see why they cannot achieve enlightenment like anybody else and share their wisdom with others. To be a woman in this village means hard work, hungry winters, illiteracy, and the task of raising children who will move away to go to school. Women's main role here is still to be the conduit of life by bringing children into the world and nurturing them. Will the nunnery change the women's position in the village? Or will they absorb these nuns into the patriarchal Buddhist system as a subsidiary addition, without giving them a real say in societal matters? My money contributed to a system that I'm not so sure I support any more. I enjoy seeing, however, that by establishing a nunnery the educational standard for the women is being raised here.

Not only do they educate nuns here in Lingshed. There's a primary public school in the village and girls can attend. Maybe the school will be more a ticket for change than the nunnery. I'll ask Tondup if we can also visit the school today, so I can see for myself.

As I'm absorbed in my thoughts, I realize that the nun is waiting patiently behind me. I get up and turn to her. She smiles and motions for me to follow her. She walks me to a room next to the hall where a few monks sit and work on thangka paintings. No nuns are painting thangkas—not yet. It's obvious that they create the decorations for the nunnery on site. I watch one monk for a while, as he dips his brush and delicately lays the paint on the canvas, creating images of devas, buddhas and religious icons in celestial settings. I wonder when secular art will find its way into these regions as I haven't seen any indigenous art in the mountains. The art sold in Leh is mostly related to monastic life, silk hangings, religious items, such as *dorjes*[40], bells and bowls. The monk stops to clean his brushes and addresses me in broken English to ask if I want to see some work he's completed. He points me to an elaborate thangka of Tara, green Tara, and I take a close look at her many arms, her teeth and wrathful expression. *Well done*, I think, *the expression of intensity and threat is palpable.*

"Beautiful!" I tell the monk. He bows and accepts my praise as if it were a religious offering. I straighten and the nun beckons me to follow her again. We walk past the section of the nunnery that holds sleeping quarters to the other end of the building where I enter a room

40. *Dorje*: A religious object known as "diamond" or "thunderbolt", connected with enlightenment.

with several tables and a few daises. I'm invited to sit on a dais near a low table. From her gestures I deduce that lunch is in the making. A young nun comes in with a tray with cups of tea and the older nun sits next to me, after she's offered me a silk scarf, the traditional gift for honored guests.

I take out the photos of my friends who have visited Lingshed several times. A smile of recognition spreads over the nun's face and when I clarify she can keep the photo, she beams. While we're drinking tea and waiting for lunch, I take a few pictures with my camera and we figure out each other's age. The nun shakes her head in disbelief when I say that I'm 58 years old. Apparently she's 48 and looks 70. She points at her leg and lets me know she has pain. She says the word "medicine" in English. I let her know I'm not a doctor. I don't know what's wrong with her leg, but I rummage in my pack and show her a tube of cream for sore muscles, which I haven't used much on the trek. She eagerly checks out the tube and I let her have it. This medicine can't hurt her, and who knows, her mental power may create the placebo effect.

Lunch arrives and with it two young nuns, with ruddy, shiny cheeks and dark eyes. They serve rice, dhal and greens. As we enjoy our lunch, they ask questions:

"Memsahib from where?"

"America." A nod of understanding follows. "How old are you?" I ask waving my hand in the nuns' direction, not sure that pointing is culturally acceptable.

"Sixteen," answers one and, "Thirty," answers the other.

"How many nuns are here?" I ask.

"Many not here now," is the answer.

I figure that more will show up when the group I met at Senge-La arrives. There were at least six young nuns in the traveling group. They must take turns walking out for supplies. I wonder when the book learning takes place, as the work for survival takes up a big part of the day. I didn't see a garden near the nunnery, but I'm sure that work in the fields is part of the curriculum here. Since nuns still have a lower status than monks, I can't imagine that the village will supply both the monastery and the nunnery. An image of a woman I saw late yesterday afternoon on my valley walk, as she straightened up from bending over in the field, crosses my mind. I saw the dark grooves in her face, the hand on her back to stretch her tired muscles as she took a rest from weeding and gave me, the stranger, a pondering look as I passed her plot of land.

Being among these women brings it home to me that we know so little about each other, we can only see each other's faces, bodies, what we carry and what we eat. We are worlds apart when it comes to what lives in our minds. I wish for a better life for them than what I am observing, but don't know at this point what "better" means to them. I wished I could know more about them, but that would require a longer stay, learning the language and taking part in their daily life. That would mean a much more radical change in my life than figuring out what to do with my marriage. I will have to satisfy my curiosity by reading and relying on others who have worked with these women. Even my friend Carol, who has returned to Ladakh several summers in a row and worked with the Women's Alliance, has only been a financial supporter for the women's cause.

Tondup returns from his village errand just about as we finish our lunch. "We go to health clinic and school," he says with little expression. Is he proud of his community? Does he want to show what's going on here, or is he just doing his duty as a guide when he takes me around?

"Oh, good." I'm happy to find out as much as I can about this remote place.

We finish our lunch with Indian-style tea, say our goodbyes and make promises to send pictures.

The weather has cleared a little; the drizzle has stopped, and the air smells rich with the fragrance of summer dampness. We follow a path leading down to the village, which doesn't have a center with houses clustered together. There are just small houses next to plots of land connected by a network of trails. No need for roads, since there are no cars, no bicycles, just foot traffic from animals and humans.

The school is sitting on a terrace. It's another rectangular, mud-brick building, with a series of rooms next to each other. Children are sitting in an open area, some on a low wall, some just on the ground. They have composition books and pencils in their hands. There are no adults around. When I raise a questioning face to Tondup, he tells me, "Today is holiday."

"Is there school going on?" I ask him,

"No, but children try to learn when there no school."

Such a difference when compared with children in the West, who avoid academic work on days off. Children here must realize the value of education much sooner, as education is hard to come by and points to a way out of poverty.

Tondup climbs to the low building, past the children whose big eyes follow us with curiosity. I peek in and see what must be a classroom, because there is a blackboard on the wall. There are no desks, just bare ground and what looks like a small teacher's table. The door stands open and the windows are a hole in the wall. Another room next to it looks the same. We come to a room with a closed door and small glass windows. Tondup knocks, the door opens, and a man greets us. Tondup explains why we're here.

"I'm the teacher, and my wife is too." He speaks understandable English and motions us to come inside. Inside is a small room, only eight by twelve feet, with a stove, a bed, some shelves and a low table. A woman is squatting by the stove and making tea. I'm invited to sit down. A baby is sleeping on the bed.

"How long have you been teaching here?" I fold my legs under me as I sit down next to Tondup on a dais which may be a bed at night.

"Two years." He raises two fingers and smiles.

"Where did you come from?" I wonder if teaching in remote villages is some kind of local program for raising the education standards in the country.

"We came from Leh," the woman answers. "Teacher college is there, but we like it here." The woman nods her head in the direction of the man while picking up the baby, now awake. like rural women in other developing countries, she manages the fire, baby in her arms, and pours the tea.

"Can you tell me a bit about the curriculum? What do you teach here?" I accept the cup of tea the woman hands me.

"We teach reading and writing, math and some general science," the man answers. "Learning is slow, because there are few supplies and the children don't have much material for reading." He picks up a little book and shows it to me. I recognize the book, I saw it at the Women's Alliance cooperative in Leh. It's written by an American woman who works in Ladakh to promote Ladakhi culture by illustrating and writing stories about Ladakhi events.

"I'm here to check on the progress of the nunnery for a friend back home who's visited here as well." I take another sip of my tea, feeling the warm liquid energize my body. "I hope that women in Lingshed will have access to more education. Research shows that if women get educated, progress in the family's life follows." I look at the man to see what his reaction will be to my statement. His wife sits opposite me and feeds the baby a little of the milky tea.

"Yes, I know," smiles the man as he motions to his wife and the organization of the living space. "She runs our life here very well." Does he mean this and does he assume that his wife is happy with the role of servant-mother-teacher?

"How long is your contract?" I ask.

"Two years, but we can renew," the man answers.

I wonder how they meet their intellectual needs in this isolated place. Without a library, without internet, it must be hard to find information and mental stimulation. We drink our tea, but before I can ask, Tondup motions *time to go*. The clinic is still on his agenda.

"Can I take some pictures before I go?" I ask.

The baby is crawling on the dirt floor now, working his way to the door which the man opens. I step outside and get a few picturesque shots of the baby in the doorway, colorful wool hat and jacket around his rosy-cheeked face with big brown eyes. This child is luckier than others. He has two educated parents looking after him. With a *"Julley!"* we part. I have another address in my little book and another promise to send pictures.

The health clinic is located along the path a few fields over from the school. It's a small house where a female nurse lives and practices.

Tondup knocks and when a nurse opens the door, he explains our visit. The nurse nods and welcomes us into the entrance space where a few shelves hold supplies. She leads us into the clinic space which appears to double as living space as well from the furnishings and cooking set-up. The nurse appears to be of middle age, with a smooth face in which brown eyes smile at me. Despite her traditional Ladakhi female outfit she carries herself with authority, sitting erect with relaxed hands in her lap, waiting for me to start the conversation. In the living space there's a table that serves as a desk and treatment table. The nurse motions for me to sit at the table. Tondup stands against the wall.

"I'd like to know a little about health and medical issues here," I start. "What diseases are common?" As I say this, I wonder how much English she knows, but I'm pleasantly surprised to hear her answer in clear English.

"Infections, eye problems, kidney problems because of vitamin deficiencies. People don't get very old here, winters are hard, food is sometimes scarce and vitamin-rich food is scarce in the winter." She looks out the window that overlooks the terraced land, and sighs.

"I met a nun at lunch who had what seemed an arthritic knee." I hope to help a bit.

"Yes, I know who you mean. Infection in the knee. She didn't come in for treatment when the infection was acute. Now she has a bad joint and more pain. She wants medicine, but it's too late." The nurse frowns.

"I gave her a tube of salve for sore muscles. She liked it." Maybe the power of belief can do wonders here. "She's only forty-eight," I add.

"Forty-eight is old here," the nurse replies.

"How do you get medical supplies in the winter?" I ask

"I try to stock up before winter, but as you know we have to carry everything in on our back or on pack animals. If it gets cold enough, the river freezes and we can walk to Phalangi on the ice for supplies. That only happens a few times in winter, it's dangerous and very cold."The nurse pulls her wrap-around dress a little tighter and smoothes her skirt as if to assure herself of her clothing and opens a ledger that's laying on the table.

I imagine a group of locals, bundled up, making the journey slipping and sliding on ice with their yak fur boots while carrying a load. I can no longer think of the picture Helena Norberg-Hodge painted in her book about life in remote villages as a romantic picture of happy communal living. Communal, yes, but short lives by our western standards, and now that I have an idea what winters are like, I imagine happiness freezes over as well. Maybe it doesn't matter how old we get as long as we feel that we belonged and have had some enjoyment from our lives.

The nurse puts the ledger in front of me and points at a list of medicines that apparently have been dispensed over the past months. It's a long list, but then I am no medical person and I can't judge what is a lot among such a small population.

"This is how much we give out medicine," she says with a sense of pride, "it does help."

"Yes, I'm sure." I give her an encouraging smile.

Tondup and I soon say our goodbyes and leave the nurse to her important work in this village. I wonder what it must be like to live in the little office, set apart from the regular population because of status and education. This woman knows more about medicine than Karma's wife Dolkar, a health educator, but she doesn't get to use her knowledge because there's a lack of medication and the primitive beliefs among the local people. I feel bad for her and hope she gets a lot out of what little she can do here. I walk back with Tondup to my tent by the monastery. If I had been raised in a small village like this, would I choose family life over progress in another part of the world? Or would I go off, as Tondup did, and try to learn and improve my chances? After a lifetime of living away from my family and community of origin, I have a longing for what looks like communal living and belonging. But is it really? Will this village lose its communal feel once a road connects them with the outside world? Tomorrow I'll start walking back to the world of technology, fast travel and economies that rely on entrepreneurship and profit. A world that tears communities apart in pursuit of economic progress. I'm caught in the web of that world.

As a young girl I lived on an island with a large family. My parents left their community for the sake of progress, to give the children a better education; they wanted to give me a better life. I left my country for the sake of discovery; to find new values to live by. For me where I live doesn't matter so much anymore as long as I feel I can belong. Home is where the heart is. I gave my heart to a man whom I lost to a cruel disease. My children are scattered in a vast country. I have family on another continent. The ties of the heart pull on me. How will I ever feel at home anywhere, with ties scattered across the globe?

Chapter 20

The next morning Tondup meets me with a horseman and his horse. Our donkey driver is standing by. He is returning with us to Photaksar. Traveling in company when going in the same direction is the safer way to travel. My body, well-accustomed to the altitude and lean from the limited diet, moves easily. A drizzling mist sets in as we hike out of Lingshed, a rain so mild and soft it seems innocent and without consequence. I look up at the patches of lighter clouds and hope for clear skies. After packing up my belongings and loading the horse with it, it feels strange not to set off with a walking companion.

Tondup turns around and says: "Follow, Memsahib, we go up together. Horseman and donkey boy travel with animals."

I'm relieved about this new walking arrangement. Now that Wouter isn't keeping me company, at least there is companionship even if we can't carry on much of a conversation. I follow and match my pace to Tondup's.

Soon we reach the ridge above Lingshed. We stop and look back at the lovely green terraced valley below, the small houses tucked among the fields. Even though I'm not sure that a nunnery and monastery are helpful for economic progress, their presence on the ledge of the mountain does tap into my childhood notion of churches as protectors of society[41]. Once the road to this village is complete, will technology, food, medicine and modern conveniences enter people's lives, extending their life span? Will they remain a rural village or are there mineral resources in these mountains that can bring industrialization? If only for a day, I've felt the pulse of this community.

---

41. "On my return to Lingshed in 2019, the road Nepali guest workers had been working on in 2005 had finally reached the village. I watched how an old monk with breathing or heart problems was given passage in the truck that brought me there to get medical help, now only a day away. He would not have been able to make the five-day walk and so his life may have been extended by having a road into Lingshed.

I've shared their meals and heard their stories. I've turned the prayer wheels and listened to the mantras, as the monks chanted in the great hall. I left a few items with them from the world I came from. The people of Lingshed will have a memory of me and I carry their smiles, their hospitality and respect inside me. I don't know what I'll do with what I gathered in Lingshed, but I do know being here has helped me let go of wanting to run away and hide from the life I have.

As I turn to continue on the trail two western women come around the bend. We exchange greetings and I find that they are from Austria and are on their way to Lingshed to work with the school and to develop a women's cooperative. I ask if I can help, and we exchange addresses. Possibilities that may or may not turn into realities.

Tondup and I walk on; the rain continues, soft and steady. What feels like a facial moisturizer at first turns us into a drenched group by mid-afternoon. Constant slow drizzle has a way of soaking everything. My raincoat can handle a light rain but isn't up to the task of protecting me from hours of drizzle; at least my fleece sweater is another barrier which keeps my undergarments dry. Tondup's coat is a sodden pink mess, his baseball cap a ledge for raindrops falling down. The endlessness of drizzle puts my body into a trance. I don't feel my muscles, just the rhythmic motion of putting one foot in front of the other. I'm surrounded by wet, black rock. My vision narrows to the trail in front of me and my mind turns inward.

I think about the Austrian women who have given themselves a purpose in this remote part of the world. So did my friend Carol who connected me with Karma and through him with Tondup. I wonder about the effect of being a tourist who inserts herself into a foreign culture. People have done it as long as they've been traveling, but it's hard to say if bringing the conveniences and ideas of another culture is a blessing or a curse for the indigenous culture that is there. Cultures change for good or bad because of foreign interaction. Karma wants a laptop. Tondup wants gear like mine to keeps him dry. By spending time together we change the indigenous culture and form a more homogenous world culture.

While I'm musing about how long it will take before the road to

Lingshed will bring in the outside world, Tondup calls for a halt. I stop and notice how heavy my wet clothes feel on me. My boots have kept my feet dry, but the wet leather weighs heavy on my feet. I look around from under the hood of my raincoat. We're in a lunar landscape: there is no vegetation and rocks are everywhere, black granite boulders shining wet against the low-hanging clouds that hide a gorge to our right.

"We stop here," Tondup says. "Not go up today to pass, snow on pass."

I hadn't realized that this rain meant snow at higher elevation. My friends in Ashland had told me that it hardly ever rains in summer in the mountains. They didn't tell me about the possibility of snow. When will we be able to cross Senge-la, I wonder? The uncertainty of it all, the lack of a common language with my guide, and the desolate landscape leaves me feeling isolated.

The horseman and the donkey boy arrive and stake out the animals. They set up my tent and create a lean-to with a tarp for themselves and Tondup. When I unpack my bag, my sleeping bag is dry and I find some dry clothes too. I'll be warm tonight. Tondup, the horse man and donkey boy aren't faring as well; they huddle together under the tarp, while Tondup prepares dinner. Night comes early wrapped in wet clouds. Alone in my tent, I'm surrounded by wet clothes hanging on a rope I strung up, creating a steamy cave. Sleep and its unconscious state come as a blessing.

I shine my light on my watch, it's three o'clock in the morning. It's cold outside my sleeping bag, but the pressure of my bladder is relentless, and I prepare to go outside the tent. No sense in putting off the discomfort any longer. I find my rain jacket, put on a fleece sweater first, a hat, then just the long johns will have to do. I listen, is it still raining? I don't hear pitter patter, but then again, even last night the rain was more like wet mist enveloping the tents, the horses and the black granite boulders. We have to wait for the rain to stop, rain which means snow higher up. Will we be able to move over the pass today?

I open the tent zipper; icy cold wetness makes me shiver. Now even more I have to relieve myself. Flashlight in hand, I venture out into this cold black uninhabited moonscape, feeling my way on the ground with my feet to an area a little away from our camp. Even at this short distance I can't see my tent. I don't hear the horses. I hope they haven't wandered off too far. The misty wetness all around me muffles any sound. There is nothing to eat for them here in the rocky gravel.

After I relieve myself I grope my way back to my tent and find the inside of my sleeping bag still warm. Lying down, I wait and fill my time thinking. I fall back asleep; when I wake up again, the tent has the orange glow which means daylight. I go through the routine of getting dressed to go outside. I can see Tondup, the horseman Lapsang and donkey boy wrapped up in a blanket together under the open tarp. Steam comes off the blanket. It must be wet and their combined body heat creates steam in this cold, drizzly morning. Tondup opens his eyes and when he sees me, he says: "Memsahib, breakfast soon?"

"No hurry, I'll get back in my sleeping bag to stay warm, I say. Even though I'd rather get moving, my sleeping bag is still my cocoon of comfort.

When Tondup delivers breakfast, he tells me we have to wait today, too much rain, meaning too much snow higher up. What will I do with a day in my tent? Daily housekeeping, little as it is with just my personal hygiene and the tidying of the few possessions I have, won't fill the time. I can write in my journal and I have the last chapters of a rather dense writing guide to spiritual journaling to read. I have finished all other trek reading. I have my mind to play with. I can meditate. As I sit up in my sleeping bag eating a breakfast of porridge and tea, I imagine life as a nun, living in solitude in a cave. In contrast with living in the world, lay-people would provide me with food. All my attention could go to the simple tasks of daily living and my mental upkeep. Was this how it was for Milarepa, the Tibetan saint of the Middle Ages, when he lived in these regions? I remember his timeless poetry, speaking to me of awareness and feelings. I would have to live in a cave to know what it's like, a day or two in a tent doesn't really give me a chance to taste the hermit's life. Today, when light allows, I can write—an activity that replaces companionship. It feeds the endless hunger of my mind for knowing, understanding, and hearing myself. Does the quest for being known dissipate when living in solitude? So far I don't see any sign of it, but then again a few days on an adventure in the high mountains isn't going to tell me much about this.

After finishing breakfast and putting the dishes outside the tent, I start my day with Vipassana meditation, sitting in my sleeping bag, focusing my mind and scanning body sensations to stay in the present. Meditation over, I turn to housekeeping, rearranging my possessions, rotating wet clothing from the line I've strung up to the warmth of my sleeping bag to finish drying. My socks are almost dry. After doing my household tasks I do some reading and note taking. The morning passes and Tondup brings lunch. The afternoon follows the same pattern as the morning. I realize that having a schedule prevents my mind from spinning out, from worrying about what will happen next if we don't get over the pass soon enough. I soothe my worries with the thought that I can miss my plane; it will be a hassle but I do have another week set aside for a side trip to Nainital to visit Maharaji's temple. If need be, I can miss the side trip and catch my plane in Delhi. I pretend I'm on a three-day retreat and follow the schedule I've set for myself. Day two passes this way; I feel that I've achieved something by maintaining an engaged state of mind and sleep comes early as darkness falls.

The third morning, when I go out to relieve myself, it isn't raining and the mists have become lighter. Tondup is up and about making tea.

"Good morning!" Our smiling faces greet each other.

"What do you think? Can we go today?" I ask, shivering as my sleep-warm body meets the chill of the wet morning air.

"Not sure, Memsahib. Rain stop, much snow." He points up toward where the pass must be.

The cold fog drifts around the wet black boulders. Tondup looks cold and wet.

"Did you sleep?" I ask.

"Yes, sleep together to stay warm," he answers. I saw them

yesterday afternoon, Tondup, Lapsang, and the donkey boy, huddled under a blanket in the plastic lean-to. It must not have been a comfortable night.

"Can we try to go over the pass?" I don't know if I have any say in the hiking schedule, but I can try. Even though I've had to surrender to the trail circumstances, I still don't want to stretch this trip any more than necessary.

"Donkeys short legs. Snow deep." Tondup holds his hand at waist level.

I hadn't thought of the practical aspect of getting the animals across, and I guess Tondup isn't leaving donkey boy behind. I myself was ready to tackle the snow, even if I had to crawl.

"We make breakfast and after, look." Tondup turns to the lean-to, squats and grabs a pot.

"OK, I'll get ready, just in case we go." I walk to my tent.

Hope fuels our activity. I want the possibility of making it over the pass. *Mind over snow* will be the name of today's game. Soon Tondup brings tea. I drink it, slurping and delighting in the warm liquid. It could have been warm water and it would have felt good in my body. After I finish my tea, I get up and put on more layers of clothing. Two days of hanging on a makeshift clothesline inside the tent, my clothes have dried somewhat from the little body heat I've given off. Breakfast is cream of wheat with some milk, hot, steamy and warming my insides some more. Being in the cold has increased my appetite. As I sit eating and looking out of my tent opening, Tondup waves his fist with thumb out.

"Lapsang will walk up with horses and see," he announces.

Relieved that they're at least willing to try, I keep my thoughts on making it over the pass. I start packing.

A half hour later, Tondup gives the go-ahead. We will pack up and try to make it. I feel a surge of energy as I get to shift into activity. Wet tent, wet gear, it all gets rolled up and packed away as is. The horses' dark, wet coats drip under the load. Tondup's bright pink coat clings wet to his body, small patch of bright wildness against the gloom of black rock and fog. We set off on the trail. Soon rock turns to snow and the pace slows. My boots are sinking in a foot of wet snow; soon it's up to my knees. Both the donkey boy and Lapsang are leading their animals, pulling them to make them move forward. Tondup scouts ahead to find the best way to get up to the pass. The horses follow him, they must want to keep moving. The donkeys, however, stop, they're up to their bellies in the snow. The donkey boy pushes them from behind while the horse man pulls on their halter rope. One hoof slowly finds its footing after the other. I put my boots inside the holes made by the animals in the snow, trying to keep my feet as dry as possible. After a little while, my boots are wet and heavy with snow and I'm breathing heavily with the effort of raising one leg after the other high into the next hole. The donkeys and horses bray and whinny, but they keep going, pushed along by Lapsang and the donkey boy. I take another deep breath and my nostrils flare with the earthy, wet-fur animal smell. I can't see Tondup, mountain goat that he is; he's forging ahead. I'm cold, the fog stings my face, my hands are turning to ice as I put them down for support on the snow. I've tied my trekking poles to my pack. They're useless without snow baskets. Why didn't they warn me about this unseasonal summer snow? I could have brought some gloves. I follow in a stupor, focused on each hole in the snow in front of me. Snow is creeping up my legs, icy, wet. Steamy breath mixes with wet fog. I'm enveloped in fog, a tunnel of whiteness. Will I see clear sky again today?

Finally, the gray foggy sky turns lighter. I see big lumps of snow with stones sticking out up ahead of me. Those must be piles of prayer stones. That means we're approaching the pass. My lungs are searing with the cold, thin air. Just a few more tired steps, a few more breaths, I think, you can do it! Then I see that what was a stone *mani* wall with flags waving in the sun and wind five days ago, is now a snow fort with drooping flags. I had thought the hard part of the trek was over when I reached Lingshed. I thought when I had done this stretch of trail once, the second round would be easier. Now I understand that the return can be as hard or harder when climbing mountains. There is snow everywhere. Clouds are hanging low, obscuring any view. July in the Himalayas wasn't supposed to be like this. Summer weather predictions had been for dry weather with occasional rainfall. A surge of contempt for the weather runs through my body and the energy lifts my legs for the last steps to the top of Shenge-La, appropriately named Lion Pass. This weather was surprisingly forceful, not quite a roaring storm, but I can only imagine what it can do here in winter.

Tondup and Lapsang are waiting for me on the snowy *mani* wall. I plonk myself down next to them, exhausted, and wait for my breathing to slow down.

"Memsahib OK?" Tondup looks at me inquisitively as if to search for any failing of my system. He doesn't look the worse for wear. He is wet but relaxed.

"Yes, I'll be OK, give me a moment to catch my breath. Maybe eat something." I don't know how much hard climbing we must do to get down and I need energy to do whatever is ahead. We share the last energy food bar I brought from the States and take pictures of our "expedition crew". Gratitude for accomplishing this part of today's trek fills me. I look at Tondup and say, *"Tashi delek*, thank you, for getting me here, you are a good guide."

Tondup nods, and says, "We lucky, gods are with us. Memsahib strong of mind and body."

I could hug him right now for saying this, for knowing me. I put my hand on his, sharing a moment of warmth and say, "You are a friend, you care about my well-being. The gods aren't always so friendly."

Tondup grins in return, maybe my comment isn't too insulting to his religious beliefs. Then he says, "I come to your country someday, you care for me."

"Yes, I will. I will be happy to do that." Our eyes connect briefly across customary deference and I can feel Tondup's warmth and his youthful hope for new adventures. We're connected in spirit. I'll try to help him in his search for progress.

"We go on, get cold here." Tondup changes to the task of the moment.

We cut the downhill trail. Going down is easier on my breathing, even though keeping my balance as I'm post-holing and my trekking poles sink deep into the snow isn't easy. The animals are eager to move now. They must know there's grass somewhere. Sun is shining through the cloud cover and breaking it up into fast-moving clouds. I drink in the vast range of snowy mountains against the blue and white sky. This is a vision I want to keep, a picture I want to take home with me to remind me I stood tall and conquered the elements, conquered adversity; dealt with the harsh elements of wind, rain and snow at high altitude. That I am strong and can overcome difficulties.

As we come down to where the snow is less deep, we see people moving in our direction. A man is climbing up to the pass. When we meet, he tells us in Swiss-accented English how he's been waiting for four days to get over the pass.

Other people, locals, are moving in our direction. A young boy breaks away from a group of school-age youth and runs excitedly to our horseman. *"Da!"* His voice rings out. Lapsang and the boy embrace. This must be his son. The boy wears regular city shoes, and thin clothes, too thin for this snowy weather. They pat each other on the back, and grin widely. After speaking with Lapsang, Tondup tells me the boy will go with us to Phalangi. He just walked three or four days to get here, and now he'll turn around and walk back with us? What a way to spend his summer vacation.

After an hour of walking, my clothes are drying out. The sun feels warm again, and the dark, snowy, rainy experience is behind me. I jump over the little rivulets which will form the bigger river down below. We walk until we find a dry piece of ground where we can spread out, dry some of the camping gear and eat lunch.

I lie down on the ground, smell the musty, spongy earth and smile. All's well, right here. My breath deepens with sweet relief as I look up at the towering, snowy peaks around me, the blue sky dotted with puffy clouds above me. The steady beating of my heart contrasts with the quick rippling of the water around my little dry island.

This is what life is. Good days and bad days. Cold snow and warm sun. People who care for me and each other, close by. People who love me, far away. I'm a child of this world and I feel the life force pulsing through me, a life force that keeps on giving answers. This life force gives me my place of belonging; it comes from deep inside me, a belonging to myself and the world around me. Living in that belonging is what my life will be about from now on.

Chapter 21

After lunch we hike downhill to Bhumitse-La Pass and on to Photaksar. As we pass the big *mani* wall I touch the warm stone and repeat *Om Mani Padme Hum* to invoke the power of the Jewel in the Lotus, to foster spiritual transformation for me and to thank the greater spirits that have guided me on this journey. Donkey boy, all smiles in red cheeks, takes his leave on a side trail that leads to the village hanging off the mountainside. We stay on the main trail, cross the rickety bridge over the stream and make camp near a nomad encampment.

We set up our tents uphill from the stream. While I'm sitting in the opening of my tent waiting for Tondup to make dinner, two children with runny noses and dressed in dirty woolen clothing appear and stare at us. A joke from Tondup produces smiles. Since I can't talk with them (we do not share a spoken language) I motion for them to take a peek inside my tent. They giggle and the oldest boy takes the daring step of looking inside. They run away as quickly as they came, back to their camp, laughing. Night falls and the mountains disappear in the darkness; cold air settles in and I put on my warm fleece. We eat our food and warm our innards, and Tondup suggests we join the nomads around their fire. We walk over and reach with our hands for the warmth of the fire after a long day on the trail. Tondup says something to the herders and they motion to us to come closer. Aside from the people I met in Lingshed, these are the first people on the trail we interact with. I feel the awkwardness of not being able to speak with them and having to learn about them through watching. Tondup and Lapsang are carrying on a lively conversation, energized as they are by the company of locals. Having company feels good to me also after three days of wet, cold camping on the other side of Senge-La Pass even if I can't converse. The women of the nomad group are busy in their tents with washing pots and organizing what few belongings they have. Every family sleeps together under a heap of blankets. The nomads may not stay clean, but they have a way of staying warm. Tondup and Lapsang must look forward to a dry sleeping place tonight.

The next morning the sun is out, and temperatures are moderate. Tondup makes me chapatis and scrambled eggs for breakfast. Where did he get these, I wonder, maybe from the nomads? I won't ask, I will enjoy the extra protein. Lopsang tightens the loads on the horses. Sitting here at the bottom of the valley and eating breakfast by myself out in the open, since my tent is packed up already, I feel my aloneness in the spaciousness of the landscape. An aloneness that doesn't scare me—I have learned on this trip that even total strangers care for me—but an aloneness of being that doesn't dissolve in the company of others, actually often gets accentuated by the differences between people I meet and myself. Tondup aims at earning money and getting a job; he can barely think about creating a family. His aloneness is temporary; he has a community of people in Leh, and his family back in Lingshed. Lopsang is doing his contract work so he can support the family he already has. I'm at the other end of life, my family doesn't need my support, and then there's Doyle: will he want my support when I return? Whatever comes after this journey, I can handle my aloneness.

"Memsahib ready to walk?" Tondup calls out as he collects his pots in a basket which he hands to Lopsang.

"I am, in a minute," I say as I scrape the last eggs from my plate and drink the last of my tea.

"We hike up to next pass. Sir-Sir-La, it's the last one." Tondup points in the pass's direction and moves his head in an upward motion. "You start; I will come soon."

I put on my daypack, apply some sunblock, take my hiking poles and set out on the trail. Snow covers the surrounding mountains; clouds are racing in the sky and the light feels intense. When I hiked down from Senge-La in the sun and snow yesterday without sunblock, I burned my face badly. I didn't think about sunblock because the sun was only partially visible and it was cold. It doesn't take much at

this altitude to burn your skin. Today, even with sunblock, the sting-
ing is intense. I put a handkerchief around my face to avoid the wind
that would irritate my sensitive skin even more. As I stop to do this,
Tondup catches up with me.

"Memsahib OK?" He peers at me with concern.

"Yes, but my face is sensitive from sunburn. I have to take care
of it," I say.

"You are white woman, you need cover up." Tondup nods in
agreement. "You go on, I check with horseman." He turns back.

As we're climbing Tondup keeps moving between Lapsang who
is driving the horse and me. His constant attention and encouragement make me feel we're like family. Will I be able to care for Doyle
when I return? Will he let me? I want to help him without interfering
with his free will. Maybe I can help manage his caregivers if he'll let
me. As I put one foot in front of the other, I realize that in my mind I'm
already at the end of this trek. The path in front of me is just that: a
path to travel on. No longer a path to discover myself. I have found my
psychological footing on the way out to Lingshed and now I have the
confidence to offer help without losing myself. Just as Tondup divides
his attention between Lapsang and me, I can take care of myself and
offer my care to Doyle without losing myself in the process.

Traveling with a horse and a smaller party makes the going faster.
Still, I'm no faster going uphill than before; I do my breathe-step-
breathe routine while Lapsang and the horse overtake me. I remember
the happiness I felt coming down from this pass a few days ago. Only a
few days and yet such a difference in my view of my world. Letting go
of Wouter, feeling my connectedness with myself and accepting whatever may come down the path has been a sobering and freeing experience. Retracing my steps on this trail in the opposite direction brings
it all home to me. Tondup waits for me on the pass, while Lapsang is
already on his way down.

"I have to catch my breath," I say, breathing heavily.

Tondup raises his eyebrows, not understanding. "Memsahib have
wrong breath?" he asks.

"Oh, no" I laugh, "Breathing difficult, not wrong." My breathing calms as I stand and take in the next mountain range and the valley toward Hanupati.

Tondup smiles, pulls down his cap and as he turns to start down the trail, says, "All good then?"

"Yes, all good," I answer and start my easier hike down. When we get to Hanupati we stop for lunch, at least Tondup and I do so. We sit on a low wall in the small village while we eat our sesame seed butter chapatis. I'm glad I found the sesame seed butter in Leh, it's good protein and keeps well on the trail. Even though Tondup hasn't touched it till today, he seems to enjoy this new food. A few local men drive a couple of yaks through the narrow street and I have to swing my legs up on the wall so as not to get them squashed by the animals who fill up the street. It's good that Lopsang moved the horses along toward the gorge so we don't have an animal hold-up. As the yaks and their drivers pass, Tondup says:

"Move yaks to new land for eating. Not much food here."

I nod as I look back at the barren valley. People must cover a lot of miles to graze their animals and can't have big herds for lack of food. The whole food chain so depends on the terrain. People here have to diversify their farming practices, grow crops *and* graze animals to get enough food for their families. And then they have to take on jobs as porters, just as Lopsang is doing, for us to supplement his income. My being here is adding to the local economy and the people's survival and yet also changes it.

"Memsahib ready to go on?" Tondup pulls me out of my reverie.

"Yes, I am." I brush the crumbs off my shirt, put my hanky around my face again and pull my hat down. Here at lower elevation the sun is warm and I need all the protection I can get. "Let's go!" I say as I jump off the wall. Tondup is already standing. We hike on to the gorge which doesn't look so imposing coming from this side. Or is it because I've become accustomed to the environment? Do the people who live here have a sense of the enormity and transcendent quality of these mountains? Probably at times, but I think most of the time they're so involved with day-to-day tasks they don't dwell on the bigger picture. They have their religious rites and rituals to take care of that aspect of their life. I recall the herder who gave me a piece of juniper, a token of the bigger picture for him, a mere twig for me.

When we get to the gorge, I ask Tondup to take my picture with hat and hanky covering my face. This high-altitude garb makes me look like the road construction workers we met on our way out on the bus. As we pass through the gorge and enter the wider road, I still don't see the workers who work on the road that needs to go all the way to Lingshed. There must be a hiatus in the project. The workers may have gone home for the monsoon season in their home country. I'm just guessing and such unspoken questions make me feel the limitations of language between Tondup and me again.

We get to the campground in Phalangi by late afternoon. One more night of camping, a bus ride back to Leh tomorrow and the trek will be complete.

I had expected that my self-imposed mission to go to Lingshed and contact the nunnery would give me insight and compassion for women of another culture, I've gotten much more than that though; the journey has given me back myself. My body feels strong, my feet feel connected with the earth, my breathing is easy. I can face whatever will come when I return home.

The bus ride back to Leh is uneventful. When I phone Dawa at the guesthouse, she regretfully tells me she has no room available. My assumption that there would be room when I returned was wrong, the summer tourist season must be in full swing. I wished I had made reservations but then I didn't know exactly when I would be back. I find lodging at a tourist guesthouse in town, a place without the feeling of being part of the family, a place that will do. Tondup delivers my luggage to the guesthouse and we say goodbye after I make arrangements to find him the next day in his Lingshed compound and settle our accounts.

It feels strange to be alone in a room without people around who know me and care about me. I take a hot shower, the first after twelve days on the trail, and put on some loose pants and a cotton shirt. With clean body, clean hair and clean clothes I go out on the town to find a meal. Cleanliness doesn't make up for the lack of company and I end up in bed at an early hour. The next morning I visit Dawa to return the tent she loaned me. When I walk into the guesthouse Dawa greets me with a smile and says:

"Come in our family room and tell about trek." She opens a door across the hall from the kitchen where she was working, and motions for me to go inside. The room has windows along one side with a view of the mountains and fields to the west. On the opposite wall are shelves with gleaming copper and steel vessels of bulbous shapes and different sizes. Shiny steel trays line the wall and a copper tea kettle perches near a wood stove. The wood stove is vented through the wall opposite the entrance with a bench next to it. I sit down. To my left are a dais and a small low chair facing a television. The old man— Dawa's or Chandar's father, I don't know which—and a young girl are watching a Bollywood show on an Indian station. Dawa introduces me to them by name and they both bow their head and say: *"Julley!"* I respond in kind. I express my admiration for the kitchen items on display and Dawa says with a shy smile:

"Yes, beautiful, family treasures."

I deduce that these items have been in the family for a while and belong in the family room. Dawa offers me chai and we chat about my trek. When I tell her about the snowy climb over Senge-La, her eyes get bigger and she says:

"You brave woman. You lucky not get stuck." I agree. Chandar walks into the room, says something to the old man and nods to me with a *Julley!* Dawa hands him a cup of chai which he throws back in one gulp before turning and leaving again. Dawa shakes her head and says: "Men busy; always busy." I can't tell if she's irritated or proud and respond with: "Summer busy time."

I take my leave after a short while, telling Dawa that I have to meet Tondup. We say our respectful goodbyes with hands held in a gesture of respect and Dawa tells me to come back soon. I feel I have made a friend in her and tell her I will be back.

That afternoon I find my way to Tondup's living quarters in the Lingshed outpost in the south-west quarter of Leh. I enter a plastered compound painted white, into which several doors open up. The doors are open and people are milling around the compound or hanging out in the rooms. I ask for Tondup and someone points to the last door to the right. When I peek in, Tondup jumps up from his settee and invites me to sit down. Once I am seated, he introduces me to several monks dressed in robes and looking at some documents lying in their laps. They smile at me and one of them grabs a white silk scarf from a pile near the door. He offers it to me and when I bow in acceptance, he drapes the scarf around my neck. The silk feels cool against my still warm, sun-burned face. I'm now officially an honored guest. Tea is served and I ask them about their duties as off-center monks, while Tondup does the trek administration, adding up all the expenses in his notebook.

"How often do you go back to Lingshed?" I ask the monks while fingering the soft, silky scarf.

"We go back one time a month to talk with head monk," they tell me, their smooth faces smiling.

"What is your work here?" I question further.

"We do ritual for villagers who stay here. We help with paper-work." They point at the documents in their laps.

"Do you meditate and do pujas for everyone here?" I'm trying to figure out their spiritual status.

"No we not have time for that; we have to buy supplies to send back to Lingshed. The monks in Lingshed meditate for all of us." They wave the documents to emphasize their worldly duties. It seems to me their role is more of economic agents than spiritual advisers. Even though I've slowly been figuring out the functioning of the Buddhist order here in Ladakh I'm still surprised by the worldly role the clerical community has. I'm disappointed that the Buddhist principles of non-attachment and reducing suffering haven't gone beyond giving up of personal property in exchange for food, shelter and being trade agents. Again, the monks being the more educated class, they have power over the uneducated lay population. They buy supplies to send back to Lingshed, keep records and apparently sit and drink tea.[42] An

42. On my return to Lingshed in 2019, the school had grown into a K-14 school with fifteen teachers. The monastery didn't have youngsters running around in monastic robes. It seemed that the only young monks had injuries

interesting communal approach to spiritual well-being I think as I sip my tea. I shift my knees and smooth my wrap-around skirt, a skirt I've used for meditation in retreat settings for its modesty and the ease of sitting cross-legged. So different from my own personal quest for spiritual insight and enlightenment. I feel tension in my chest as I realize again there isn't a linear path to enlightenment, that I don't have to meditate for hours and years to attain enlightenment. I have had my moment of enlightenment, the knowing that *this is is it—there's no place to go* on the trek. Who knows, now that I've experienced a sense of universal connectedness in these arid mountains, individual spiritual achievements may just be a contribution to the larger goal of raising consciousness for all beings. My quest is just a tiny cog in the wheel of *Dhamma*. I take a deeper breath and let go of the tension on my out-breath.

My attention back on the monks, I nod, and smile in understanding of their monastic tasks as part of the Lingshed community. I'm a little closer to unraveling the question of what life is all about.

Tondup sits down next to me and shows me his accounting. It all looks good and we settle the accounts. Aside from money I offer him my Swiss Army knife as a bonus. He holds it in his young and weather-worn hands, a treasure. I have little in the way of gear I can part with at this moment, but I resolve to help him financially with his education once I return to the States. I'm not ready to sever our relationship and sponsorship is an accepted way of life here. I ask him for his address, so I can contact him. He shakes his head, points at the simple compound and says: "No address." Hmm, no address, no phone. I'll have to find another way to communicate with him. I suppose there isn't a postal service here. Maybe Tondup can set up a postal box, I must speak with Karma to make arrangements for his nephew. Karma has an email account, I know that much. I feel better deciding I will do something for Tondup besides giving him a Swiss Army knife.

"I will stay in touch with you through Karma," I tell him.

---

or were developmentally delayed. The power of education had shifted to lay people and the role of the monastery was changing to performing rituals only.

Tondup wrinkles his brow and says:

"Memsahib write letter, I will write letter." He smiles a worried smile about our postal relationship. Has he ever written letters to someone? I wonder. He'll have the monks to help him, I reassure myself.

"Thank you, Tondup, I will write and expect a letter back from you. Thank you for taking care of me so well on the trek." I bow with my hands pressed together. No hugs allowed here.

"Yes, Memsahib, I happy to take care of you, thank you for knife." Tondup fingers his new treasure and puts it in the pocket of his vest.

I wish I could tell him how much his wild and comfortable outdoors nature has reassured me and guided me to find my belonging to the wildness in these mountains. I cannot tell him about the profound experience of earth and origin in the rocks near Senge-La. I cannot tell him how I resolved my relationship issues by leaving Wouter behind. I get up to take my leave. I say my *Julley* greeting to the monks, turn to Tondup and look him in the eyes. We both smile. Our relationship is not of words. Ours is a relationship of being in nature, breathing and walking together, a relationship of caring for one another, and a knowing that whatever we encounter passes. Our friendship is here now, and will pass eventually, but the knowing that our memories connect us in this vast realm will stay with me. We will carry each other's essence in our heart. We will both share what we gained from this trek with others.

Before I return to the West, I visit Mahara-ji's ashram in Kainchi. I make the overnight trek from Delhi into the foothills of the Himalayas by train and bus and end up in Nainital tired and travel weary. I find the hotel where we stayed in 1972, and book a room with a view of the lake. Nainital is more built up but in essence not that different. It is still a hill town where tourists come to get away from the Delhi heat and monsoon. The monsoon is in full swing now and it rains almost every day I'm there. I walk around the lake, visit the chai shops, buy a new meditation shawl. On my third day the sun comes out and I take a taxi to the ashram in Kainchi. I try to remember the surroundings, but can't. I arrive at the ashram and enter the long walkway into the compound. The buildings are whitewashed and painted with bright orange roofs. Chanting music is coming my way as I approach. I open the gate and ask the first person I see if I may enter. The man shows me a guest register in a small office, where photos of Mahara-ji and books are on display. I tell the person I've come to revisit the ashram after 34 years. He nods. "Many come and pay their respect to Guru-ji." I ask if I can walk around the temple grounds. "Sure, yes," he answers.

I walk a few yards and recognize the little house Mahara-ji stayed in, the porch with the dais, empty now save for a blanket and flowers. I sit down again in front of the dais and close my eyes. Within no time I'm crying, remembering and feeling the inexplicable energy of what happened here so long ago. I can't explain what happened then, and I feel a sudden letting go of the need to know. I can just be here and experience the energy. I open my eyes, a person is walking up to the dais and adding fresh flowers. I didn't bring any flowers. Everyone has their own way of connecting with Mahara-ji, I think, mine hasn't been the outward devotional connection. Despite living with my rational mind I've held on to that moment at Mahara-ji's feet so long ago as a gift; I haven't negated it. As I get up to visit the rest of the ashram grounds, I feel connected again with the things that are unnamable, just as I felt connected in the high mountains of Ladakh. Meeting Mahara-ji long ago was a beginning, an opening for a lifetime of learning about the unknown.

I walk toward the small Hanuman temple; someone is chanting and playing the harmonium. I let the music fill me as I stand and listen. I recognize the melody and start chanting silently in my head. The years of gathering with friends and chanting are no longer in my life, as so many things have come and gone. The people who take care of the ashram are honoring the meaning of life in their own unique way. I turn to leave, and say my goodbyes at the gatehouse. The ashram is not my place to be, never was. I will go home to find my way.

The next day I pack and book a train ticket for my return trip to Delhi. The long journey home can begin.

The Journey Home

Chapter 22

I return from Ladakh to face my husband. A week at home, confined to bed, thanks to an intestinal travel bug, gives me time to think how I will tell him I want to hold up my end of our marriage vows and care for him or make sure he's cared for. One afternoon I ask him to come over to talk. The sunlight is coming in through the plate-glass windows in the living room. Doyle enters through the back door which makes its familiar creaking sound and clang when he pushes it shut. I'm sitting in a comfortable chair looking out toward Grizzly Peak through the windows. He sits down on the couch next to me and looks out. It feels funny to have him here as a visitor. This is still his home too, but it doesn't feel that way any longer. I have been lying on the window bed, nursing my health this last week, the same bed he spent so much time in ten years ago after the accident. Doyle unzips his fleece vest but doesn't take it off. He's not here to stay, I guess. I might as well get to the matter at hand.

"I want to care for you, help you deal with the illness." I wait to see if he will ask questions before I elaborate.

Face gaunt, eyes fixed—Parkinson's is taking its toll, I can see that—he tells me, "I want to stay married, I just don't want to live with you. I want to do what I want."

"What do you mean?" I sit up in my chair.

"I don't want you to have a say in what I do." Silence hangs between us. The cherry tree outside moves in the wind and ripples the light in the living room. I feel my shoulders tense up with the notion of him having carte blanche. Do I care enough to give that to him?

"You don't want me to say something when you come home with twenty tubes of cortisone cream you can't use? When you buy a brand-new car, without consulting me? When you risk falling, a return to the hospital? How can I care for you and stand by? That's not what I call being married." I sound shrill, the fear of being at the mercy of his disease rises as a blob in my throat.

His torso wavers, his face is tight. He crosses his legs. Is it fear? Or is it the tremor of the disease? I don't know this man, my husband, anymore. We haven't talked about his illness in a long time; I don't know how he's coping, what his daily struggle is. A flash of Wouter's dispassionate face against the mountainside as he told me, "I'm just traveling, discovering what my guru has in mind for me," crosses my mind. Doyle may be on a different journey than Wouter, but he has a connection with his higher self to help him figure out how to go about it. He's always found ways to cut cost by going around the system when he did building projects. Is he trying to keep emotional cost down by living separately, and financial cost down by staying in the marriage, I wonder. I get up from my chair and walk toward the hearth, from where I face him.

"If you want to stay married because you need the health insurance I get from my job, I can arrange that, you don't have to be married to me for that." Will he accept this offer and let go of us as an "us"? Or does he still have feelings that make him want to stay married? My chest feels heavy, numb, the air stale between us, it feels like our life together is bleeding out. The yellow leaves on the cherry tree outside the window drift down in the soft October breeze.

"Yes, I need the insurance," he answers with a stiff voice.

"You want a divorce then?" I say the words, a heavy word crushing apart a life of being together.

"Yes, I do, no attorneys, we can do this ourselves." He gets up and says, "I need to go, we can talk more later." He walks toward the door, opens it and doesn't look back nor does he say anything more.

I just stand there, stunned over his abrupt departure. Does he not want to face the tearing apart of our relationship? Does he not want me to see how he feels, or is his medication running out and he doesn't want me to see him falter? I watch him walk away, unable to call him back, unable to take back the words spoken. What if I refuse to divorce him? Take care of him no matter what? It will be the same as it has been for the last eighteen months, separate lives, joint accounts, no say in how he spends *our* money.

I know I can't go on like that. Not if we're not connecting, not talking, not if there isn't an acknowledgement of our relationship, an acknowledgement of a new relationship. I worry how we will fare financially if we stay married, considering Doyle's decline and the impulsive buying tendencies that seem to get worse. A divorce will guarantee my part of the settlement and I can work toward a stable financial future for myself. I can help Doyle better if I don't have to worry about losing all assets to his care and increasing financial irresponsibility. If we stay married, will that turn our relationship around? Can our eyes meet again without fear? I enter the kitchen and heat up water for tea. It's hard to figure out what to do when I can't talk it over. When he's not listening to my side of the story. I pour myself a cup of tea and pace around the kitchen stirring the cup, waiting for the tea to cool so I can drink it. Options keep tumbling through my head.

Am I hanging on to a vow that has lost its value? I can love without a vow, without a contract. I can care for him as much as I want, as much as he will allow. A divorce will let me care for myself. I owe that to our children. They need not end up with a financially destitute mother. My head hurts with all the conflicting thoughts about my options. I put my cup down and rub my head, pace some more, feel the knot in my gut. Then it hits me, he hasn't changed his stance in the last year regarding us, he's had the opportunity to make amends and hasn't, he hasn't even asked to talk it all over. I'm on my own in this decision, I can't make him be what I want him to be. The moment with Wouter when he didn't want me to stay with him when he needed to rest after Senge-La flashes through my mind. This is the same, Doyle doesn't want me to stay with him. I know what to do—I must go on without him. I'll go ahead with the divorce proceedings. We'll see what happens in that process.

I'm faced with the remnants of a marriage that is a marriage no longer. I get the do-it-yourself divorce papers, which we fill out, each doing our part in our separate home. Neither one of us pulls back on the decision. Where is the magic that can overcome the crevasse between us? But there are no magic words, no gestures to bring us together.

I go to work. I engage a lawyer to help look over the divorce papers and advise me on how to separate our assets. We visit a paralegal who makes the paperwork official. It's a dreary afternoon in November, with a touch of snow in the air, when we have our appointment. The office feels cold. I feel cold inside. Doyle signs the papers first, he doesn't hesitate. I follow. The paralegal tells us there's a waiting period of three months before the divorce will be finalized. A period in which we can still undo this. We leave when the signing is done and stand on the sidewalk.

"That's it then," I say, "are you OK with this?"

"Yes, it's better this way." He makes his gyrating hand motion, his Parkinson's signature.

"Three months' waiting time before we finalize," I add. Will we change our minds? Is three months enough?

"I'll see you around." Doyle turns and walks to his new car. I go to mine. We drive away separately. The choice, to stay with him and care for him, or to care for myself, isn't mine.

As I drive home, I reiterate what I know. Like Wouter who didn't reach for relationship, Doyle doesn't want me in his life any longer. In the grip of his disease, he doesn't seem to be able to express why he doesn't want my care, but he does need the economic advantages. Has he admitted to himself that he can't be a partner any longer? Does the relationship with his disease usurp all his relational energy? Does he want to set me free?

I park and enter the house that will be all mine after the divorce is final. A house that has so much of both of us in it, the attached apartment that will give extra income, the window bed for lounging, the light that tracks around the house all day, the growth marks of the children on the support post in the kitchen, but also the leaking windows, the lack of good kitchen lighting in the evening, the lack of a bathroom in the upstairs bedroom, the buckling plywood siding, the funny roofline that causes water to puddle and seep in. I walk around still in a daze over the finality of what we just did at the paralegal's office. I tell myself, this house will be mine and I will have to care for it, change it, make it whole. That thought makes me feel good, it's something solid I can put my hands on. Re-building the house will be the start of re-building my life. The almost trite expression, *We are born alone and we die alone,* spins through my mind with new meaning. I sit down on the couch and move the paperwork and books on the coffee table around into orderly piles. My piles of stuff, items that I can keep or toss. My life to make meaning of. I think of the hopes I had for becoming enlightened through relationship. My marriage to Doyle has given me moments of bliss, given me the taste of wholeness and oneness the spiritual masters talk about. The end of my marriage isn't the end of the road toward enlightenment. I'm awake to that now.

Chapter 23

I couldn't stop caring. I cared for him from a distance. I gave him the medical insurance. I arranged for my daughter to help him sort out his paperwork as it became clear his ability to track transactions was failing. The slow road to mental decline was a couple of years of what I call "living in the gray zone"; it was unclear if his decisions were his, or aberrations of a mind that doesn't remember. Only in hindsight do the early stages of dementia show themselves. A cognitive competency test didn't confirm the daily faltering; his intelligence got him through the test with the help of his medication. As his physical decline continued I arranged for caretakers, a home where he had some supervision, until he decided to move to San Diego into the care of his daughter from his first marriage, a nurse, a grown-up child, who was less demanding of relationship.

I began the journey of rebuilding myself, to belong to myself instead of *us*, a self I'd found on a grassy knoll high in the Himalayas. I'll never know what went on in Doyle's mind. He lost his capacity for speech two years later when he fell and broke his jaw. Because of the long inactivity of his jaw and throat muscles during recovery he lost his ability to speak and swallow. I believe that despite the changes, he never stopped loving me. I never stopped loving him.

When Doyle moved to San Diego in the care of his daughter, our relationship was reduced to occasional meetings in the care home. My visits would enable him to get out, take a walk in a park. Conversation was one-sided. I would tell him things about the children, he would nod and occasionally write something down in response. He never refused my visits, he never asked for more than help with a walk in the outdoors. During those visits I found that I could love from my heart and not lose myself. I know that marriages can end before we're ready to have them end. The journey it left me with was a journey of loving myself enough to live my life out with passion and embrace all that's worth loving.

When the time came for Doyle to pass out of this world, I gave him the words from Suzuki Roshi we spoke to each other on the day of our marriage:

The way-seeking mind is the conviction to fly as a bird in the air, to enjoy our being in this vast world of freedom.

I told him: "Fly free, my love."

A half hour later, Doyle took his last breath and left this world, leaving me to live in my belonging self.

And so my journey of living with the awareness of *nowhere to go, nothing to attain* continues. A journey I have always been on but that has became clear and more poignant during the time of losing Doyle. Being in Ladakh had awakened me to the knowing that *this is all there is*. There is no special realm or state that will set me free through endless hours of meditation. It's already there when I pay attention— whether as I often do when sitting in meditation, or in the living of life itself. When I lost Doyle I had to come to terms with the unwanted freedom he left me with; I learned that love transcends relationship.

I turned to nature to experience connection and found a deep happiness on the trail. I found the blessing of having a physical body, as I reached for the edges of my physical abilities, living to the bone. A way of living I discovered in the high Himalayas in my search for meaning.

Walking in the mountains frees me from attachment to daily comforts and gives me a sense of being connected, belonging to the universe.

Loving people that cross my path sets me free to belong with anyone. It's been a slow awakening to the truth with every step I take, every mountain pass I climb, every person who enters my life and everyone that leaves my life. I sit in meditation to touch base with the emptiness of things. I'm on my journey to nowhere, a journey to an all-encompassing belonging. And one day I too will fly free, free as a bird in the air.

Thank you, my love, for letting me find the wholeness of my heart. You'll be with me always.

Afterword

My story is not unusual. It's a story of belonging and of loss in the wake of degenerative disease and dementia.

In the USA 10,000 people reach retirement age every day, and 80% of older people have one or more long-term illnesses. In the US, Parkinson's disease (PD) is the second most common degenerative neurological disorder after Alzheimer's disease. It is estimated that PD affects 1% of the population over the age of 60, with an onset of dementia after 10 years; at the time of writing one in eight people over 65 have a diagnosis of Alzheimers disease or other form of dementia in the USA.

Stories of cognitive impairment abound. At a time when there is much publicity about these illnesses and how they affect the sufferer, the story of the partner, the caregiver, needs to be told. Many women raised in an era of women's emancipation are struggling with the choice between caring for self and caring for a person who no longer can relate to or share emotional intimacy with her. Of course, men, too, have similar stories, but statistics show that men are less likely to be full-time caregivers to women with cognitive deficits. The difficult question is how to sustain, or how to end, a marriage when the partner no longer lives in a shared reality.

If you have found yourself in a similar situation with a partner, I hope *Fly Free* has offered you a helpful perspective on partnership and marriage and the bigger search for meaning and belonging. I'm grateful that my journey led to an ability to transcend the choice between belonging to a relationship or a spiritual teacher and myself. Whatever your journey, I wish you peace and a true connection with yourself.

Dear Reader,

I want to say a thank you for choosing to read *Fly Free*. If you enjoyed it and want to keep up-to-date with my writing, just sign-up at the following link. Your email address will never be shared and you can unsubscribe at any time: www.transformation-travel.com

You can imagine how difficult it has been to put the events of my marriage onto paper. And yet, I was compelled to do so to make sense of what happened. Writing this memoir has been part of reclaiming myself. I hope that my story will help others find the courage to face difficult situations with honesty and awareness. My Facebook page includes a closed group, "The Examined Life", where we post experiences, ideas and moments that foster awareness and compassionate living.

If you are a hiker and enjoyed reading about trekking in the Himalayas, you may be interested in my "WalkingWomen50plus" page on my website and Facebook. I administer a closed group for walking women over 50. Members join for inspiration and to share hiking and walking moments and hiking and walking events.

In the meantime, if you loved *Fly Free*, I would be enormously grateful if you could write a review. I'd like to hear what you think, and it makes a real difference helping new readers to discover one of my books for the first time.

I welcome post and mail from my readers—you can get in touch on my Facebook page @damiroelse and @walkingwomen50plus or via email: transformation-travel@ashland97520.com

Thank you,
Dami Roelse

1. Do you think *Fly Free* is more a love story or more the story of a spiritual journey? Do you think spiritual seeking and marriage/love hamper the development of one or the other?

2. The title *Fly Free* is from a quote of Suzuki Roshi, a Zen Buddhist teacher: "The way-seeking mind is the conviction to fly as a bird in the air, to enjoy our being in this vast world of freedom." Do you think this quote applies to Dami's whole life or does it come to bear after she and her husband use the quote at their wedding? Why?

3. In your opinion what does it mean to have a "way-seeking mind". Who in this book, either Western or Asian, displays the way-seeking mind and how does it affect their life?

4. *Fly Free* presents the devastating effect degenerative disease can have, not only on the ill person, but also on everyone connected with them. What caused the breakdown of the marital relationship in *Fly Free*? Do you see a way that breakdown could have been avoided?

5. Dami accepts her husband's request for a divorce, even though she married Doyle taking the vow of "until death do us part". Was the impossibility of a full-fledged relationship the death that parted them? Or do you think Dami should have refused a divorce and stuck to her vow until Doyle died?

6. Doyle's brain and his thinking were affected not only by the disease but by the prescription medications which enabled him to function more effectively. Should a person be held accountable for his/her actions when those actions are a result of the illness and the side effects of medication such as, in this case, increased impulsivity and increased libido?

7. Both Dami and her husband embraced the Buddhist philosophy that the path to freedom from suffering is being equanimous when faced with pain and hardship. Do you think that either or both of them practiced their Buddhist philosophy? How would you have handled the situation?

8. When Dami is trekking with Wouter she analyzes his spiritual aspirations and his past actions and compares them with her own. Does this help or hinder her own spiritual journey?

9. Dami hires a local guide and porter for her trek. How does the Western rich tourist, local poor worker and servant continue to affect the divide between the West and the East?

10. Do you think Dami is right to go her separate way from Doyle and let Doyle "fly free". What would have or could have happened if she had refused?

CONVERSATIONS ON AWAKENING

Interviews by Iain and Renate McNay

Conversations on Awakening features 24 unique accounts of Awakening all taken from transcripts of interviews made for conscious.tv.

Some of the interviewees are renowned spiritual teachers while others are completely unknown having never spoken in public or written a book.

These conversations will hopefully encourage you, inspire you, and maybe even guide you to find out who you really are.

Conversations on Awakening: Part One features interviews with A.H Almaas, Jessica Britt, Sheikh Burhanuddin, Linda Clair, John Butler, Billy Doyle, Georgi Y. Johnson, Cynthia Bourgeault, Gabor Harsanyi, Tess Hughes, Philip Jacobs and Igor Kufayev.

Conversations on Awakening: Part Two features interviews with Susanne Marie, Debra Wilkinson, Richard Moss, Mukti, Miek Pot, Reggie Ray, Aloka (David Smith), Deborah Westmorland, Russel Williams, Jurgen Ziewe, Martyn Wilson and Jah Wobble.

Published by White Crow Books.
Available from Amazon in ebook and paperback format and to order from all good bookstores.
Part one: p.282, ISBN: 978-1786770936
Part two: p.286, ISBN: 978-1786770950

www.conscious.tv

Books in print from New Sarum Press

Real World Nonduality—Reports From The Field; Various authors

The Ten Thousand Things by Robert Saltzman

Depending on No-Thing by Robert Saltzman

The Joy of True Meditation by Jeff Foster

'What the...' A Conversation About Living by Darryl Bailey

The Freedom to Love—The Life and Vision of Catherine Harding by Karin Visser

Death: The End of Self-Improvement by Joan Tollifson

2020 Publications

Glorious Alchemy—Living the Lalita Sahasranama by Kavitha Chinnaiyan

Collision with the Infinite by Suzanne Segal

Transmission of the Flame by Jean Klein

The Ease of Being by Jean Klein

Open to the Unknown by Jean Klein

Yoga in The Kashmir Tradition (2nd Edition) by Billy Doyle

The Mirage of Separation by Billy Doyle

Looking Through God's Eyes by Han van den Boogaard

The Genesis of Now by Rich Doyle

www.newsarumpress.com

Made in the USA
Monee, IL
26 September 2020